LAWYERING

LAWYERING

Helene E. Schwartz

Farrar, Straus and Giroux 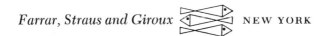 NEW YORK

Library of Congress Cataloging in Publication Data

Schwartz, Helene E.
    Lawyering.

    1. Schwartz, Helene E.   2. Women lawyers—United
States—Correspondence, reminiscences, etc.
I.   Title.

KF373.S346A32   340'.092'4   [B]   75-22451

This book is dedicated to

Ethel, Mel, and Bee,
my eccentric, volatile, loving family

Contents

Preface

I am a lawyer. I practice, teach, write about, and lecture on the law.

A lot of what I do is in the area of constitutional law. My clients have spanned the political spectrum, from hippies, Yippies, Zippies, and other anti-war protesters to Bill Buckley, Bill Rusher, *National Review*, and various committees to preserve, protect, and defend the crack in the liberty bell. Among the issues I've dealt with are freedom of the press, selective prosecution, illegal wiretapping, use of informers, abuses of the grand jury, deprivation of the right to a fair trial. This book is partly about some of these issues and the cases in which they arose.

It is also about the art of lawyering. When I tell people that I am a litigator, they tend to think that I spend every day in the courtroom. An appearance in court is the tip of the litigation iceberg. Perry Mason never cracks a book; but the strategic decisions and paperwork that precede courtroom appearances are the heart of litigation. This book attempts to describe what the daily work of a constitutional lawyer is like.

In one major respect, it is different from most comparable

books. This time, the lawyer is a woman. My being a woman is not the central focus of this book, but it is necessarily a leitmotif. I can't discuss my cases without writing about the effect that my being a woman has had upon my career as a lawyer.

I have gone through all the classic stages in the life of a woman who has a career in a profession that has traditionally been considered the exclusive domain of men. I was held back because I am a woman. Worse yet, I did not recognize that I was being held back or that I had a right to expect a greater role as a lawyer: that writing briefs and carrying papers to court should reasonably lead to participation in courtroom argument. The growth of the women's movement led to an awakening in me of what I might hope to accomplish as a lawyer, and for this the movement has my everlasting gratitude. I then had to fight for the new role I saw for myself, and it was during the time of my work on the Chicago Eight case that this struggle took place.

Once I realized that I was being oppressed, I got angry, which is only natural. Some of the anger remains, particularly insofar as the present continues to be rooted in past discrimination. But, in all fairness to ourselves and to our potential, we women cannot let anger set our mood for the future. We have to stop dwelling on past difficulties and start talking about the achievements that have accompanied our new self-awareness.

Which is why this book is not about a woman who is a lawyer but about a lawyer who happens to be a woman.

LAWYERING

1

Pauling versus *National Review*: Pre-trial

My first case made newspaper headlines and legal history. It was the sort of case most lawyers would give a lot to be involved in. Like almost everything else of importance in my life, I had the good fortune simply to fall into it.

When I graduated from Columbia Law School in 1965, the job market was not good for women attorneys. At a mandatory interview with the law-school placement director —a woman—I was told: "You'll never get a job on Wall Street and you probably won't be able to get a job in New York. You certainly won't be able to get a job in any litigation department. In fact, I doubt whether you'll be able to get a job at all." With such encouragement as I received from her, buttressed by my natural inertia and self-doubt, my attempts to find a job combined naïveté with confusion.

I heard that President Johnson was looking for brilliant, young, new faces to help formulate the Great Society, so I sent a telegram to the White House offering my services. I think I expected appointment as counsel to the President. Two weeks later, an unimaginative Presidential assistant sent me an application for the civil-service test. I halted all attempts to aid Lyndon.

Then I read that John Lindsay, who had just been elected to his first term as mayor of New York City, was seeking "bright people" to work in his administration. I went to Lindsay headquarters and presented myself. When the politicos learned that I had not worked on the campaign staff, I was politely dismissed.

I was almost convinced that I was fated to be a member of the hard-core unemployed, but I knew I wasn't going about this job-hunting business in the right way. Taking a clue from my classmates, I sent one hundred letters, together with my résumé, to firms listed in the legal directory. Of these, only forty-seven bothered to reply (a fairly standard response, my friends told me). Most of these were form letters indicating no need of my services. Twelve seemed interested in meeting me, but five of these changed their minds before I had a chance to arrange an interview. Three I crossed off my list because they were offering sixty-five dollars a week. My male classmates were making one hundred and fifty dollars a week and I was not willing to accept so much less.

One firm fell by the wayside when the managing partner admitted over the phone, with an unwelcome display of candor, that he "just wanted to see what kind of women the law schools are turning out these days." I declined to traipse down to Wall Street to satisfy his curiosity, and he had the nerve to sound offended.

Then I got a call from a lawyer named C. Dickerman Williams, a partner in one of the firms that had received my résumé. "I'm preparing for the trial of a very important case and I need your help. Can you come down here tomorrow?" he asked.

The following morning I, a native New Yorker, journeyed to Wall Street for the first time in my life. Williams's office was on Exchange Place, one block below Wall Street itself and far narrower and more cavernous than its famed neighbor to the north. I arrived at the firm's offices a few minutes early and was asked to wait. A red sofa and several hard chairs surrounded the receptionist's cubbyhole. I eyed the sofa suspiciously. It was large and soft. There was no way I would be able to sit in it or rise from it gracefully. Reluctantly, I chose one of the wooden chairs. I sat next to a table covered with copies of a magazine called *National Review.* I vaguely recalled that this was an ultra-conservative publication and I wondered whether that was a none-too-subtle hint of the politics in this office. I was beginning to feel uneasy. I was probably politically unfit for this office, too. I shifted listlessly in the hard chair and tried unsuccessfully to read *National Review.*

Eventually, a tall, slender, darkly elegant young woman, not much older than I, came into the hallway. She introduced herself as Corrine Schade, Mr. Williams's secretary, and I followed her to a corner office in the back of the suite. "Mr. Williams, this is Miss Schwartz," she said as she left his office, closing the door behind her.

Williams and I nodded warily at each other. There was another red sofa in his office and without invitation I sat down and we looked each other over. He was an elderly gentleman with wispy gray hair, sharply defined features, and intelligent eyes. His shoulders sloped and he was thin, but he looked fit for his age, which I correctly judged to be somewhere in the mid-sixties. He was very active. As he spoke, his hands flew in all directions, his eyes darted about, his voice rolled up and down the scale. At first I thought his mannerisms were due to the urgency and complexity of the case he was describing, but I later learned that he was always like this. I was unsure what to make of him. Then I noticed that he was wearing suspenders, and I had the irrational thought that any man who wore suspenders might be slightly reactionary but couldn't be all bad.

Our mutual perusal completed, he began to speak. "This is only a temporary job," he told me. I raised an eyebrow and started to get up and leave.

"Look, look, look," he said, and for the first time I heard

that repetitious phrase which was his favorite way of getting attention. "Sit down and listen for a minute. It's a very interesting case. Let me tell you about it." Just to be polite, I relaxed on the sofa.

"This case involves William F. Buckley, Jr.," he said with great pride. For a second, the name meant nothing to me. Then I remembered that a few months ago he had been the third-party candidate for mayor of New York. The only thing I could recall about his campaign was that he wanted a separate roadway for the use of cyclists, and that when asked what he would do if he won the race, he announced with Pooh-Bah dignity that he would "demand a recount."

"Buckley is being sued in his capacity as editor of *National Review*," Williams continued. Ah, I thought, that explains all those magazines in the waiting room. "The magazine is also being sued," Williams said, "as is its publisher, William A. Rusher. We represent all three defendants. The suit is being brought by Linus Pauling." A fragment of my mind told me, "Chemist. Nobel Prize."

Williams showed me the *National Review* articles that were the basis of Pauling's claim that he had been libeled. Then we began to discuss some of the legal issues involved in the case. He told me that my job would be to prepare testimony, organize exhibits, do research, and write memoranda of law. He offered me the job. I was flattered by the offer, but unresponsive. A few months was not my idea of job security. Williams mistakenly assumed that I was hesitating because of money. He said that he would pay "the going rate on Wall Street," which was one hundred and fifty dollars a week. I told him that my hesitation had nothing to do with money. He looked nonplused. Perhaps he shouldn't have offered me the full rate. After all, I was only a woman. I explained that I was not happy about the temporary nature of the job and said that I would let him know whether or not I was interested.

"Look, look, look," he said in that agitated voice I came to know so well. "I've got to know immediately. Can't you tell me now? I have to find someone right away. We go to trial in a few weeks and there's a tremendous amount of work to be done." I stalled and finally agreed to call him within twenty-four hours. My problem was that the job was only for the duration of the trial. Still, I seemed to have the choice of a temporary job or no job at all. The few firms that wanted to see me didn't look promising and I was discouraged by the thought of more job hunting. The real reason why I accepted Williams's offer, though, was that I was dazzled by the case. Linus Pauling, Bill Buckley, libel; the people and issues involved were fascinating. To someone who had been told that she probably wouldn't "be able to get a job at all," it seemed like a miracle. So that was how I got my first job, a "temporary" position that lasted three and a half years, until Williams retired from Wall Street and I did too.

My first three weeks as a Wall Street lawyer were hectic. Nothing—not studying for senior comprehensives and finals, not even cramming for the bar exam—had prepared me for the pressures of litigation. For twenty-one straight days I was at the office. Weekends and any other semblance of a personal life vanished in a mélange of briefs, affidavits, exhibits, newspaper articles, and law books. I would be a useless appendage until I learned about the factual basis of the Pauling case and the legal proceedings that had taken place up to this point. I buried myself in an office and began to read.

The suit was based on two articles, the first of which was written by James Burnham, a member of *National Review's* staff. Although I was to meet him numerous times, I never got to know him well and he remained for me a courteous but shadowy figure. He had once been associated with Communists and active with the Trotskyites, but finally had "seen the light." Now he pursued the conservative cause with a convert's zeal. I was told that during the 1965 blackout in New York (which occurred two months before I joined the firm) he had stood at our office window, looked at a strangely darkened Manhattan from the heights of the twenty-third floor, and proclaimed in solemn tones: "Gentlemen, I have no doubt but that we are witnessing the beginning of World War III." Fortunately for us all, Burnham turned out to be a better researcher and writer than he was a prognosticator.

Burnham's article, published in July 1962, was titled, "The Collaborators." It began: "What are we going to do about those of our fellow citizens who persist in a course of collaboration with the enemy who has sworn to bury us?" The article then discussed the public political activities of several prominent people, including Linus Pauling. The section relating to Pauling read:

> Take second, Professor Linus Pauling of the California Institute of Technology, once more acting as a megaphone for Soviet policy by touting the World Peace Conference that the Communists have called for this summer in Moscow, just as year after year since time immemorial he has given his name, energy, voice and pen to one after another Soviet-serving enterprise. . . . Pauling and a dozen others, attached their signatures to one more in a decades-long series of Communist-aiding fronts: this time, an Open Letter not only calling for the liquidation of South Vietnam's President Ngo Dinh Diem but condemning the presence of American personnel in that country as imperialist aggression (hence, by implication, more than justifying the Vietcong for killing Americans).

These were the only passages where Pauling was mentioned by name. But other sections of the article were equally important to the case because they made generalizations about the class of people being discussed, and it was undeniable, because of his specific identification in earlier parts of the article, that Pauling was considered by the author to be a member of that class. From a legal point of view, this meant that even if the sections of the article which discussed Pauling by name were not defamatory, the entire article could be considered a libel. Two other sections of the article were considered particularly controversial:

> Are such persons Communists? Some such undoubtedly are, but there is not publicly at hand the full proof, of the kind demanded by the courts, that they are Communists in the total, deliberate, disciplined organizational sense. But whether they are Communists or not in the legal sense, the objective fact is that these persons we have named, and many others like them, have given aid and comfort to the enemies of this country. They have done so not once or twice, by what might have been a special impulse, quirk or personal attachment, but time and time again, over a period of years and decades; and some of these acts are saved from falling under the constitutional definition of treason only by the historical chance that our government has not yet decided to give direct legal recognition to the fact that our present enemies are our enemies, and that we are at war.

> This soft and complacent public attitude toward the collaborators amounts, at bottom, to a general collusion in the sabotage of the nation's will, and in the moral nihilism that their actions express. If our standards have so far dissolved that there is no longer *anyone* on whom we will turn our backs, then we as a people are ready for suicide.

The article appeared on an editorial page of *National Review* and, as is the custom with editorials, it was unsigned. However, as the magazine's files showed, the article had been written by Burnham, not Buckley. But Pauling's lawyer was sure that Burnham was merely a front man and that the article had actually been written by Buckley. He was so certain of this that he named Buckley (as editor and "author"), Rusher (as publisher), and the magazine itself as defendants, without mentioning Burnham. This showed how little he understood Buckley, who was always mobilized for a good controversy, would probably have been delighted had he written the Burnham article, and would certainly have admitted it with alacrity.

I think Buckley would have been disappointed had he been sued only in his official capacity as editor of *National Review*—like Rusher, named only because as editor (and publisher) they had nominal responsibility for whatever the magazine printed. As it happened, although he had not written the first article, Buckley did write the second. The occasion of the second article, another unsigned editorial published a couple of months after the first, was what is known in the trade as a "lawyer letter." Pauling's attorney had written to *National Review* complaining about the first article. Like most such letters, this one included a threat to sue unless there was an apology or retraction or payment of damages. It was meant to be intimidating, but it apparently amused Buckley. He wrote an editorial entitled "Are You Being Sued by Linus Pauling?" After noting, with glee, "We are (or so his lawyer tells us)," Buckley went on to detail some of the other libel suits in which Pauling had been involved as plaintiff.

(Pauling's libel suits against the York County Anti-Communist League, the *Bellingham Herald,* and the Hearst Corporation were settled out of court for a fraction of the amounts sued for. His suit against the Australian Consolidated Press Ltd. was discontinued. Prior to the *National Review* case, Pauling had gone to trial only in his actions against the *New York Daily News* and the *St. Louis Globe-Democrat;* he lost both cases.)

According to Buckley, Pauling had "litigious goosepimples" and seemed to

> be spending his time equally between pressing for a collaborationist foreign policy and assailing those who opposed his views and who question whether this country can simultaneously follow Dr. Pauling's recommendations and remain outside the Communist orbit.

The article ended:

> Dr. Pauling is chasing after all kinds of people, even the
> formidable Sam Newhouse, owner of twenty-odd daily news-
> papers. His victory signal is the check or two he has wrested
> from publishers—who may indeed have libeled him, in which
> case they should pay up; but who may simply have been too
> pusillanimous to fight back against what some will view as
> brazen attempts at intimidation of the free press by one of
> the nation's leading fellow-travelers.

When I read this second article, it seemed to me that Buckley was determined not only to endorse Burnham's article
(witness what must have been his intentional use of the
word "collaborationist," a variation of the Burnham title)
but to do it one better. Undoubtedly, the single phrase in the
two articles which gave us the most trouble was Buckley's
description of Pauling as "one of the nation's leading fellow-
travelers." Burnham had hinted around the issue; Buckley's
piece was a premeditated clash. In May 1963, after several
fruitless months of negotiations over apologies and retrac-
tions, Pauling instituted suit for one million dollars in damages.

When I joined the case, in January 1966, the pre-trial
diddling around had consumed three years, which is typical
of the delay of the trial of civil cases in New York City. Now
the pre-trial motions and examinations were over and we
were nearing trial. In order to learn what the legal issues
were, I hunted for several hours until I located Pauling's
complaint at the bottom of one of dozens of office files.
Written in the usual legalese, it alleged that the defendants,

> recklessly, wrongfully and maliciously intending to injure,
> stigmatize and destroy the good name, fame and reputation
> of the plaintiff, and wrongfully, wantonly and maliciously
> intending to hurt, injure and damage the plaintiff, and to
> expose and in fact exposing the plaintiff to public scandal,
> hatred, contempt, infamy, obloquy, ill repute, disgrace and
> serious financial injury, and holding him up as an object

of contempt, scorn, ridicule, derision and aversion among his
friends, acquaintances, colleagues, neighbors, associates, and
the public at large, and to deprive him of the companionship
and friendship of respectable persons did wrongfully and
maliciously circulate, distribute, publish or cause to be published [the articles in question].

Simply stated, in a libel action for punitive damages, the
plaintiff must prove that something untruthful has been published with ill will toward the plaintiff, and that as a result of
the publication the plaintiff has suffered damage to a previously good reputation in the community. Notwithstanding
all the legal double-talk, this was what Pauling was claiming
in his suit. *National Review*'s answer alleged the typical
defenses in libel actions: that the articles published were
true, that they were published without any malicious intent,
and that the magazine was entitled to make "fair comment"
on Pauling's public activities. The factual heart of the case
was whether what was said about Pauling was true. Was he
"one of the nation's leading fellow-travelers"? There wasn't
any legal definition of the phrase, so we adopted a working
definition. To prove the defense of "truth," we would try to
show that Pauling supported the same positions as the Communists and was a member of Communist-front organizations.

How do you prove that a person holds the same public
political positions as the Communists? Getting the Communist position was easy. I became an avid reader of old *Daily
Workers*. I had lists of organizations Pauling had belonged
to and some twenty years of his publicly voiced political
statements. For instance, Pauling had been a director and
vice-chairman of the Committee on Peaceful Alternatives,
a group that opposed the North Atlantic Treaty Organization. It wasn't too difficult to find a *Daily Worker* article in
which the Communists denounced NATO, thereby proving
the parallel in positions. Pauling had supported Henry Wallace for President of the United States in 1948; so had the

Communists. Pauling had repeatedly urged that Mainland China be admitted to the United Nations; so did the Communists. And so on.

Of great importance to the factual defense was a 1961 Senate Internal Security Subcommittee report concerning Pauling's sponsorship of a world-wide petition to stop nuclear testing. Among other things, the report concluded:

> Dr. Pauling, in the course of his career, has been connected with various pro-Communist or "Communist-front" political activities and with a significant number of persons whose affiliations with the Communist Party, U.S.A., are matters of record.

> Dr. Pauling has figured as the No. 1 scientific name in virtually every major activity of the Communist peace offensive in this country. He has participated in many international organizations and international conferences sponsored by the Communist peace offensive. . . .

> In his statements and his attitudes, Dr. Pauling has displayed a consistent pro-Soviet bias.

These conclusions by a congressional committee could not be used at the trial to prove the truth of the statements made about Pauling in the *National Review* articles; but they were important to show the reasonable basis of the belief of the authors of the articles that what they wrote about Pauling was true.

After a week going through the mounds of papers in the files, I felt I had the basic thrust of the defense case on the facts fairly well under control. Now I would be able to join the daily conferences on the case. At the time I did not appreciate how important such conferences were. They enable lawyers to exchange ideas on strategy, examine each other's legal reasoning to see where it is weak or faulty, and identify possible ramifications of problems that had not been considered or precedents that had been missed. Years later

I realized how dependent I had become on legal conferences when I found myself alone in a strange town, preparing for trial. I had given considerable thought to an evidentiary problem in the case and I was fairly sure I had the solution. But I felt uneasy and wanted to talk it over with another lawyer. A friend of mine, who was associated with a local law school, arranged for me to meet with the man who taught evidence. The evidence expert confirmed my own analysis of the problem, and the hour-long discussion we had reassured me.

At those first conferences on Wall Street, however, I was afraid to open my mouth. I sat quietly on the sofa while Williams did most of the talking. Occasionally, he would ask for my opinion. "Maybe you have a different view. You're new to the case and we're all stale," he would say, looking at me expectantly. Instantly, I had an all too familiar feeling. It was just like class at law school. I was being called upon to recite, and whatever I said, I was going to be destroyed. My initial answers were mumbled and hesitant. After a while on the job, I got to know Williams better and I became friends with the other two lawyers on the team, Robert Makla and Alfred Koller. I gained confidence and soon I began to rival Williams as the most frequent and voluble participant. Our conferences were generally intellectual and volatile. Both Williams and I loved a good fight and we both liked to be right. Unfortunately for me, discussions often ended with Williams saying something like "Well, you may be right, but it's my client and the decision is up to me."

During the course of these conferences, it became obvious that the central legal issue in the case was the question of "malice." To get punitive damages, Pauling had to prove that the defendants published the article with "malice," which had always been understood in the dictionary sense of the word; legal "malice" meant "ill will." In an attempt to show that *National Review* had been activated by "ill will" in publishing the articles, Pauling intended to introduce evi-

. dence that the articles were part of an on-going campaign against him by the editors of the magazine, as shown by numerous similar references to him of the same ilk. What made this legal question crucial was that the Supreme Court had recently turned the law upside down in certain types of libel cases. In a historic decision in the case of *New York Times* versus Sullivan, the Court had held that in order to recover for libel a public official had to show that the defendant had acted "with knowledge that [the publications] were false or with reckless disregard of whether [they were] false or not." A finding of falsity alone would not "strip protections from the publisher." If the *Times*-Sullivan stand-ard applied to our case, it meant that even if Pauling could prove that the articles were untrue, he would still have to show that the defendants had actual knowledge of their falsity when they were printed. It made Pauling's case infinitely more difficult, especially in light of the evidence available showing reasonable grounds for belief in the truth of the statements, such as the conclusions of the Senate committee and the parallels between the public positions taken by Pauling and the Communists.

The problem was whether the *Times* case applied to Pauling at all. The new requirements for recovery were restricted in the *Times* case to suits in which the plaintiff was a public official. The Court's rationale had been that criticism of public officials was so crucial to an informed electorate that it was necessary to narrow the circumstances under which a public official could recover for libel, by requiring proof of "actual malice" as newly defined. Pauling was not a public official. However, there were indications in the Court's opinion that its rationale might be extended to cover cases involving people other than public officials. In the *Times* case, the Court had expressed

> a profound national commitment to the principle that debate on public issues should be uninhibited, robust and wide open. . . .

And in another case, which came down only a few weeks
before the Pauling trial began, the Court had said that the
thrust of the *Times* case

> is that when interests in public discussion are particularly
> strong . . . the Constitution limits the protections afforded by
> the law of defamation.

In this latest opinion, Rosenblatt versus Baer, the Court had
pondered, without deciding, whether the *Times* standard
should apply to a plaintiff who had

> thrust himself into the vortex of the discussion of a question
> of pressing public concern.

The basic legal argument in the Pauling case was that the
Times standard should be extended to apply to Pauling because he was a public figure who continually "thrust himself
into the vortex" of public discussion of controversial issues.
He should therefore be required to prove that the articles
had been published "with reckless and wanton disregard of
the truth," a much harder burden for him than the pre-*Times*
libel standard.

Even at the time, I realized how lucky I was to begin my
legal career in a case involving such intriguing people and
issues. But there was always something about the Pauling
case that just escaped my grasp. As someone who had been
too young to appreciate the political problems of the fifties,
someone to whom Joe McCarthy was merely an enigmatic
figure mentioned in passing and dismissed in history classes
as an aberration, there was a part of me that never understood what the shouting was about in the Pauling case. In
the political arena, people were always calling each other
names. Buckley himself had been called a Nazi, a Fascist,
and worse in the recent mayoral campaign. So what if somebody said Pauling might be a Communist. Who cared? What
difference did it make?

Only someone who was an adult during the fifties could

really understand why the parties got so riled up in the Pauling action. As for me, I secretly felt that both sides should just shrug their shoulders, accept the slings and arrows as part of the price of political activism, go back to their own corners, and start again. I never understood why Pauling brought the suit in the first place.

(Buckley had almost as many "litigious goosepimples" as Pauling. While I was his lawyer, I worked on libel actions he brought against Artie Shaw, Gore Vidal, and *The New York Post*. Some of the things that were said about Buckley were vicious. Still, when one considered his own acid tongue, I thought that for a public figure he was amazingly thin-skinned.)

Nor did I think that Pauling was a "collaborator." One of the other people involved in the case was convinced that "Pauling takes his orders directly from Moscow," that he was "Moscow's puppet," but I never saw it that way. Now I marvel at the foresight of a man courageous and knowledge-able enough to have condemned American involvement in Indochina as early as 1962. When working on the case four years later, I had barely heard of Vietnam, let alone become active against the war there. To me, Pauling was a liberal; if his public political positions were often the same as those of the Communists, that could merely be coincidence.

Irrespective of my personal opinion of Pauling (which I never voiced, for fear of losing my job), I was equally convinced that *National Review* had the right to draw its own conclusions from Pauling's public record. If *National Review* saw more than a coincidence, *National Review* had the right to say so. That, to me, was the essence of the "uninhibited, robust and wide-open" debate on public issues to which the First Amendment's protection of free speech committed us.

Their conversations invariably began in the same way.

"Hello, Bill," Williams would say in a jovial voice. "How's the greatest editor in the world?"

"Fine, Dick," Buckley would reply. "How's the greatest lawyer in the world?"

I had been working on the Pauling case for only three or four weeks, but it seemed like years. I was beginning to think that I had made a mistake in taking this on; it was too much work. And I'd missed what I had thought would be one of the best parts of the case: meeting Bill Buckley. He was in Switzerland writing a book and, so far, all contact with him had been under the auspices of the overseas operator, with me (at Williams's request) listening on the extension.

I consoled myself with the certainty that I would have to meet him someday. A decision had been made to put him on the stand as a witness for the defense. Along with my other work, I had been given responsibility for preparing Buckley's testimony. To do this, I'd had to pore through his scrapbooks—beginning with his term as editor of the Yale newspaper—looking for material which might be relevant to the case. Among the "political" documents were personal mementos detailing his marriage, army career, and the like. From them, I got a skeletal idea of what Buckley was like, and I was curious enough to want to meet him.

One Saturday morning I was in the office doing research. Williams was not in that day, but he called to check up on me. "I'll see you tomorrow morning," he said. I groaned. Another Sunday on Wall Street. Then he added the teaser. "Bill is flying in from Switzerland tonight and he'll be at the office at ten. Since you're preparing his testimony, of course it is essential that you be there."

At last! Saturday scampered away because I was so looking forward to Sunday. It arrived with a cold, gray winter wind that made the deserted streets seem drearier than usual. I rode alone in the elevator to the twenty-third floor, entered the firm's suite, and walked down the hall to Williams's office. The door was open. A broad back, encased in a white shirt, blocked my view of Williams. Was it the greatest editor in the world? "Oh, here's Helene," said Williams.

The back twisted and I examined the man facing me. His eyebrows were raised, his mouth open in a tiny, questioning circle. Yet somehow his face looked detached and devoid of expression. He was a large, well built, handsome man. He looked younger than the pictures and television views I'd seen of Buckley. For a moment I wasn't sure. Then I realized this person was definitely William Buckley: he was chewing on the ubiquitous pencil.

He acknowledged the introduction with a slight nod in my direction and turned his attention back to Williams. They continued to discuss the case as though I were not there, which was probably just as well, because I could not concentrate on their conversation. I was mesmerized by the gesticulations of the man sitting not two feet from me. "Gosh," I thought, "he really does make those faces, maul that pencil, and talk through his nose, even in private."

Lunchtime finally arrived. I was pleased, partly because I hoped we could relax and get to know each other better, but mainly because I was starving. On previous Sundays I had brought my lunch to the office, but today I figured that the presence of an august client would mean we would lunch in a restaurant. It turned out that Wall Street restaurants were closed on Sundays. The sophisticates knew this, but no one had bothered to inform the lowly associate. I watched with rising dismay as Williams and Buckley pulled out their brown paper bags. My hunger apparently showed. Buckley sympathized and offered to share his lunch with me.

I was impressed. I have brown-bagged it in my time, but never in my life have I seen anything like this. William Buckley had class. In addition to the delicious tuna-and-turkey combination sandwiches, the bag contained real Swiss cheese that he had personally flown in the day before from Switzerland. But the pièce de résistance was a bottle of red wine. How many people did I know who brought wine in their lunch bags?

I warmed to Bill, a feeling to which the wine made no small contribution. In fact, after two glasses of this wonderful surprise, I was just plain warm. I rarely drink anything alcoholic, and I would never have accepted the wine if Williams had not proposed a toast to a successful defense. In the presence of the client, it seemed churlish to refuse. (I've never had any capacity for alcohol. When I graduated from law school, one of the men in my class gave me a sterling-silver thimble from Tiffany's, with a note: "To be used as your jigger." Since that time, "Thimble Schwartz" has been one of my more enduring nicknames.)

Heavy legal dialogue swirled around the room, but I was oblivious. I sat on the edge of the red sofa, thinking to myself through a haze of red wine, "I will not fall off the sofa; I will not fall off the sofa," as though will power alone could keep me upright. My first job was only weeks old. What would the client think if he suspected that I was smashed? The room wobbled. I smiled a wide, silly grin. I held on tight and did not fall off the sofa, but it was truly a heroic effort.

2

Courting Justice

The trial had originally been set for February 1966, but it was postponed because of a number of procedural problems. One delay was caused by a motion by Michael Levi Matar, Pauling's lawyer, that the judge assigned to the case recuse himself, that is, step down from the case. Prior to his appointment to the bench, Judge Irving Saypol had prosecuted Ethel and Julius Rosenberg and Morton Sobell. Among the public positions Pauling had espoused which *National Review* alleged were similar to those of the Communists was his support of the Rosenbergs and Sobell. Pauling's lawyer suggested that Saypol should disqualify himself from presiding at the Pauling-Buckley proceedings because his relationship to the Rosenberg-Sobell case might somehow prejudice him. Since justice must always give the appearance of justice, Saypol reluctantly withdrew.

The case was then assigned to Judge Samuel J. Silverman. In a way, it is unfortunate that he was the first judge I ever appeared before, because he set standards in my mind which too few jurists I met later could fulfill. Many judges have such poor temperaments that they make it difficult for the parties to have a fair trial. They seem to forget that they are the people's servants, not their masters, that they are only first among equals. Compounding the problem is that some of them are ill-versed in the law. I once saw a judge make a ruling, on an evidentiary question, which we all knew was wrong. One of the lawyers showed him the statute that made it clear that his ruling was erroneous. The judge contemptuously pushed the book away and said, "I don't give a damn what it says. In this courtroom, I am the law."

Sam Silverman is a rare exception to the mediocrity of much of the bench. He has a reputation for writing well-reasoned and thoughtful opinions. In addition, although he runs a tight courtroom, he is always gracious and polite to counsel and the parties. Even though we had fought to retain Saypol, we regarded it as a good omen that Silverman would be governing our trial.

Another cause of delay in bringing the case to trial was that counsel for the parties had taken the adversarial process outside the courtroom and had imposed it upon their own relationship, which could only be characterized as wildly antagonistic. Each party passionately believed that it had right and the gods on its side and was sure that a win was necessary to save the American Way of Life. On a more mundane level, Williams and Matar did not like each other. I liked Matar and he appeared to like me, so I was often the emissary between the two clashing sides when it was necessary to exchange papers or get an agreement to a stipulation.

One result of my experience in this case was to make me conscious of how important it is to keep up the professional façade in relationships with opposing counsel. It is emotionally draining to make a client's cause your own to such a degree that your courtroom opponent becomes your own personal enemy. It does the case no good.

Worse yet is the effect the adversary system has on one's private life. The characteristics that make a good lawyer—contentiousness, a definitive way of speaking, undoubting confidence in one's cause and one's ability—are less desirable in a friend or daughter. The very skills I have cultivated as a lawyer are the ones I've fought to keep out of the private person who has finally matured into a woman I can live with and sometimes even admire. But the conflict between the private and professional personalities can make you feel schizophrenic if you dwell on it.

During the Pauling case, it was too early in my career for me to be conscious of these problems. Anyway, I had no difficulty in getting along with Matar, and although I wanted us to win the case, it wasn't a life or death matter for me.

Matar was assisted in court by his wife. She wasn't a lawyer, but she was an integral part of his team. Even Williams had to admit that she was a "gracious lady," and he occasionally nodded genially in her direction, while wondering under his breath what she could see "in a fellow like Matar." The Matars were Orthodox Jews, a fact which came to light during the trial, when Matar asked for an early adjournment because of the Passover holidays. For the next week, he and his wife remained in the courtroom during the luncheon break, munching on matzoh and hard-boiled eggs. They won me over completely when they offered to share their matzoh. And as we left the courtroom that day, Pauling walked toward me with a friendly smile and wished me a "happy Seder." He mispronounced the name of the festival meal, but I was glad that he too thought the animosity that occasionally surfaced in the courtroom was inappropriate.

Because the Matars were Jewish, Williams was anxious to introduce me to the prospective jurors and keep me visible during the trial. At least half of the venire (that is, the group of people called for jury duty) was Jewish, which is not unusual in New York. Williams was sure that the jurors would be surprised and unfavorably impressed if there was no Jew on the Buckley team. He seemed to fear that the Jewish jurors would associate Buckley and the right wing with Fascism and anti-Semitism and he hoped that my presence would ameliorate this problem. I was uncomfortable being singled out for this reason, but there was nothing I could do about it. Attorneys are customarily introduced to the venire to find out whether any of the prospective jurors know any of the lawyers, which might be a disqualifying factor. With a name like mine, the jurors could guess that I was Jewish.

As it turned out, Williams's ideas were outmoded. My best friend on the jury was undoubtedly Mrs. Avila, the graceful Puerto Rican woman who fearlessly closed her eyes during the most tedious testimony. My feeling that we had good rapport was borne out after the trial was over, when she told me: "I loved your different-colored hair ribbons. Every morning, I would look to see what color you were wearing. They cheered up this dull courtroom."

Dear Mrs. Avila! Little did she know how happy I was to hear of her appreciation of those much beleaguered hair ribbons. They were symbolic of a running battle I'd been having with Williams over my clothing. This was long before the advent of pants suits and my wardrobe tended to be rather conservative anyway. I wore dresses or suits, stockings and heels to work. My first few weeks on the job, I had been confined to the office. When the pre-trial hearings began, I asked to accompany Williams to court, where, if I was not allowed to speak, at least I could listen and learn. He agreed, but as we were leaving for court, he suddenly noticed what I was wearing (a red jersey dress), and from that moment on, my appearance was a source of extenuated irritation to him.

"You can't wear a short-sleeved dress in court. You have to wear a jacket."

"Don't you have any gray dresses? Or black? Or navy? Must you wear red?"

"Look, look, look, you can't wear ribbons in your hair. It's undignified."

As Mrs. Avila's comment made clear, everyone notices what women wear in court. Nobody notices what a man wears, unless it is extreme. My brother, who is also a lawyer, gets away with a wardrobe of three suits, which he alternates wearing when on trial. Women in the public eye need a much larger wardrobe. It must be fashionable without being outlandish. It can't be too sexy, or it might alienate the women jurors. If it is too drab, it might alienate the men. Or maybe the men will think you are a better lawyer if you *are* drab. Who knows? Proper courtroom attire is a constant problem for women.

Once, I began my argument with the traditional opening, "May it please the Court." The judge interrupted me to say, "Oh, it does. But don't you think it's a little short?" The men in the courtroom thought this was funny. I was embarrassed by the judge's comment, but he was right. I hadn't expected to be in court that morning and was just covering for an associate who couldn't make it at the last minute. I knew my attire wasn't exactly proper, but I couldn't help thinking that if I had been a man wearing dungarees and a sports jacket instead of a suit, nothing would have been said.

Women witnesses or defendants have the same problem. One of my clients customarily wore short, tight dresses and walked with a pronounced wiggle. I supervised the buying of two new "courtroom" dresses and told her to "get rid of the wiggle when you walk to the witness stand." The men might like it, but the women wouldn't; or maybe it would be vice versa. But she was facing twenty years in jail and we couldn't take a chance.

I once had a witness who wore a ring through her nose. We were not in a big-city courtroom (where jurors might be accustomed to such a sight). She was annoyed by my request, but she finally agreed to remove the ring while testifying. Sometimes, even spectators have to be carefully dressed if they are known to be associated with a party to the case. (See page 44, where Mrs. Buckley's clothing was a source of concern to us.) I've told male clients to wash and trim their hair, get clean shirts, change the dungarees for a suit and the army boots for shoes. Juries like clean-cut defendants and witnesses. It may seem dishonest, but would you go to jail for ten years for a pair of dungarees?

The point is that it is horrible to have to worry about something as silly as this when you're involved in legal proceedings. I'm not usually a clothes-conscious person, but I can't run the risk that the judge or jury might be antagonized by my attire. The discretionary power of judges is so broad that even the smallest prejudice might influence the outcome of the case. And jurors have the final say. So the mini-skirts, maxi-skirts, gypsy blouses, sun-back dresses, and dungarees stay in my closet when I'm in court. But the flowers and ribbons remain in my hair.

The struggle over my clothing receded as we faced the problem of the jury. Picking a jury in a case involving volatile political differences is not an easy process. The candidates were asked what they had read or heard about the parties, all of whom were relatively famous. Particular emphasis was laid on what they had heard about Buckley, who had been on the receiving end of some nasty attacks during the recent mayoralty campaign. The jurors were also questioned about their political ideas and associations which might influence their verdict.

It was during the voir dire (questioning of prospective jurors to see if they will be impartial) that I discovered that others ascribed to me political leanings that I had never voiced. As each prospective juror was seated in the box, Williams would lean in my direction and ask, "Well, Helene, what do you think of him [or her]? You're the house liberal. What's your opinion? Think we should keep juror number four?" As far as I knew, I had never given him any reason to think of me as a "liberal." Sure, I disagreed with some of

what was written in *National Review;* but I had said nothing
about this. In the back of my mind, I think I feared I would
be fired if anyone realized that I was not a conservative;
indeed, that I was not a particularly political person at all.
As long as I worked with Williams, I was eternally damned,
or saved, by the label "house liberal."

On the second day of jury selection, Williams requested a
chambers conference. He asked that juror number six be
called in to join us. "Mr. Plotkin," he asked the juror, "are
you related to a Barbara Plotkin?"

"Yes," the juror replied. "My wife's name is Barbara."

"Is she the same Barbara Plotkin who signed a petition last
year for peace in Vietnam?"

"She may be," Plotkin replied. "I know that she is against
the war, as I am."

I was puzzled. How had Williams obtained this information overnight? I did not learn until weeks later.

There was some consultation at the defense table as to
whether we should get rid of Plotkin, "an obvious liberal
who will probably idolize Linus." It was decided not to
challenge Plotkin or any of the other jurors, who included a
large number of women and several members of minority
groups. Williams feared that challenging any of the blacks or
Puerto Ricans would only confirm the jurors' possible suspicion that Buckley and his associates were prejudiced.

After the jury was selected, Judge Silverman gave it a
warning that showed his sensitivity to the issues and personalities involved in this case. "We all have political views," he
told the jurors. "This is not the forum to strike blows for
whatever side we happen to be on."

Then came the opening statements by counsel. Matar referred to Pauling as a "magnificent American," setting the
tone for his argument throughout the case. "If you call
someone a Communist-fronter or a fellow traveler, or pro-
Red," he said, "for all practical purposes the reader treats

them the same as he would a Communist. He takes them
to be pro-Soviet, anti-democratic, and their patriotism is
subject to question."

Williams responded with an equally impassioned opening
in which he defended the necessity for a free press and open
debate on public issues. He stressed that "there can be no
doubt the purpose of this case is to get Buckley." Each side
objected vehemently to the opening remarks of the other,
with little success.

Plaintiff Pauling then began the presentation of his case.
Normally, the words "the plaintiff's case" are a misnomer,
for it is the plaintiff's lawyer who presents the case. Not so
here. Linus Pauling, a gangling, friendly fellow with an
untamed bush of angelic white hair and a wide, endearing
smile, sat at the counsel table actively participating in the
presentation of his case. He passed notes to Matar, conferred
with him, and was obviously enjoying himself.

The first witness was Ava Helen Pauling, the plaintiff's
diminutive wife. The tactical reason for calling her was to
win the jury's sympathy by showing that this likable, gray-
haired woman totally supported her husband's defense of his
good name. On the day Ava Pauling was to testify, Matar
came into the courtroom lugging two enormous suitcases.
When they were opened, there was a gasp of awe from everyone present. Pauling tried to look nonchalant as we gazed
open-mouthed at his more than twenty-five honorary de-
grees, some thirty medals, and two Nobel Prizes. It was
Matar's intention to have Ava Pauling identify these for the
record, as evidence of her husband's high standing in the
community, which the *National Review* articles were alleged
to have damaged. Each medal and degree was carefully removed from the suitcase and brought to her on the witness
stand for an account of the circumstances under which it had
been awarded.

The effect on the jury was devastating, and we knew it.

Williams made numerous objections to the cumulative nature
of the testimony and offered to stipulate to Pauling's good
reputation as a scientist. At first, Judge Silverman was as
hypnotized as the rest of us; finally he agreed that Matar had
made his point and ordered an end to Ava Pauling's testimony. But the damage had been done. We were in the
presence of an intellectual giant, and I was totally cowed. The
next morning, I took my Phi Bete key from the drawer and
wore it for the first time since my election to membership.
To this day, I cannot explain what I hoped to accomplish
by wearing it. Pauling most certainly didn't notice the key
and wouldn't have been impressed if he had.

Then Pauling himself took the stand. He was an articulate
and ingratiating witness and the jurors clearly liked him. But
to defense counsel, particularly on cross examination, he was
infuriating, devious, coy, tediously ingenuous, and too clever.
I had already decided that I admired Pauling the man; but
Pauling the witness was a killer.

On direct examination, Pauling admitted that he had
been an active supporter of many of the groups and causes
which *National Review* claimed were sympathetic with the
Communist line. He testified to his involvement with the
1948 Wallace campaign, his efforts against the Rosenbergs'
death sentence, his vocal opposition to congressional committees investigating alleged Communist activities, his participation in international peace conferences which some
claimed were Communist-dominated. In each instance, he
explained that his involvement was motivated by humani-
tarian feelings or that a particular activity was one "that
should help the cause of international understanding and
world peace." More damaging to our case, he also testified
about occasions when he had publicly denounced Communist positions, such as his statement about the Soviet nuclear
test in October 1961, which he had characterized as an act
that was "the most horrifying and immoral in the history of

the world." He insisted throughout that he was not a Communist.

After being on the stand for several court sessions, Pauling
was turned over to the defense. Al Koller, who had devoted
months to preparation of the Pauling cross examination, came
to court laden with copies of the *Daily Worker*, congressional
reports, and hundreds of pages of proposed questions. With
respect to each activity in which Pauling had admitted his
involvement, he was shown evidence of the Communist
support of the same position, such as a *Daily Worker* editorial, and asked whether it was not a fact, or at least a
reasonable inference, that he had been following the Communist line. He repeatedly answered that "on a very few
issues" did he "know what the Communist line has been over
the last eighteen years." When asked whether he allowed
the use of his name by Communist organizations, he replied:
"Not to the best of my knowledge." He also testified that he
had "never associated with any persons who were—with any
persons that I knew or even suspected of being dedicated
Communists or of being Communists."

I wasn't sure that this sort of questioning was going to
impress the jury favorably. In so many instances, the causes
that Pauling espoused were also supported by other famous
Americans—such as Eleanor Roosevelt and Adlai Stevenson—
who certainly were not Communists. I still thought that the
coincidence between Pauling's positions and those of the
Communists could have been fortuitous, and that the jurors
would possibly view it that way and decide against *National
Review*, particularly since they were obviously enamored of
Pauling as a person. I hesitantly voiced my thoughts to the
rest of the defense team one evening, but was overruled. I
didn't push the point, because I didn't see any alternative to
the strategy being used. It wasn't a queston of fact so much
as a question of law. We didn't have to prove that Pauling
was actually a Communist. But we had to convince the jury

that *National Review* had the right to draw that conclusion from his publicly stated positions.

On only one occasion during our cross examination did I vociferously oppose a line of questioning. Williams insisted on asking Pauling about a meeting he'd once had with Nina Khrushchev. As "house liberal," I objected. "Everyone likes fat, grandmotherly Nina," I said to Williams. "If I were traveling in Russia, I'd love to meet her. The fact that Pauling met her doesn't make him a Communist or a Communist sympathizer." Williams looked at me with disappointed eyes, as though there were something important I failed to understand. I continued to press my point, urging that this series of questions could only backfire, but again I was overruled.

"While you were in Moscow—did you go to Moscow on that trip?" Williams asked Pauling the next day.

"While I was in the Soviet Union, you mean. Yes," Pauling replied.

"The trip began on or about November 18, 1961?"

"Yes."

"And did you receive an invitation to tea from Madame Khrushchev?"

"No," Pauling answered.

This was a totally unexpected response. We had a photograph of Pauling and his wife with Mrs. Khrushchev, which had been taken on that trip. What was Pauling up to?

With a frown, Williams pressed on. "Did you see Madame Khrushchev?"

"Yes, I did."

"And wasn't it at tea?"

"Well, I—no, it wasn't a tea. But tea, I believe—"

"—was served?"

"Tea was served, and vodka, if I remember correctly."

"At any rate, you received an invitation to visit her at the Kremlin?"

"No, I didn't. I didn't receive an invitation to visit her in the Kremlin or anywhere else."

"Well, you did get together with Mrs. Khrushchev at her suggestion, did you not?" Williams asked.

"Is this about my moral behavior?" Pauling asked ingenuously.

Judge Silverman interrupted the cross examination at this point, to ask: "I take it you did have a meeting with Madame Khrushchev?"

But Pauling would concede nothing. "Well, I was not invited by her," he said.

My colleagues were pleased by the cross examination, and especially by this series of questions. They felt it showed that Pauling was sneaky, but I wasn't sure. The jury had been Pauling's rapt and devoted audience. I thought his performance had been impressive and I was glad when he left the stand.

Matar then surprised the legal strategists by calling defendant Bill Rusher to the stand. Rusher is a handsome, self-contained man whom many describe as Napoleonic in physique and temperament. Others say he is "Bill Buckley without the sense of humor." Anyone who knows him at some depth realizes that neither of these characterizations is apt. Rusher often demeans himself playfully by saying that "if they can't get Buckley, they call me." That might be true, but audiences get their money's worth with Rusher. He is an intelligent, articulate proponent of conservatism. On a personal level, he is warm and thoughtful, and I found it easy to appreciate and respect him.

Rusher had been named as a defendant in the suit, not because he had written either of the articles, but because as publisher of *National Review* he was nominally responsible for its content. We were surprised at Matar's tactic in calling Rusher to the stand, because of the legal rule that one cannot impeach one's own witness. By calling Rusher,

Matar was forced to vouch for his credibility, which was a strange position for a plaintiff's lawyer to have to take with respect to a defendant. In fact, Matar tried numerous times to impeach and attack Rusher, but he was prevented from doing so by the judge, who reminded him that Rusher was his own witness.

Matar's purpose in calling Rusher was to show that *National Review* had published the articles with "ill will," that is, the old-fashioned "malice," toward Pauling. His basic approach was to question Rusher about what he knew or had heard about Pauling at the time the articles were published. This was a mistake. Bill Rusher had been counsel to the Senate Internal Security Subcommittee before he had joined *National Review.* He was an old hand on the anti-Communist front and was well versed in Pauling's activities. He also testified that he had relied on Burnham's judgment as author of the first article, "because of his great knowledge of the material." Matar tried to undermine Rusher's reliance on Burnham by showing that Burnham had been a Trotskyite during the thirties, but this did not rattle Rusher, who had great respect for his colleague. Burnham had published a number of books, including *The Managerial Revolution,* and was highly regarded in conservative circles.

Matar had Rusher on the stand for days. Rusher may have been a bit pedantic at times, but he never lost his cool. The worst that can be said about this portion of the trial is that it was boring, often consisting of the lawyers reading long passages to the jury from the examinations before trial or from congressional-committee reports. Juror Avila's head nodded, and at one point Judge Silverman showed his irritation when he wearily announced: "If the jurors should happen to hear both sides say they rest, remember it's April 1."

There were times when I didn't go to court but stayed in the office to do research on legal issues that came up during

the trial. I remember one of these was the question of how Pauling could claim his reputation had been damaged by the alleged libels, in view of the fact that after their publication he had been awarded a second Nobel Prize.

Researching these points was fun. My biggest problem was getting a secretary to type the briefs and memos I had drafted. During my first months in the office, I could not seem to do anything to make the secretaries like me. I knew this was a problem women executives frequently faced, but that didn't make it any easier for me. I blamed myself and tried hard to please the other women in the office. Years later, one of them told me that they thought I was "very snobby, like you were used to being the boss's daughter."

"I was shy," I told her. "And you all frightened me. You never even said hello."

The barriers between the lawyers and the secretaries in the office were exacerbated for me because I was a woman. To some of the secretaries, no doubt I was little more than a snippy child. They were middle-aged and had been legal secretaries for more years than I had lived. They obviously resented "taking orders" from someone half their age. But I wasn't any more popular with secretaries my own age. They made no secret of their preference for working with the men. Working for a woman lacked prestige. Besides, who would want to work for a woman when there were bachelor associates around?

Williams, Makla, Koller, and I shared the services of two secretaries. The first was a young woman with a sharp mouth and a noticeable dearth of secretarial skills. She was asked to leave several months after I joined the firm, and was not much missed. The other was the gem of the office, Corrine Schade. She was the best legal secretary I've ever met. Unfortunately, she took an instant and strong dislike to me. Naturally, Williams had first call on Mrs. Schade's services. The rest of us fought for her and were completely dependent on her good will, of which, for me, there was little. Unwittingly, Williams often put Mrs. Schade and me in conflict. He would insist that I finish a crucial memo for him. Then he would call Mrs. Schade in to dictate a letter. He would ask her to type up his letter and then complain because my memo wasn't typed. The resultant session of recriminations gave Mrs. Schade further reason to dislike me.

After six months as an unsuccessful contender in the battle for secretarial help, I gave up. Reluctantly, I admitted to Williams that I knew how to type and asked him to get me a typewriter. For the duration of my stay on Wall Street, I typed all my own memos and most of the first drafts of legal papers I was asked to write. Because of this, I never learned how to give dictation, but at least I could get my work done.

Still, I was hurt that the other women resented me and the fact that they had to work with me. Sometimes I think I tried harder to please them than I did to please my boss. There was no miraculous breakthrough, only a gradual acceptance of the obvious fact that I was there to stay and that I was harmless and perhaps even nice. And eventually the hostility disappeared. It was replaced by mutual respect and friendship one day when, in my never-ending campaign to make Mrs. Schade tolerate me, I took her to lunch.

On my return, I was confronted by one of Williams's partners. "It has come to my attention that you have gone to lunch with one of the secretaries. Is that true?" he asked. I said it was. "Surely you know that there is a difference between lawyers and secretaries which must be maintained at all times," he continued. "As a woman lawyer, you must make added efforts to maintain your distance from the secretaries. You can take them to lunch on special occasions, such as an engagement or Christmas, but otherwise I must insist that you refrain from eating with the secretaries. You have to remember your place."

"Sir," I said, "it's awfully hard to snub women you meet three times a day in the ladies' room. There is something very democratizing about the toilet." He glared at me and told me not to lunch with the secretaries again. When I told the women what had happened, they didn't say anything. But, from that day on, they were my friends.

When I left the firm, the women invited me to join them at dinner every other month. "The only reason we are having these dinners," one confided to me, "is that we want to keep seeing you." I bloomed.

The courtroom had always been filled with spectators, drawn by the fame of the parties. Even they began to desert us as the trial dragged into its fourth week. "It isn't as exciting as Perry Mason, is it?" Judge Silverman asked a group of school children as they fled from the courtroom.

After Rusher, the rest of Pauling's witnesses consisted of a procession of scholarly men who testified to his good reputation in the academic community, the blackening of which was the basis of his claim for damages against the defendants. Williams grimly remarked that one, George Wald, appeared to be the only Pauling character witness who had never won a Nobel Prize. Two weeks after the trial, Wald won the accolade. "No doubt because of his brilliant testimony on behalf of Linus Pauling," Williams commented dryly.

This parade of the distinguished provided me with a job I did not like. As each man was called to the stand, Williams would hand me a dime and I would head for the phone booth outside the courtroom. I would dial a number, and when a woman answered, I would give her the name of the witness. "One moment," she would say. Seconds later, she would return to the phone and give me a list of the political causes the witness had espoused. "Supported Wallace in 1948. Signed petition on behalf of the Hollywood Ten. Testified before the Senate Internal Security Subcommittee in 1957. Signed civil-rights petition in 1961. Marched with Martin Luther King in 1963. Attended Vietnam protest rallies." I would return to the courtroom, hand the list to Williams, and then listen to him "attack" the character witnesses on cross examination, in an attempt to destroy their credibility by showing that they were just as "liberal-pinko" as Pauling himself.

The mystery woman's name was Ruth Matthews, and she had also been the source of the information about juror Plotkin. I knew little about her then, but I later learned that she was the widow of J. B. Matthews, who had been on the staff of the House Un-American Activities Committee. Rumor was that when he resigned from the committee staff, he took with him copies of most of the papers in the committee's files. These became the basis of an enormous library he accumulated for use in anti-Communist activities. After his death, his wife continued his work. Though I never met her, I did have much contact with her by phone and letter, none of which made me any more comfortable about the idea of private citizens having so much information about the activities of others. It was bad enough for the government to gather this type of information; somehow, it seemed even worse in the control of private interests.

Toward the end of the trial, something happened that almost brought an early end to my budding career as a Wall Street lawyer. Although everything turned out all right, the incident explains why I have since been uncomfortable in my relations with the press.

Every day of the trial, the press section was filled, and there was extensive newspaper coverage. This was not only because of the colorful characters involved in the trial but also because, as a matter of enlightened self-interest, the press is generally attentive to First Amendment cases. Much to my dismay, Williams told me that I was to be in charge of press relations. The idea that I might be quoted in permanent print made me cautious about what I said. My job was further complicated by the fact that Judge Silverman had issued a so-called "gag order," which forbade the lawyers

and parties from talking to reporters. This meant that my
task was little more than to smile pleasantly at the reporters
and be evasive about why we were not talking. They were
unaware of the gag rule, as it had been issued in chambers,
with the further injunction that the press was not to be told
that the judge had "gagged" us. Perhaps Judge Silverman
realized the incongruity of a gag rule in a First Amendment
case.

My work as public-relations coordinator went fairly well
until the sixth week of the trial. As I was leaving the courtroom, I was stopped by a reporter from *The New York
Times*. "How come Buckley hasn't been in court up to now?"
he asked me.

Since this question did not relate to the substance of the
case, I was able to reply without violating the gag order.
"Because he's been in Switzerland writing a book about
his mayoral campaign," I told him. Buckley had flown in for
the conference at which I'd first met him, and then returned
to Europe.

"Come on now," he said to me. "I can't believe that Buckley would stay away from a trial where he's a defendant.
What's the real reason?" I hesitated to answer. The real reason
was related to the fact that Pauling's lawyer had taken the
unorthodox step of calling defendant Rusher to the stand as a
witness on behalf of the plaintiff. Normally, a defendant
doesn't take the stand, if at all, until the defense presents its
case. But Matar had kept Rusher on the stand for over a week,
asking him time-consuming and repetitive questions. Why
should Buckley be subjected to this? Besides, when the *Times*
motion was renewed, Matar might try to reopen his case in
order to call Buckley as a plaintiff's witness. To avoid this possibility, Buckley stayed out of court until it was time for him
to appear as first witness for the defense.

However, this was a strategic decision and not something
for publication. Matar might have suspected this, but he
didn't know it for sure and it would be grist for his mill to

see it confirmed in print. I told the reporter that I had no comment. "Oh, come on now," he said again. "You can tell me. It's just for my own curiosity, as background information so I can write my story. I certainly wouldn't print it if you don't want me to." I believed him. He was a young fellow whom I'd come to know over the last six weeks. Also, I naïvely assumed that a *Times* reporter would be honorable. Trusting his promise not to print what I said, I told him the reasoning. He thanked me and wandered away.

That evening, I bought a copy of the *Times*. And there it was, in bold black print:

> Mr. Buckley had deliberately stayed out [of the trial]. It was understood that his lawyer, C. Dickerman Williams, was fearful that if he appeared, Mr. Matar might try to have him testify in the hope of re-opening [Pauling's] case.

As I read these words, I felt an odd combination of extreme calm and horror. "I'm going to be fired," I thought. "Williams will never forgive me for this." The story made us look terrible, as though we had something to hide. The newspaper's readers couldn't know that Buckley *was* going to testify, as the first witness for the defense.

I was afraid to go to work the following morning. I thought of pretending to be sick (which was true emotionally, if not physically), but I knew I'd have to face this sometime. When I arrived at the office, everything was in turmoil and Williams was furious. "Did you see this? How did they find out? Who told them that?" he asked.

I had no choice but to admit that it was my fault. Hesitantly, I told Williams the whole story. "He promised that he wouldn't print it," I said, "and I was stupid enough to believe him. But he was from the *Times*. I thought he would be honest."

To my surprise, Williams was not too hard on me. In fact, seeing how abject I was, he was even gentle. I then got my first, albeit belated, lesson in lawyers' relations with the

press. Williams explained what I should have known in-
stinctively—that there are some things one told reporters "in
confidence" and there are others one never told reporters
under any circumstances. My little exposé fell into the
second category.

After Williams reassured me that I had not caused the
whole case to go down the drain, he called Buckley to tell
him that I had been the source of the story. Buckley's reaction startled me. As a journalist himself, he was incensed
when he heard that the reporter had promised not to print
what I had told him. He regarded it as a breach of journalistic ethics and he wanted to call A. M. Rosenthal (one of
the *Times*'s editors and his personal friend) to see to it that
this fellow got fired or at least severely reprimanded. Like
Williams, he told me that no harm had been done by my
gaffe. He was warm and sympathetic. In his eyes, the fault
was with the *Times* reporter. He was so vehement about
it that I began to feel sorry for the reporter. I asked Bill not
to call Rosenthal, and when he calmed down, he agreed. I
was touched by Buckley's loyalty to me and I shyly told him
so. I was beginning to see what a special man he was and
why his friends, many of whom were publicly his political
adversaries, were personally devoted to him.

When someone asks me if I have ever made a bad mistake
as a lawyer, this incident always comes to mind. Given how
disastrous it could have been for me, I was fortunate and
grateful that both Buckley and Williams supported me. It
was a hard lesson and one I never did learn well. Though I
now have considerably more experience in dealing with the
press, I still seem to suffer from a chronic case of instant
foot-in-mouth disease with reporters. I've found that the best
course is usually to let one of my co-counsel be our liaison
with the media, while I hide somewhere behind a law book.

3

Making New Law

When Pauling rested his case, we made a motion to dismiss on the ground that, as a public figure, Pauling was covered by the stringent libel rules in the *New York Times* case, and he had failed to prove that the articles were published with "reckless disregard" of whether they were false or not. It was a *pro forma* motion which we did not expect to win because we had made similar motions at various times throughout the trial and they had been denied. This time, Judge Silverman reserved his decision.

We were now ready to begin presentation of our defense: that the articles about Pauling were true and that they were fair comment on his public record. Bill Buckley was to be our first witness. I was excited because I had spent weeks working on his proposed testimony. In addition, I had tried to anticipate how Matar might cross examine Buckley, so that Buckley would know what to expect. I had written a memo entitled "Preparing for Possible Pitfalls: Testimony of William F. Buckley," which included the following warnings:

> Buckley should be prepared for a line-by-line analysis of the articles, similar to the one experienced by Rusher. This is

certain to be the procedure for the two articles [in suit] and may also be the case for the additional articles introduced on the question of malice, particularly those written by Buckley.*

Buckley and Rusher have different interpretations of several things in the two main articles, but this is not important because Buckley is the author of the second article and is the only one who knows what he intended. In any case, the impact of the words is up to the jury, regardless of what the writer actually intended.

In the second article, watch out for:

a—"newspaper accounts." Rusher testified that this is a reference to the *Faulk* verdict (Direct, 837). Buckley said this refers to accounts of Pauling's litigious activities. (Buckley EBT 352)†

b—"litigious goose pimples." Rusher said on direct (835) that this refers to Pauling's threatened suit against *National Review*, not his suits against other publications.

c—meaning of "pusillanimous." Matar is certain to tease Buckley about his use of the English language and his impressive vocabulary. Matar himself sometimes misuses or mispronounces words, and it is our hope that Buckley's reaction to this will be characterized by a lack of hubris.‡

---

* Pauling's theory was that, motivated by ill will (the pre-*Times* definition of "malice"), *National Review*'s editors had been conducting a campaign against him, intending to vilify him. He tried to prove this by introducing other articles which named him, published in the magazine both before and after the articles in suit. Some of the other articles had been written by Buckley.

† "EBT" stands for "examination before trial," a pre-trial deposition which is intended to apprise each side of the other's position, to avoid surprise and make for speedier trials. If there is a conflict between someone's testimony at an EBT and trial, that can be used to impeach the witness's credibility. The Faulk case to which Rusher referred is a leading libel case in which the plaintiff recovered damages from a defendant which named him in an anti-Communist blacklist.

‡ Although this memorandum was written in the third person, it was meant for use by Buckley and I knew he was going to read it carefully. As you can see, we were worried about the jury's reaction to the customary demeanor of our star client. This was intended to be a not-at-all-subtle reminder that, hard as it might be, he should occasionally look humble.

d—Buckley's understanding of the meaning of "fellow traveler" "collaborationist" and "Communist front organization." Buckley might make reference to the International Security Act, SISS and HUAC reports, as well as his own daily use of the words.

e—What other suits brought by Pauling did Buckley know of at the time he wrote the second article?

Matar's second line of questions will concern the particulars of Pauling's associations. To understand how he does this, see Rusher Direct, 556 and following. His style is to ask questions in these categories:

a—How did you learn of these associations? (e.g. letterhead, newspaper story, etc.)

b—What was Pauling's particular activity in connection with this group? (e.g. signed petition, member, etc.) It won't hurt to admit ignorance on some of these, if that is the case. Buckley is not claiming to be a walking library.

c—Matar is sure to ask questions about "numerous other subversive activities." See Rusher Direct 607.

Matar will probably try to show that the first article was written by Buckley. Throughout the trial he has accused Burnham of being a front-man for Buckley and has attempted to discredit any testimony relating to Burnham's authorship of the article.

One big problem with both Buckley and Rusher is that each has independent knowledge of Pauling's activities; things would have been simpler if they had just relied on Burnham's knowledge as an expert. However, in case the jury buys the "Trotsky-Burnham" theory that Matar is pushing, Buckley's independent knowledge may be helpful.

See Buckley EBT 142. He says that he made the statement that Pauling was a "fellow traveler" on the basis of his own knowledge of Pauling's career in politics. Buckley should be prepared to name the committee reports which he has read which deal with Pauling's activities.

Buckley should be prepared to name and prove by documentation the people with whom Pauling associated whom he should have known were Communists. See Buckley EBT 301.

I had consulted with Buckley numerous times about his testimony. He was understandably frustrated at being excluded from the courtroom by order of his lawyers, but he appreciated our reasons. Now he was like a thoroughbred at the gate, anxious to have his day in court.

On the morning we were scheduled to open the defense case, I called for Bill and his wife Pat at their East Side town house. Trial tactics demanded Pat Buckley's appearance at her husband's side. If Ava Pauling had shown her support of her husband, Pat could do no less. Besides, after six weeks of trial, I was tired of being asked by the press and spectators if I was Williams's secretary. It would be good to have another woman at the defense table. (Several reporters had asked me if I was Buckley's wife. My presence seemed a continuing mystery. No one thought to ask me if I was a lawyer.)

Although I had never met her before, Pat Buckley and I had had several telephone conversations about what she should wear in court. We didn't want her to alienate the jurors by overdressing, or to give them the impression that she and her husband wouldn't miss the one million dollars for which Pauling was suing. I had consented (sight unseen) to what she described as "a simple blue suit." When I saw her that morning, I groaned inwardly. Her idea of a "simple blue suit" was a silk ensemble with matching pillbox hat and white gloves—an outfit that looked straight out of *Vogue* when worn by that chic, slender woman who was almost six feet tall. I hoped that the jurors would be impressed rather than alienated. I suspected that, if anything, their sympathies would be aroused by seeing her on crutches, the result of a serious skiing accident.

As it turned out, the jurors never got to see her. They were out of the courtroom when the Buckleys made their first appearance, because Judge Silverman was asking for a delay in the proceedings. "I have some thinking to do," he said in essence. He then recessed court for two days. None of us knew what it was he wanted to think about, but we hoped that he might change his mind and rule favorably on our motion based on the *Times* case.

The following Wednesday, April 19, 1966, the courtroom was packed with representatives of the media, people from *National Review* and our office, and members of the public. Among the spectators was a tall, stately woman. I poked Al Koller, who was sitting beside me. "That's the judge's wife," I said. "I met her when I delivered papers to the judge at his home."

"What's she doing here?" Koller wondered aloud.

"I think it's a good sign," I replied. "I'll bet she came to hear her husband give the most brilliant decision of his career, the dismissal of Pauling's case." Koller smiled hopefully.

We rose as the judge entered the courtroom, holding a sheaf of typewritten papers in his hands. The room was silent as he announced: "I have decided to grant the motion of the defense and to order the dismissal of the plaintiff's case." There were murmurs of surprise from the spectators. As Judge Silverman banged his gavel for order, I watched Mrs. Matar, who was sitting at the counsel table, reach over and take her husband's hand. It was a poignant gesture and made me realize how hard he too must have worked on this case.

We listened attentively as the judge began to read his decision. First, he detailed the content of the articles in suit. Then he said that "the critical question on the present motion" was whether the doctrine of the *Times* case "should be extended to apply to the present case, and, if so, whether plaintiff has proved a prima facie case under the doctrine." He noted that Pauling was not a public official, which was the express situation to which the *Times* doctrine applied, so that the threshold question was whether the *Times* doctrine "has any applicability to his case at all." Matar had been arguing that it did not.

Judge Silverman then explained what he understood to be the heart of the *Times* decision:

> In determining the relative importance and protection to be given to the interest in public discussion, on the one hand, and the safeguarding of individual reputation on the other hand, the Supreme Court, in the *New York Times* case, has shifted the balance sharply in favor of the freedom of public discussion.

After stressing the importance of the "freedom of public discussion," Judge Silverman got to the heart of the matter:

> These considerations, stated by the court [in the *Times* case] with reference to public officials, would seem to be equally applicable to a private person who publicly, prominently, actively, and as a leader, thrusts himself (however properly) into a public discussion of public and exceedingly controversial questions.

In other words, Judge Silverman held that the *Times* rule applied not only to public officials but to public figures as well. The question now was whether Pauling fell into this category. This Judge Silverman dealt with by outlining some of Pauling's testimony about his participation in numerous public political activities. "It is clear," the judge concluded, "that if any private person has, by his conduct, made himself a public figure engaged voluntarily in public discussion of matters of grave public concern and controversy, Dr. Pauling has done so." He then went on to explain the consequences of his characterization of Pauling as a public figure:

> Accordingly, I hold that, in order for Dr. Pauling to recover, it would be necessary for him to meet the standards of New York Times Co. v. Sullivan.

> The basic principle of New York Times Co. v. Sullivan is that, in the cases to which it applies, there can be no recovery for even a defamatory falsehood unless the plaintiff proves that the statement was made "with knowledge that it was false or with reckless disregard of whether it was false or not."

This was the "actual malice" which we had discussed at length. Judge Silverman held that in this case there was "no real evidence that defendants knew that the statements they made were false." For this reason, the complaint had to be dismissed.

He could have stopped there, but he did not. After six weeks in the courtroom, even Judge Silverman was impressed with Linus Pauling the man. In an unusual step, he included in his legal decision a paragraph which emphasized his own feelings about the plaintiff and his activities.

> Lest there be any misunderstanding, I do not hold that the charges against Dr. Pauling made in the articles, are true or justified. It is clear that in all his actions, Dr. Pauling acted well within his legal rights. . . . Dr. Pauling has added the prestige of his reputation to aid the causes in which he believes. I merely hold that by so doing he also limited his legal remedies for any claimed libel of his reputation. And perhaps this can be deemed another sacrifice that he is making for the things he believes in.

The defendants and their supporters were delighted with the decision, and as soon as the judge left the courtroom, there was loud applause and much hugging. I had mixed feelings. I was happy that we had won, but disappointed that, after so much work preparing the defense, we weren't going to get a chance to present it. And worse was the knowledge that my temporary job was at an end.

When the jurors were dismissed from the box, at least five of them ran over to Pauling for his autograph. I was tempted to do the same thing myself. Makla, Koller, and I meandered toward the jurors and tried to engage them in conversation, to discover how the case might have gone if Judge Silverman hadn't taken it away from the jury. Indications were that about half the jurors were for Pauling and about half for us, which wasn't bad, considering that we hadn't presented our defense yet. Even so, Mrs. Avila was the only juror who was openly friendly.

I have in my scrapbook a photograph taken that day. It shows the jubilant victors standing outside the Supreme Court building. I am looking toward Williams, who is standing directly to my left and whom the news photographer undiplomatically cut out of the picture, causing no small consternation in our office. On my right is the greatest editor in the world, giving forth a superlative version of the famous gleaming smile. With the eyes of the world upon him on this momentous occasion, his fly is open.

The morning after the decision was announced, I received a telegram from Buckley: "Thanks for all you did to help win this case." I learned that he had sent a telegram to every person in the office who had been connected with the case, including all the secretaries of the lawyers who represented the defense. And he had taken the time to word each telegram differently. It was a lovely thing to have done, so typical of him.

Williams gave a victory party and Bill sent over a case of champagne. Plentifully refilled with the bubbly stuff, Mrs. Schade's mouth began to move. "Miss Schwartz didn't agree with a lot of Mr. Williams's tactics," she announced generally to the assembled revelers, at least ninety-nine percent of whom were dedicated conservatives. "She doesn't think Pauling is a Communist."

I tried to muffle her. Free speech was one thing, but I still wanted a decent recommendation from Williams to attach to the second hundred letters I would soon have to send out. Happily, victory brought euphoria, and if anyone heard Mrs. Schade, her comment was allowed to pass.

The trial was over, but there was still much work to be done on the case. Since Judge Silverman made new law, it was likely that the decision would be appealed by Pauling. So we had to organize the voluminous files and exhibits and attempt to translate the piles of illegible notes we had taken at the trial. In the midst of this turmoil, Al Koller left the firm, went to Germany, and got married. With the connivance of his co-workers, I sent a telegram of congratulations over the names of all the junior partners and associates—and Linus Pauling. Not that our recent adversary had agreed to lend his name to this totally apolitical cause, but I thought he wouldn't mind.

A year later, the Pauling case came back into our lives. It was now on appeal. Pauling had switched lawyers and was represented in the Appellate Division by Louis Nizer's firm. We were unsure why Nizer had taken this case. It was certainly a hard case to get reversed on the law, because Judge Silverman had written a good opinion. And, politically, Pauling was on the side of repression in that he was seeking to narrow First Amendment free-speech protections. I'd always thought that Nizer was a liberal, so I was surprised that he agreed to handle the case. Maybe he took it out of respect for Pauling, or perhaps because of the publicity attached to the case. It would be a coup if he could beat Buckley and company.

We received a long legal brief on behalf of Pauling. The crux of the argument in it was that Judge Silverman's extension of the doctrine in *New York Times* versus Sullivan to "these defamatory, personal attacks" on Pauling, "a private person who has never been a public official or candidate," was "unwarranted, improper and unsound." The brief urged that the application of the *Times* principles to "private individuals in the course of discussions of public matters . . . would not encourage, but would gravely impair freedom of speech."

Our answering brief in support of Judge Silverman's decision was equally long and rich in rhetoric. Its theme was

summarized in a paragraph I wrote that succinctly expressed
my own feelings about the case.

> Appellant [Pauling] and respondents [*National Review,*
> Rusher, and Buckley] may disagree as to the motivations
> behind appellant's activities, but disagreement is the essence
> of free speech. We question whether the spirit of the First
> Amendment is served if Pauling, himself a legitimate object
> of polemical comment, is permitted to voice his views with
> impunity, and his political opponents forced to hold their
> peace for fear of retaliation by means of costly libel suits.

It was afternoon and we were at the Appellate Division
on Twenty-fifth Street in Manhattan, waiting to be called
for argument of the appeal. There were a number of other
cases before ours. I figured we would be on in about twenty
minutes. An associate from Nizer's firm had been waiting
in the anteroom, but I knew he was not going to argue the
case and I wondered where the senior partner was. I wandered out to talk with him.

"Where is your man?" I asked.

"He is staying in the office uptown until I give him the
word. He'll come down when I telephone."

"But argument is in about twenty minutes," I said. "He'll
never have time to get here."

He looked up with dismay. "What do you mean? I thought
it wouldn't be for another hour or so." He added up the
amount of time each of the cases before us on the calendar
had requested and discovered that he had miscalculated. He
slapped his hand to his forehead and frantically ran toward
the nearest phone booth.

The case was called and Nizer's firm was still represented
in court only by the associate. With his odd, shuffling walk,
he approached the bench. "Your Honor," he said to the Presiding Justice, "the lawyer who will argue this case on behalf
of Dr. Pauling isn't here yet." He explained why, taking the

blame on himself. He asked the Court to wait ten minutes for the partner, who was on his way by taxi.

The Presiding Justice asked the associate why he didn't argue the case himself. But the associate didn't have the courage to do this. For the next year of his life, he would castigate himself for his cowardice. "If only I'd argued the case, or at least begun argument and carried the ball until the senior partner arrived, it would have made my career," he would say.

I tried to console him by reminding him that if he had begun argument and it hadn't gone well, it would have finished his career; you don't take over a senior partner's case without permission, especially if you're an inexperienced associate. Anyway, he hadn't done it. He told the Court that he couldn't take the responsibility for argument and again asked the judges to wait.

The Presiding Justice refused his request. Instead, he made a speech on the duty of lawyers to be prompt and the necessity of courtesy to the Court. He was annoyed and he showed it. The associate stood before him looking desolate, convinced that this would ruin his career (it didn't). The Presiding Justice asked us if we wished to argue, in the absence of adversarial dialogue.

"Your Honor, we are urging that the decision below be affirmed. No argument has first been made that it should be reversed, so there is nothing for us to answer. We are willing to submit the cause on the briefs, without argument."

The Court ordered the case marked "submitted." This meant that the case would be decided on the briefs, without any oral argument. We were amazed that this had happened. Submission of a major case like this was unheard of. "Let's get out of here," Williams said, "before someone from Nizer's firm shows up."

Pauling's case had been immeasurably prejudiced by what had happened in court and Williams didn't want any of us

to be around for the inevitable disturbance when Pauling's
lawyer finally arrived. We left, I with a sad backward glance
at my fellow associate, who was still pacing in the anteroom.
A few months later, Judge Silverman's decision was unanimously affirmed without an opinion.

Another year passed, and like the tides and seasons, the
Pauling case returned once again to consume our time and
interest. It was now in the highest court in New York State,
the Court of Appeals.

It wasn't clear to me why Pauling continued to fight an
almost certain losing battle. His position was now even more
difficult than it had been before. Not only had two courts
dismissed his claims, but a couple of months after the Appellate Division's affirmance the Supreme Court of the United
States had come down with two important cases in the field
of libel: Curtis Publishing Company versus Butts and Associated Press versus Walker. Both involved plaintiffs who
were not public officials but, like Pauling, were definitely
public figures. In Butts and Walker, the Court held:

> A "public figure" who is not a public official may also recover
> damages for a defamatory falsehood whose substance makes
> substantial danger to reputation apparent, [only] on a show-
> ing of highly unreasonable conduct constituting an extreme
> departure from the standards of investigation and reporting
> ordinarily adhered to by responsible publishers.

In other words, the *Times* doctrine had been extended from
public officials to public figures, who would also have to
show "actual malice" before recovering for libel. The Court
even cited with approval Judge Silverman's opinion in Pauling versus *National Review*.

I suppose Pauling continued to appeal his case in the
hope that a higher court would hold that he had met the
Times standard—that he had proven *National Review* had
published the articles with "actual malice," in disregard of

"ordinary" standards of investigation. I thought he had a tough case. *National Review* hadn't said anything much different from what other publications and semi-official government sources had said about Pauling. Under those circumstances, how could Pauling show that the magazine's conduct constituted "an extreme departure" (Butts-Walker) from journalistic standards?

The briefs submitted by both sides were essentially the same as those we had filed in the Appellate Division. The date of argument was set, and Williams and I flew to Albany, I to perform my usual function as chief book carrier and note taker, to sit next to Williams during oral argument, passing him small yellow papers with suggestions, comments, reminders, citations, and the like.

Nizer took no chances; he was in court at least an hour before argument. I introduced myself and we exchanged small talk. I had expected a blustering, overbearing fellow, but he was very pleasant—especially considering the fact that most lawyers are tense and short-tempered before argument and want to be left alone.

The case was called. Before argument commenced, Judge Kenneth Keating began to speak. "A letter has been received by this Court from Mr. Nizer, asking that I disqualify myself from hearing this case," he said.

"What letter?" Williams whispered to me. I shrugged my shoulders. I had no idea what Judge Keating was talking about. It is basic procedure that when any communication is made to a court, copies are sent to opposing counsel. But we had received no copy of this obviously important letter which Nizer had sent to the Court of Appeals. This was probably no more than a clerical error by someone in his office, but it was still awkward.

Judge Keating revealed that the ground upon which he had been asked to disqualify himself was that when he was a senator from New York, he had been a member of a committee that had investigated Linus Pauling. Nizer had suggested that the judge's background might prejudice him in this case. "I don't think that I would be prejudiced," Judge Keating said. "But to avoid even the appearance of prejudice, since the possibility of my prejudice has been suggested, I am disqualifying myself." He then rose from his chair and left the courtroom.

We were stunned. Although there were a number of other judges on the bench that would be hearing the case, we had been counting on Judge Keating and were sure he would vote with us. Williams was so unprepared for this development that he forgot to tell the Court that we had not received a copy of Nizer's letter. After argument, he remedied this oversight by writing a letter to the Court (copy to Nizer), pointing out that we had not received timely notice of Nizer's request that Judge Keating recuse himself. As things turned out, it didn't matter.

Nizer began argument from a high stack of legal pads, each page of which had only a few lines of writing on it. He combined the factual and the emotional for what I thought was an articulate argument but one that wasn't as exciting as I'd expected. Williams's argument was not as punchy as I'd hoped it would be either. That was probably because of overconfidence, an understandable feeling even in the face of Judge Keating's unexpected recusal. After all, we had an unbeaten record in this case and the decisions in Butts and Walker made it almost certain we would win the appeal.

The confidence was justified. Several months later, the decision in our favor was again unanimously affirmed. The Court's opinion was extremely short.

> We agree that the complaint before us was properly dismissed. It is unnecessary to decide whether the charges leveled by the defendants against the plaintiff are true or justified. The statements which they made concerned one

who, concededly, was and is a "public figure" [citing Curtis Publishing Co. versus Butts]. Accordingly, we need to go no further than to say that we find, as did the courts below, that the plaintiff failed to establish the fact, essential to the cause of action, that the defendants published the statements in question either with "knowledge" of their falsity or with "reckless disregard" of whether they were true or false [citing *New York Times* versus Sullivan], or with a "high degree of awareness" of their probable falsity or that the defendants "in fact" entertained "serious doubts" as to their truth. The order appealed from should be affirmed, with costs.

Here was one case Nizer wouldn't devote any space to in his next book. (Which isn't meant to demean Mr. Nizer. The only lawyers who never lose cases are lawyers who have no cases.)

Pauling decided not to petition the Supreme Court. He had thrice been unsuccessful and was probably unwilling to spend any more money on this litigation, the outcome of which appeared predictable. After two years of being an important part of my life, the case of Pauling versus *National Review*, William A. Rusher, and William F. Buckley came to a lazy close.

4

The Six-Day War and Other Office Battles

One may ask how I parlayed what was supposed to be a temporary job into one which went on for over three years. During the several months it took to organize the files after Judge Silverman's decision in the Pauling case, I expected each day to be my last. Instead, Williams asked me to stay on for another two or three months, to help him work on a case involving allegedly substandard sugar that the company we were defending had sold to the United States government. It wasn't exactly on a plane with the Pauling case, but I agreed to stay.

The sugar case ended in a pre-trial settlement and I was given miscellaneous small tasks around the office. Then, one hot July day: "Helene," said Williams, "I've spent the last three weeks arguing with my partners about you."

"What do you mean?"

"I've been satisfied with your work and I want to hire you on a permanent basis. But there has been opposition because some of the partners don't like the idea of hiring a woman lawyer. However, I'm happy to say that I've won and I hope that you will stay with me."

My immediate response was to accept. Security at last!

Perhaps this was unfortunate. In retrospect, I should have given more thought to whether I, both because I am a woman and because of my distinctive personality, was meant to be a Wall Street lawyer. In too many ways, I wasn't; but it took me a long time to get out.

Like many women, I have often been told by men that women have characteristics which make them unsuitable as lawyers. This sort of attitude has always seemed strange to me. I've never thought that characteristics can be categorized as "male" or "female." For example, I happen to be a volatile creature, a trait which most people think is "typically female." But in this respect both my brother Barry and I take after our father, not our mother, she being one of the most even-tempered people I've ever met. Gender doesn't necessarily determine personality and it certainly has little to do with the ability one brings to the law.

Naturally, I do have personal characteristics that influence my work (and so does every man). Among these is a refusal, call it stubbornness, to be cowed by people or institutions of authority. I have to be shown that authority is worthy of respect and I unhesitatingly attack it when it is not. This is a good attitude to have when you're a lawyer. Law is one field in which it does one no good to be cowed by dogmatic respect and knee-jerk responses to authority, particularly if that authority is the law itself.

I've always thought that was one way in which I was much like Williams, and was a reason why we got along so well. As a lawyer, he was definitely of the old "bulldog" school: pugnacious and undaunted by the fact that the law might be against his client on a particular point. His attitude was that if the law was against him, it was probably wrong and should be changed. The books are filled with cases in which he "shaped" the law on behalf of his clients. Sometimes, like all lawyers, he made "good" law, sometimes "bad." But even when the law he made was "bad," he fulfilled one of the most important functions of the lawyer: to find the holes in the law, so they can be plugged up. The best lesson I learned during my years with him was the value of straightforward attacks on "wrong" law. It was a lesson I learned well and easily because it fit so comfortably into a facet of my own personality.

In other ways, though, I was singularly unsuited for life as a Wall Street lawyer. I chafed at the long hours in an office where brittle silence was the rule (even Muzak would have been an improvement) and the occasional whispered joke which produced a raucous laugh was followed by a reprimand. I couldn't get used to my own nervousness when the receptionist marked me present at 10:10 in the morning, instead of 9:30. I felt like a cheat when I began leaving the office at 6:01, so that the daily sign-in sheet would show me as still "here" when the receptionist left at 6:00; perhaps some senior partner would be misled into thinking I'd worked until ten that night. I hated dressing like Jane Eyre when I wanted to be wearing fishnet stockings or one of the newly fashionable pants suits. It was against my grain to sit politely and listen to a senior partner pontificate about a case to a client or a judge when I, who had done the research, knew more about the case than he did. I resisted the impulse to stand up and yell, "Garbage!"

No, I have never been a good follower, which sometimes made me less than the perfect employee. On the whole, I did what I was told, but occasionally I lapsed. My revolts, when they took place, were generally trivial. For example, I discovered that if I turned the back of my big leather desk chair toward the door of my office, I could slink down and disappear in its confines. In this position, I would sometimes take an afternoon nap. When I awoke, I would be faced with the problem of accounting for the lost hour on my time sheets. I'd usually pick the most aggravating client of the week and let him pay for my siesta. "Research, Doe case, one hour." This might be accounted eccentric behavior for a Wall Street associate, but I never felt it was dishonest. I spent so much time working beyond normal hours that when I was tired, I figured I deserved a rest.

Two or three times a year, my temper surfaced. Once, Mrs. Schade and I were Xeroxing and collating twenty-four copies of an eighty-page memorandum to a client. It was a tedious job and we'd been at it for five hours when Williams came into the library (where we were working) and announced that he did not like the way the covers were attached to the front pages. I guess I was already overwrought by the idea that nineteen years of schooling had ill prepared me for this drudgery, because I erupted. On the verge of a screaming tantrum, I left the office. Ten minutes later, after purchasing some frilly lingerie, I returned to the library and continued sorting the memo as though nothing had happened.

Only once did I lose my cool completely and take a stand against the law of absolute obedience. It was a difficult time for me because I, who fight hard on behalf of others, am often strangely unable to protect myself. But in this instance a confrontation was necessary to preserve my own self-respect, which had been slowly diminishing while I tried to fit the mold of the Wall Street regular. I had to struggle or the person I had known all my life would disappear altogether.

It began during the Six-Day War in June 1967, on the day I learned that the Israelis had captured the old sector of Jerusalem. I had already been to Israel twice: once in 1963 (a summer's respite from law school) to teach English to immigrant children from Arab lands; and a second time, in 1965, after the bar exam, to visit the children and my cousins who lived in Israel. Each time, I'd taken the train to the Israeli sector of Jerusalem. I'd climbed to the top of Mount Zion, the highest point in the city near the Jordanian border. From there, I would stare in the direction of the Old City of Jerusalem. I longed to see the Wailing Wall, the Dome of

the Rock, the other ancient sites. But Old Jerusalem had
been in Arab hands since the 1948 war and the Jordanians
had persistently refused me a visa. Now, for the first time,
the entire city was within my reach. I was obsessed; I had
to get to Jerusalem.

The fighting was still going on and the State Department
had temporarily invalidated American passports for travel in
the war zone. In addition, Jerusalem was off limits to all but
soldiers and journalists. "Do you think Bill Buckley would
give me press credentials?" I asked Williams. I explained
why I wanted them, and Williams agreed to think about
what Buckley's reaction might be to such a request.

The next morning, I got a phone call from Williams. "I'm
having breakfast with Bill," he said. "I just asked him
whether he would be willing to give you press credentials
from *National Review* and he says that he would be happy
to do it. I thought you'd like to know."

What a surprise! When I'd asked Williams to allow me to
approach his number-one client (something one didn't do
without permission), I'd never thought he'd take it upon
himself to do the asking for me. It was a lovely thing for him
to have done, but I was so excited that I could barely tumble
out my thanks. "And thank Bill too," I said as I hung up the
phone. Then I let out a howl that had Corrine Schade running into the office. "What's the matter?"

"I'm going to Jerusalem!"

She smiled indulgently. For the past few days I'd done
nothing but think aloud and plan about how I could get to
Jerusalem. And I was still at it. My brother Barry had never
been to Israel and I was trying to think of a way to wangle
him into this trip.

I called Buckley to thank him for the credentials. "I don't
know what to say, Bill. I'm so excited about this trip that
I can't begin to express how I feel."

"Just charge it to Linus Pauling," Buckley replied. "I'm

delighted to be able to help you. I'll send you a press card and a letter of introduction this afternoon. And you'll need another letter, to the Israeli Consul General in New York. He just called me the other day to thank me for my columns and articles supporting Israel. You shouldn't have any trouble with him," he said. "Now, is there anything else I can do?"

I was again charmed by Buckley's thoughtfulness, though after several years of acquaintance it shouldn't have surprised me. And his last words gave me an idea. "My brother has never been to Israel," I began, "and I'd like to take him with me."

Before I could say anything further, Buckley anticipated my request. "Should I send a press card for him too? We can make him your photographer."

I called the Israeli press attaché. As Buckley had predicted, I was warmly received when I told him that I represented *National Review*. "Whom would you like to see when you are in Israel?" he asked me. I hadn't thought about that. In my excitement about going to Jerusalem, I'd forgotten that I was supposed to be a journalist. "I'd like to see Defense Minister Moshe Dayan, Commander-in-Chief Yitzhak Rabin, Teddy Kollek [the mayor of Israeli Jerusalem], and whoever was the mayor of Old Jerusalem before the war." The events of the past few days had given me nerve.

"I'll cable instructions to Jerusalem," he said.

When Barry and I arrived in Israel, we rented a car and drove to Jerusalem. We saw the Wailing Wall, and for some reason I was perplexed to find that it was nothing more than that—row upon row of big stones making an enormous wall. Then why were there tears in my eyes? We took our shoes off and entered the awesome, beautiful Dome of the Rock. We meandered through the Old City, saw Rachel's Tomb in Bethlehem and the traditional sites of the graves of Abraham and his family in Hebron. Everywhere, we were surrounded by ecstatic Jews, dipping and praying before the Wall, touching with reverence the ancient relics, crying at the sight of Jewish gravestones used for roadbeds in Jordan, laughing from the sheer relief and happiness of seeing the old sites and knowing that, at least for the present, they were safe and accessible.

Our instinct for pilgrimage temporarily satisfied, we became journalists. With a military press pass, we toured the restricted areas. We heard shooting at Allenby Bridge and terrorist bombs exploded while we were in Shechem and Gaza. We took a military press tour of Sinai. Thousands of abandoned Egyptian trucks and tanks of Russian origin lined the roads, as though in parade formation. We saw the Suez Canal, the hastily evacuated homes in Qantara, the pathetic boots of the Egyptian soldiers. After fourteen hours in a bus jogging over bombed-out roads, we arrived at the captured Egyptian airbase at Bir Gafgafa, where we spent the night. I have a photo of me, taken at four the next morning, standing in front of my tent. I am wearing my brother's shirt and a creased, stained skirt. My hair is in bunches and my hands are on my hips. I look tough. I am Marguerite Higgins Schwartz.

Back to Tel Aviv. Our requests to see Rabin and the former mayor of Old Jerusalem had been denied, for "security reasons." We were number 180 on the list of journalists who wanted to see Dayan and would probably be reached in several years. But Teddy Kollek, mayor of Israeli Jerusalem, agreed to see us.

"What do you want to know?" he asked brusquely when we met him at eight the next morning. The old Religious Studies major in me was moved to ask: "What are you doing to ensure the protection of the Moslem holy places in the captured areas?"

"It is obvious that you haven't done your homework. If you want an answer to that question," Kollek said angrily, "read this week's issue of *Time* magazine, don't bother me about it." Minutes later, he stalked out of his office, leaving Barry and me still sitting in front of his desk.

"Let's get out of here," Barry said.

"Yes, but let's not go through the front door. I don't want to bump into Kollek," I said.

We hastily surveyed the room, looking for another door. We saw one on the other side of the room, rushed toward it, flung it open, and ran in, only to discover ourselves in a huge coat closet. Reluctantly, we went through the front door. We never saw Kollek again.

I was mystified by Kollek's anger. It occurred to me that *Time* magazine must have done a cover story which I'd missed, entitled "What Teddy Kollek is Doing to Ensure Protection of the Moslem Holy Places in Jerusalem." I got copies of back issues and watched *Time* for the next month. Nothing. Barry and I decided that Kollek, who was working twenty-four hours a day to unify the administration of the once-divided city, had probably been exhausted when he saw us, which would justify his otherwise inexplicable behavior. But in the process he managed to squelch my burgeoning career as a journalist.

September 8, 1967

Dear Helene,

I haven't read your piece but intend to do so over the weekend—Priscilla [Buckley; managing editor of *National Review*] says it is first-rate. This is just to acknowledge with thanks your kind letter. I am delighted you had such a fine trip. My regards to your brother.

Yours faithfully,
WFB

A few weeks after I submitted the story to *National Review*, Williams called me into his office and closed the door, always a serious sign. "Helene," he said, "I've read your story [which I'd given him as a courtesy], and I enjoyed it very much. You must have had a wonderful time in the Middle East." I smiled and nodded. "But I'm afraid it can't be printed."

"Why?" I asked. "Doesn't Buckley like it?"

"He does," Williams said. "In fact, he wants to publish it. But we can't allow that."

"What are you talking about?" I asked. I hadn't even known Buckley intended to publish the article, and I couldn't figure out what Williams was leading up to.

"The article is very pro-Israel," Williams began.

"No, it isn't," I interrupted. "It's totally bland and apolitical. It just describes some scenes I saw. It's no more than a few vignettes. Priscilla told me that's what she and Bill wanted, and that's what they got."

"Well, my partners don't agree with you."

"Level with me, Mr. Williams," I said. "What's at the bottom of this?"

"Helene, I don't think your article was very political myself," he said. The trouble was one of his partners, call him Sam Hardy. "Hardy thinks that it is too pro-Israel. He represents the Indian government and the Indians haven't been in favor of Israel recently. Hardy is afraid that if the Indians see your article and know that someone in this office has been to Israel they will be offended."

"But I went to Israel on my own time, on my vacation," I said. "It had nothing to do with this office."

"I know," Williams said. "But Hardy is afraid that the Indians won't understand."

"What does Bill Buckley have to say about all of this?" I asked. I couldn't imagine Buckley being intimidated by what Hardy thought.

"That's the trouble," Williams answered. "Bill still wants to print it, even though Hardy has said that he won't allow it to be printed."

"Then it's a question of your most valued client against Hardy's?" I asked.

"Yes."

"Are you going to let Hardy win? Buckley won't stand for it."

"Hardy knows that. He says that it's up to you to stop Bill from publishing the article. Tell him you've changed your mind and don't want it printed," Williams said.

"Not on your life. No one in this office has the right to tell me what to do with my time after hours. If Buckley wants to print that article, I'm delighted. I'm not lifting a finger to stop him."

I was furious. Did Williams really think I would do as Hardy wished, without a fight? By what right did they think they could prevent me from having the article published? They could force me to dress a certain way in the office; chain me to a desk to read law books eight to twelve hours a day; insist that I fill out those insidious forms accounting for every minute of my time; hound me for long memoranda of law on subjects they just told me about twenty minutes ago; make my life tedious five days a week, six, and sometimes seven. But what little time was left over was mine and it was never more precious than now, when it was being threatened. Ordinarily, it wouldn't have made much difference to me whether the article was published or not, but this was a matter of principle. What was the sense of fighting for freedom of the press in the Pauling case if it was a freedom that didn't extend to me? What kind of life was I leading if they could interfere with it to such a degree?

I didn't want to be totally unreasonable. I was willing to compromise. Although I thought Hardy was being over-concerned about the sensibilities of the Indians, I wouldn't risk offending his client. I told Williams that I was willing to use a pseudonym, so that the Indians would never know I was associated with the firm. Hardy rejected this, too. He didn't want the article published under any circumstances. That did it. I told Williams that either the article got published or I would quit my job.

I left Williams to deal with Hardy. I knew that he was concerned lest Hardy's reactions interfere with what Buckley and I wanted to do, and I was confident that he would put up a strong fight. And he did. Several days later, he told me that Hardy had reluctantly agreed that the article could be published if I agreed to use a pseudonym. I was not fully satisfied, but at least the article would appear. And the very fact that I had struggled on my own behalf, for what I thought was right, showed me that, under the façade of the obedient associate, the spirit stirred.

5

Tidbits from the Life of a Round Peg in the Square Hole

Without Bill Buckley and his case, life on Wall Street was much less exciting. Still, it had its high points. One memorable assignment in the summer of 1966 (soon after I had become a regular member of the staff) took me to Washington, D.C., to do research in connection with papers to be filed in the Supreme Court. The case itself wasn't especially interesting. It had to do with maritime rate differentials and shipment of agricultural commodities under the Cargo Preference Act. Even so, I enjoyed wandering around congressional office buildings, meeting with senators and representatives, while investigating the legislative history of the Act. Then I got a call from Williams.

"We're still waiting for the settlement in that sugar case," he told me. "Our client has agreed to pay the government $25,000 in damages. But before the U.S. Attorney in New York can accept the check, the settlement has to be okayed by the Justice Department in Washington. Please go to the Justice Department and see what is holding up their consent to the settlement."

The next afternoon, after I'd finished my other work, I walked over to the Justice Department. I'd been given the name of a Department attorney who was supposed to know something about the case. He was a charming, languorous fellow who told me that the papers had been on the Attorney General's desk for several weeks. He didn't know why they hadn't been signed, so I thanked him and left.

The reception area in the Attorney General's office was empty. Through an open door, I saw a tall, husky man standing behind a desk. "May I help you?" he called politely through the doorway.

I entered his office and introduced myself. "My name is Helene E. Schwartz. I'm an attorney from New York. Who are you?"

He smiled at me. "I'm Nicholas Katzenbach," said the Attorney General. Just the man I wanted to see. Surely he should know why those papers hadn't been signed. I explained the reason for my visit. "What's the name of the case?" he asked.

I told him and he rummaged around on his desk until he found the file. "How come they haven't been okayed?" I asked, as though the only thing Nicholas Katzenbach had to worry about was my case. Instead of sitting on me as I deserved, he said, almost apologetically, that he had been busy testifying before a congressional committee about the latest civil-rights bill. He promised to look over the papers immediately and, if they were in order, to send the consents to the New York office by morning.

When I reached my hotel, it was after six, too late to call the office. The next morning, I called Williams. Before I had a chance to tell him of my meeting with Katzenbach, he said: "The papers in the sugar case came through this morning, so you don't have to bother going to the Justice Department."

"I know all about it," I replied. "Mr. Katzenbach promised me yesterday that the matter would be taken care of this morning."

"Mister who?" Williams asked.

"Mr. Katzenbach; you know, the Attorney General. I saw him yesterday afternoon." Perhaps I had misunderstood my instructions. "Didn't you tell me to go to the Justice Department and find out why the papers weren't signed? The man you sent me to didn't have the information, so I just looked around until I got the right answers."

"Well, I hardly expected you to go to the Attorney General," he said with increasing astonishment.

"Why not? He's the one who was holding everything up. Who else could I have asked?"

I could almost see Williams nodding his head in despair. "Oh," he said, "the glorious naïveté of the young!" A pause, and then: "Only a woman would do a thing like that." And finally, in mixed tones of grudging admiration and perplexity: "Well done, Helene. Well done."

Throughout my tenure on Wall Street, the men remained suspicious of what they regarded as my unusual double role as woman and lawyer. Their instincts told them that I had no place in the courtroom. They preferred to see me as a super-secretary: carrying files, doing research, writing memos, and generally staying in the office or library. I didn't complain much about this. I felt lucky to have a job with a law firm, particularly in the litigation department. Many of my women classmates had difficulty getting a job with a law firm. Most of those who did were stuck in the trusts and estates department, where there was little contact with clients, and if there was, the clients were either too young or too old, or dead, to be offended by having their affairs handled by a woman. The men at my firm, especially Williams, had always been generous in allowing me client contact, and to my knowledge, after the initial surprise at first meeting, no client ever complained about my being a woman. It was a situation I appreciated.

The other reason why I didn't say much about the limita-

tions on my role as a litigator was that I was only an associate
and I knew that my male classmates at other Wall Street
firms were laboring under similar restrictions. They would
write the briefs and a senior partner would stand up and
argue in court. But after a while they began answering motions, arguing cases and the like, while I remained a closet
litigator. As I grew more confident of my lawyering skills,
I became resentful of my enforced silence in court, and I
began to press for more courtroom experience. Eventually,
I was allowed to answer motions, and occasionally I was
given responsibility for minor courtroom work. I didn't push
for more because I was conditioned by the men, and I understood that I had gone about as far as I could. My male classmates would become partners and have charge of major
litigation. I would always be a super-annuated associate if I
remained on Wall Street. That's the way things were in the
sixties, and I knew my place.

Christmas was not the season to be jolly at this firm. It was
the custom for the lawyers to get together for lunch. Never
had it occurred to them that it might be nice to take the
secretaries along for this annual bacchanal, an omission that
caused needless bitterness among the women. "A bunch of
black Protestants," sniffed one of the many Catholic secretaries. "We even had to fight for permission to decorate the
office."

Unknown to me, my first Christmas at the firm provoked a
crisis. Meetings among the partners took place behind closed
doors. As usual, the secretarial grapevine got the word and
Mrs. Brooks announced with glee: "Miss Schwartz, the men
don't know what to do about you." According to Mrs. Brooks,
the Christmas lunch was traditionally held at a downtown
club which allowed women to dine only in certain areas.
What was to be done about me?

I thought it was a big fuss over nothing, so I went to talk

to Williams about it. "I've got a solution to the problem," I said. "I have no desire to go to the Christmas luncheon. I'll stay away and you can have the luncheon wherever you want."

"Look, look, look," he cried. "You're one of the lawyers. You have to come. All the lawyers always come. Don't worry. We'll work something out." And they did. The annual occasion of forced jollity and simulated camaraderie between lowly associate and senior partner was moved, with much ado, to the Downtown Association, an equally solemn men's club, which allowed women to eat in the private dining rooms. In a blaze of secrecy, the partners dragged me up the back stairs. Years later, Williams insisted this was because the front elevator was broken, which was irrelevant. The point is that these eating clubs did not allow women members, and restricted women guests to certain dining areas, which made it difficult for me to lunch with colleagues and clients. Occasionally, I consented to eat in the "women's area" at one of these places, because at the time I didn't realize how degrading it was. Now I know better.

Bob Makla, Al Koller, and the other three junior partners and associates, William Dean, Clifford Lefebvre, and Robert Atkinson, were all bachelors, which made the only woman lawyer in the office the butt of a lot of teasing. Williams often reminded me, in his blunt but well-meaning way, "what a nice young man that Bill Dean is," or "what a good catch Cliff would be for some clever girl." He was right; they were good men and wonderful to work with, but that was it. I made it a policy never to date anyone in the office.

I usually had lunch with one of the men, but I had to be careful to rotate. If I didn't, there was sure to be gossip. "Lunching with Bob Atkinson rather frequently, aren't you?" Williams asked one day.

Mrs. Schade overheard Williams's comment, and when he

left, she said to me, "You know, Mr. Williams thinks that
you and Mr. Atkinson are dating."

"It's hopeless," I laughed. "Whenever I go to lunch with a
man two days in a row, everyone thinks that we're having
an affair. Either I ignore the gossip, or I lunch alone in my
office."

Money was a painful subject on Wall Street. The associates
at our firm were making less than associates at larger firms.
The argument was that our firm was too small to pay the
going rate. I could understand that. But I was less sympathetic when I learned that I wasn't making as much money as
the male associates at our firm. When I'd first been hired,
Williams told me that I wasn't expected to last as long as the
men associates did, because "women marry and stop working." Turnover being what it was, within five months I was
the senior associate in terms of service. Given my "seniority,"
I was even more annoyed about the money situation.

"How come I'm not making as much as the men?" I asked
Williams. I could have understood it if he'd said "because you
have less experience," but he didn't.

"Well, after all, Helene," he replied, "you don't need as
much money as they do. A man has a more expensive social
life because he has to pay the bills. A man will marry someday and he needs the money to support his family. Success
is more important for a man than for a woman."

"That's ridiculous," I said. "If I don't marry, I'll need the
money to support myself. I don't want to starve either. And
if no man asks me out, I have to pay for my own social life."

"How can you compare yourself to Fred?" he asked, nam-
ing one of the other associates. "He has a wife and two children and a third on the way. He needs the money."

"Who told him to have three children if he can't afford
them? Why should he get paid so much more than I do?
I'm doing the same amount of work, if not more. We should

get paid for our work, not the number of children we conceive."

Williams shrugged his shoulders. "Men always get paid more than women. They need the money," he said again.

"And I thought you were a conservative," I teased.

"Of course I am."

"Then how come you're spouting the Communist line?"

"What are you talking about?"

" 'From each according to his ability, to each according to his needs,' " I said. "That sounds like Marx to me."

"Now look, look, look, Helene," he began. But I was already out the door.

We were once asked to represent a group of Westchester conservatives known collectively as the Committee for the Advancement of the Bill of Rights. They were being sued by a teacher who had been fired, he claimed, because of his public stand against the war in Vietnam. He alleged that the committee had been part of a conspiracy to get him fired.

Listed among the team of lawyers representing the teacher was one William Kunstler. "That name looks familiar," I said.

"He's one of those civil-rights lawyers," Williams replied. "Find a flaming liberal cause and his name will be there somewhere."

A few months later, the case against our clients was discontinued. I had yet to meet that Kunstler fellow.

In the spring of 1968, I found myself involved in one of the most difficult cases of my career—difficult not because of its legal intricacies, of which there were many, but because of the personal involvement I felt. A young couple had adopted a child, and soon after the adoption became final, they discovered that the little boy was autistic. This is a form of childhood schizophrenia about which not much is known. One outward manifestation is that the child does not relate to people but lives in a world of its own. For this and other equally tragic reasons, the adoptive parents decided to try to have the adoption abrogated.

Abrogation or recision of an adoption is a rare proceeding and must be approved by the Court. The judge was the same Samuel Silverman who had tried the Pauling case. He was now sitting as Surrogate and had jurisdiction over adoptions. I had come to know him well professionally, not only because of the Pauling case, but also because I had handled several adoptions before him. He told me that he would not consent to the abrogation unless all the parties, including the child, the adoptive parents, and representatives of the adoption agency, appeared before him.

On the appointed day, I arrived at court and was ushered into his chambers. Sitting on the floor next to the judge's desk was one of the most beautiful children I've ever seen. He was about two years old, had very light blond hair, and was dressed in maroon corduroy pants with a matching jacket and a maroon-and-white-striped polo shirt. He did not look at the people who were coming into the room, but continued to sit by himself, banging his fist against the judge's chair. I was told that repetitious behavior and seemingly unfocused attention to inanimate objects are characteristic of autistic children and that it would be best to ignore him and just let him sit on the floor.

The lawyers and the parties involved joined the judge at a conference table and we began to discuss the psychological evaluations of the child's behavior and the legal consequences of abrogation. I was engrossed in presenting a legal point when I suddenly felt something tugging at my skirt. I looked down, and there was the little boy, staring up at me with his arms outstretched. Without thinking, I lifted him up and placed him in my lap, while continuing my argument. The child huddled quietly next to me, and soon his arms slid around my neck and he placed his head on my shoulder.

It was a poignant moment for me and I found it difficult to go on with my argument. The room was silent. Everyone was watching the child. Finally, one of the people from the adoption agency said, "You know, this is the first time I've ever seen him relate to anyone like that. It's very unusual. Maybe he isn't as severely autistic as we thought."

We were all moved by her statement. With an effort, I finished my presentation while the little boy clung to me. We thanked the judge and started to leave his chambers, with me carrying the child, whose arms were tightly clasped around my neck. As I walked toward the door, Judge Silverman called to me that I had forgotten my briefcase and legal papers, which were spread out on the table where I had been sitting. With the child in my arms, I returned to get my papers.

Judge Silverman looked at me and, with a slight tease in his voice, said, "You look very nice carrying that child. I wonder why you forgot your papers. Maybe you'd rather be a mother than a lawyer."

"I'm not sure I'd take that comment from anyone else but you, your Honor," I replied as I walked from the room.

The abrogation was subsequently granted and the child was returned to the custody of the adoption agency. I don't know what happened to him, but I will never forget him and the way he reached out to me.

"How come the men are always sent to London, the Bahamas, India, and I am never allowed to go on any business trips for the firm?" I would ask Williams periodically. I loved to travel and the idea of a free trip to an esoteric clime intrigued me. "There just hasn't been any opportunity for it," he would reply.

To some extent, he was right. Most of the other lawyers were involved in admiralty work and they were always traipsing away to some far-off port in connection with a case or the sale of a ship. Williams and I did some admiralty work, but mostly general litigation, and there was no call for either of us to travel. Still, I envied the more peripatetic members of the firm, and I couldn't help wondering whether my being a woman wasn't a factor in keeping me at home. When I broached the subject with Williams, he laughed uncomfortably. "Well, Helene," he said, "maybe that's part of it. After all, you couldn't share a hotel room with opposing counsel. You'd have to get your own room and it would cost more to send you."

I grumbled every once in a while, but it did me no good. Bob Atkinson would go to London and I would continue the trek to Wall Street. Then one day Williams called me into his office and told me that depositions had to be taken in one of the admiralty cases. Since none of the men was available to go, I was being sent. It wasn't much of a victory. I was going by default rather than by choice, but at least I was going. "Where are the depositions going to be taken?" I asked.

"You'll be going to Pascagoula," Williams told me.

"Mississippi! You're sending me to Mississippi! How could you?" I howled with disappointment.

And so I went to Pascagoula, one of our nation's major Gulf seaports, a small Southern town that languished in the June humidity. I did have a nice time, though, excited by travel, my first glimpse of the Mississippi River (on a one-hour stopover in New Orleans), and a delicious meal, complete with grits and corn fritters.

In addition to the experience of traveling and taking depositions, the excursion to Pascagoula was memorable for another reason. We had hired a local stenographer to record the depositions. While we were riding to the place where the examinations had been scheduled, she and I had a conversation in the car. "Wasn't it a shame about Martin Luther King?" she asked me. King had been assassinated only a few days before. I was surprised by her question and some of my assumptions about Southern bigotry prepared to fly out the window. "Yes," I said.

"They never should have shot him," she said. I agreed. "They never should have shot him," she repeated passionately. "They should have poisoned him, made it look natural." Fortunately, she was concentrating on her driving, so she missed my horrified reaction. "Forget about India," I said to myself. "There's a lot to be done in America."

In the summer of 1968, Williams went to Divonne-les-Bains, France, for a three-month vacation. He sent me as many as two or three cables or letters a day. In return, I was expected to write detailed letters about goings on in the office: status of cases, contents of mail received, calls from clients, number of paper clips left in the supply closet, etc. Interspersed with this trivia was the nearest thing to political commentary that I ever voiced in that office. Looking back on it, I think I was "liberated" by the confrontation over my article on the Middle East. Times were changing in the late sixties, and I guess I was too.

July 2, 1968

As per your instructions, I have been reading Bill's [Buckley] columns as they come in. I have always passed them on to you sans comment. Today, for the first time, I had doubts about a column, so I took it to Bob [Makla]. He agreed with me that, as written, the column might be libelous. We revised it, and after numerous calls to the syndicator, the matter was straightened out. Bill could not be reached, as he is en route from Hawaii.

The column was on James Earl Ray. Just as we finished revising and had the problem all wrapped up, the *Post* came out with an "extra": Ray was to be extradited from London. Bill had repeatedly referred to Ray as [Martin Luther] King's "murderer," which we changed to "the accused," "suspected murderer," etc.

August 1, 1968

This morning you also received a request for funds to ensure the election of a liberal Congress in the face of a "dangerous threat" from conservatives, as evidenced by Rafferty's victory over Kuchel. I laughed in your behalf.

August 22, 1968

Paul O'Dwyer is arousing admiration (of the people) and dismay (of the Democratic machine) for his integrity. He is so anti-Vietnam War that he has refused to support Humphrey when (if?) he is nominated.

August 27, 1968

Saw Buckley-Vidal on television last night. Each of them got off some really good cracks against the other. [This exchange, during which Vidal called Buckley "a crypto-Nazi" and Buckley called Vidal "a goddam queer," resulted in counter-claims for libel, in May 1969, after unsuccessful attempts by lawyers for both sides to negotiate apologies.]

August 29, 1968

I've been mesmerized by the television coverage of the demonstrations at the Democratic Convention in Chicago. Last night, police were hitting people over the head and gassing them. It looked like we were one step away from *1984*. The protesters were shouting, "The whole world is watching." Is it? Have you read anything about the demonstrations in the European press?

6

Transition

Judging from the experience of my friends and classmates, lawyers stay on Wall Street for fairly standard periods of time. Those who discover almost at once that they dislike the atmosphere or the work or both usually remain at least six months or a year, fearing that their résumés will reflect a certain instability if they don't. Others stay for seven or eight years, hoping that they will make partner (which usually takes that long). If they don't by then, they leave. Naturally, I fell into neither of these groups. I knew right away that I didn't like the atmosphere on Wall Street, and when I was involved in almost anything other than the Pauling case, the work was less than interesting; but I stayed for three and a half years.

I had a typical Wall Street practice. I represented plaintiffs and defendants in all sorts of commercial litigation: breach of contract for failure to deliver sulphur; admiralty work, including dead freight and demurrage on shipments of wheat and rice to India and oil to all parts of the world; suits revealing internecine family warfare over who should get what share of the estate; battles over corporate profits, and the like.

But while working on these cases, I always felt as though something were missing. I didn't care which of two great corporations got the profits from the tiny electronic component over which they were fighting. I couldn't get excited over the fact that one branch of a family was complaining that another branch was inheriting three million dollars more than the first branch. I didn't think it was important whether the oil company paid $87,000 in demurrage or only $55,000. I didn't enjoy spending my time writing memos entitled "Some Differences between Indemnity and Surety Contracts and Their Applicability to the [Doe] Correspondence of March 9–10, 1965," or "Long-Arm Statutes as they Apply to the [Doe] Case," or "Improper Nautical Charts and the Question of Seaworthiness." I was restless and unhappy. I found myself looking for any excuse to avoid coming into the office.

Inertia governed my life and I remained on Wall Street for about a year more than I should have. I would probably be there still had not the *deus ex machina* which intermittently flits through my life intervened. Williams informed me that he planned to retire. The significance of this for me was that, while I sometimes worked on other partners' cases, I was associated only with Williams. Each junior partner, associate, or secretary worked with a particular senior partner. Corrine Schade and I were part of Williams's team. His retirement meant that I was out of a job. I was nervous about having to find another position, but I was also relieved. I regarded Williams's resignation from active practice as an omen: my own departure from Wall Street was long overdue.

I was lucky that my first job as a lawyer afforded continued association with someone I respected as much as I did Williams. No case he was involved in could be completely boring, because he was always investigating new methods of attack and developing new theories of law. Intellectually, it was a joy to work with him. In spite of myself, I learned a great deal. In fact, I learned what law school had never taught me: how to be a lawyer. Williams used to say jokingly that I ought to pay him for the privilege of clerking for him; though I would never admit it, there were times when I thought he was right. For if there was one thing my work as a Wall Street lawyer confirmed, it was, as I had always believed, that my formal legal education had mostly been a waste of time.

I don't remember ever wanting to be a lawyer. According to an interview in my high-school newspaper, my ambition was "to finish the *New York Times* crossword puzzle without any help from the other people at my lunch table," a goal of dubious laudability which I have long since achieved. With a more realistic aim in mind, I studied shorthand and typing during my senior year, became adept at both, and had every intention of becoming a secretary. It took one volatile family session to convince me that I was going to college. The deal was that I would go to an out-of-town college for a year and if I didn't like it I could quit and go to work. My family apparently knew me better than I knew myself; stubborn and often afflicted with a curious inertia, I would never quit anything once I had started. And so I was skillfully seduced into continuing my education.

I was accepted at Brown University and spent the next four years in Providence, Rhode Island. It was a peaceful, unaware, sheltered time in a comfortable ivory tower. The peace was shattered in my senior year, when reality hit us all with a startling crunch. What were we going to do when we graduated? Senior ring-fever, an annual epidemic which attacked those with "fifties" mentalities, had infected most of the women in my class, and each month more of them capitulated and chose the nearest eligible male. As a child, I too had always assumed that someday I would get married and have children. But that was a faraway "someday," when I "grew up." I was nineteen when I entered my senior year at Brown and a young twenty when I graduated in 1962. I did not feel ready to get married, and besides, there was no one around I wanted to marry. The amiable and natural question, "What are you going to do next year?" from a friend or member of my family was enough to raise in me the urge to kill.

I spent most of my senior year trying to answer that bothersome question. The problem was that I didn't feel I could plan my life as though I were definitely going to be a housewife, and I wanted to be able to support myself and have something to do in case I didn't get married. My major at Brown was in religious studies, which did not give me much in the way of vocational training. I might have become a rabbi, but in 1962 women did not become rabbis. I gave some thought to studying for an advanced degree in religious studies and eventually becoming a college professor, but I gave that up when I discovered that I would need seven languages for a Master's Degree in my field, which was a comparison of Biblical literature to the Koran.

I couldn't become a secretary without wasting my degree. I knew that I didn't want to teach little children. That let out the two most acceptable careers for women. What could I do? I had to do something that would involve and challenge my mind. But what? My decision to apply to law school resulted more from elimination than from any deep desire to be a lawyer. I couldn't think of anything better to do. In its favor was the fleeting thought that if I got married, my degree wouldn't be wasted, because I could always do free legal work instead of the usual club work married women did. I still hadn't given up on what was then considered to be a "normal" life for a woman.

I applied to New York University and Columbia law schools. I was accepted at N.Y.U., but had not heard from

Columbia, so I asked Dean Gretchen Tonks at Brown to call Columbia about the status of my application. "Haven't you heard from them yet?" the Dean asked me in surprise.

"No, I haven't heard a thing. Why?"

"Because the men at Brown who've applied to Columbia Law heard last week."

That was strange. I was the only woman in my class who wanted to go to law school, and I had one of the highest averages of those from Brown who had applied to Columbia. The Dean called Columbia's admissions office and then told me: "It seems that they've already made their decisions on what men to take and they are meeting this afternoon to discuss the applications from women."

"Why are they considered separately?" I asked.

"I wondered about that myself," she said. "But the person I talked to either didn't know or wasn't saying."

Dean Tonks called me that afternoon to tell me that I'd been accepted at Columbia. I bought myself a large yellow tulip plant to celebrate the occasion, though I was more relieved than ecstatic. A few days later, the official notification of acceptance came in the mail. It was a form letter and among other things it included a request that all first-year law students live in the John Jay Residence Hall for men. My reply to this fascinating communication was concise: "It is my intention to work my way through Columbia Law School, but not precisely in the manner you suggest." My letter was never acknowledged.

Columbia and I were at odds from the beginning. I was used to the "community of scholars" at Brown, the small classes, casual camaraderie between professor and student, the loafers and knee-socks atmosphere that permeated the campus. Columbia Law School was foreign to everything I had known and loved. I resented compulsory attendance at classes, mandatory jackets and ties for men, and dresses, stockings, and heels for women. I objected to being told what classes to take; on my own, I would have skipped medieval English Star Chamber proceedings and the rule against perpetuities. I found it difficult to pay attention, let alone learn, in classes held in huge lecture halls, with hundreds of dispirited students slumped in uncomfortable seats.

I was also disappointed in the attitude of the professors toward the students. The professors were all men, all white, all middle-aged or older—which is not to say that I expected to be taught by young, black women, but merely to describe what was the norm for most law-school faculties in the early sixties. In addition, most of the professors were singularly lacking in humility. Their sole joy in life seemed to be to call upon the students in class, not in order to teach them, but to make fools of them. It sometimes seemed to me that class sessions consisted of repeated sighs of relief when other people were selected to be ripped apart. I quickly learned to answer "Unprepared," whether or not I was, to avoid class recitation. Grades meant nothing compared to the loss of self-esteem at being reduced to a simpering, stammering, red-faced, apologetic idiot in front of my classmates.

On top of the generalized antipathy toward all students was the special paternalism reserved for the women. There were about sixteen women in our class of two hundred, and I should have been able to gauge the school's receptivity to women by the letter I had received upon admission. Many of the women did so well academically that it was difficult to dismiss us all as a group of frilly accessories. But there was an undoubted if mainly unvoiced attitude that any woman who went to law school was a bit freaky.

Several of the professors made no attempt to hide their feeling that any woman would marry as soon as she could find someone willing to take her off the wallflower line, and for that reason we were merely taking up precious space that rightfully belonged to men who could be counted on to make important contributions to the profession. One professor delighted in what he called "Ladies Day," a nefarious institution that I had heard was also popular in other law schools. On the designated day, he would call on all the women in the class to recite. Our male classmates, relieved of the anxiety of having to face recital themselves, watched with ill-disguised glee as the professor harangued the women. "Well, well, Portia," he would cry with mock surprise when one of the women answered correctly. Or: "Better get back to the kitchen," to someone who stumbled.

Fortunately, this man was an exception. Most of the professors and male students either ignored the women or regarded us with tolerant amusement. It was understood that upon graduation we would, if lucky, get jobs doing trusts and estates or some other equally dull work, be relegated to the back room and allowed minimal contact with clients (who, of course, wouldn't tolerate a woman lawyer). This while the men did the more "glamorous" corporate and courtroom work.

My greatest shock during these years was the idea that school—any school—could be boring. I tried to give law school a chance. I kept up with the reading, made summaries of the cases as we were advised to do, attended all my classes. This devotion lasted approximately six weeks. By then, the accumulated insults overcame my vaunted inertia. I decided to quit law school. I went to Marvin Frankel, a professor who seemed more human than the others; he patiently asked me why I wanted to leave, and I detailed my catalogue of annoyances, both petty and important. "If practicing law is anything like this, I might as well quit now," I said. "At Brown, I loved my studies. Now I hate them."

Frankel surprised me by agreeing with most of my complaints. He confessed that he hadn't liked law school either—astonishing information, since he was rumored to have been one of Columbia's all-time prodigies. "Practice isn't anything

like law school," he told me. "In fact, many people who like
law school don't like practice and return to the academic
life as professors of law." He said that if I had the slightest
desire to practice law, the only important thing was to last
out the three years at Columbia and pass the bar. I believed
him and I stayed.

Apparently, I made less of an impact on him than he did
on me. Four years later, when I appeared before the then-
Judge Frankel in the United States District Court, he raised
his eyes above the glasses perched low on his nose and asked
in disbelieving tones, "Are you a lawyer?" I mumbled that I
was and refrained from reminding him that it was his own
fault.

Clever animals adapt to even the most unnatural circumstances in order to survive. By my senior year of law school,
I had become thoroughly anesthetized. Once, one of the
great men called on me in class, refused to accept my auto-
matic response of "Unprepared," and forced me to recite.
After completely destroying me, he proclaimed in a rising
crescendo of outrage, "Miss Schwartz, will you please tell
me how you ever managed to get to your third year of law
school?" I might have hung my head, cried, or at least
cringed with embarrassment; instead, armed with the training born of long-accustomed boredom, I just stared back at
him. All I wanted to do was graduate, and when the great
day finally came, I had the feeling that I had pulled a fast
one on Columbia by getting through.

The first session of the bar-review course began the evening of graduation day. In six weeks of compact lectures, I
learned everything there was to know about the law—or so
it seemed to me. Why had my courses at law school been
so convoluted, when the bar-review course made everything
so clear? Columbia prided itself on being a "national" law
school. This meant that Columbia did not believe in teaching
its students what the law was, but preferred to talk in

esoteric terms about what the law should be. On every level, theory replaced the practical. We spent months discussing "mens rea" in our criminal-law class; no one I know has ever had a case involving "mens rea," and few lawyers could tell you what it is. We studied evidence with men who were never inside a courtroom. We spent a whole semester discussing the exceptions to the hearsay rule. Never once did we learn how to make an offer of proof, how to draft an affidavit, how to get around the best-evidence rule. Students in corporate-law classes never practiced writing minutes; our class in contracts included no instruction on how to draft contracts; we never wrote complaints or answers or any motion papers.

Given my attitude toward my own legal education, it is ironic that I am now teaching at Rutgers Law School in Camden. As I repeatedly tell my students, they are either the beneficiaries or the victims of my own law-school experience. My seminars are designed to teach the students not only what the law is but how to use it on behalf of clients. My classes are practical. It isn't enough to talk about problems engendered by pre-trial publicity, which might deprive a client of the right to a fair trial. Students must also be taught what to do about it: motions for a change of venue, requests for a continuance until the publicity abates, the drafting of voir dire questions designed to find jurors who have not been affected by the publicity, and the like. I make my students write briefs, affidavits, and motion papers and participate in oral argument. They tell me that my courses make them feel like lawyers. And that is as it should be. After all, law school is a trade school.

Happily, the deficiencies of the system under which I studied are being recognized and many students are now being exposed to the "real" law before they graduate. Enlightened law schools, Columbia among them, are allowing their students to participate in clinics or work-study programs, where, under the guidance of experienced attorneys, they learn to draft legal instruments, have client contact, and even argue real cases. Law schools have finally acknowledged that you can't learn to be a lawyer just by reading books.

I have proof of the new spirit that pervades my old law school. Not too long ago, I received a fund-raising plea in the form of a poem which read:

> Columbia, the gem of the ocean,
> Is having a fiscal commotion.
> Tuition is rising
> And we are apprising
> You of our need for devotion.

The accompanying missive was addressed to "Dear Mr. Schwartz." Shades of that admission letter. Once again, I penned a reply:

> Columbia, you gem, it's no wonder
> Your finances are messed and complex.
> I was with you three years
> And now it appears
> You've yet to distinguish my sex.

A friend of mine who was a student at Columbia at the time tacked both poems to the bulletin board of the law-school women's organization. Unlike his counterpart so many years ago, a member of the administration had the grace to write me a letter of apology.

After I left Wall Street, in July 1969, I went to the Middle East and Europe for several months. When I got back to New York, I called some of my colleagues at the firm to say hello. I discovered that in my absence there had been a major power play. Bob Atkinson, who was Sam Hardy's junior partner, had threatened to leave if he was not given a more important policy-making role. The word was that I was the prime mover behind Bob's decision to leave.

My "influence" on Bob was based on our alleged affair, which was supposed to have begun in 1968. I had gone to the Virgin Islands with three women friends and Bob was there at the same time. He gave me a call and we went snorkeling with a friend of his. We took a picture to commemorate the occasion, and I innocently showed it to Mr. Williams. I later learned that, from then on, some people at the firm suspected Bob and I were having an affair. Would I have shown anyone the picture if we were?

Now our "affair" burgeoned into a full-fledged conspiracy. Rumor was that I had convinced Bob to leave the firm (I was six thousand miles away, on the Suez Canal, when he made his decision), that we were plotting to take away Hardy's clients, and that I was having affairs with the clients, in an attempt to entice them away. Bob took the allegations in stride and eventually found them amusing. I didn't.

While on Wall Street, I'd had my share of resisting clients' advances, removing errant hands from my knee or backside, and the like. Women who work in offices learn to handle situations like that. But these accusations went beyond playful teasing, and they angered me. If I were interested in taking over the accounts, I would get them by dint of my lawyering ability, not by means of seduction. I knew of other women who had faced similar accusations ("She just got a raise. She must be sleeping with her boss"), but this was the first time it had happened to me, and I reacted badly. I even thought of bringing a suit for defamation.

My father laughed it off. "They're afraid of you," he said. "In business, if a man beats you in your own field, he's an SOB. If a woman does it, she's a whore. You'll just have to get used to it." I never have.

Sometimes the most unlikely people affect our lives in the most unexpected ways. Such a person was Corrine Schade. She was indirectly responsible for my getting involved in the work I have been doing since I left Wall Street. In 1968,

Corrine gave birth to her second son. Rather than return immediately to the firm, she decided to work closer to home until the baby was a little older. She found a job with a lawyer in New Jersey. One day she called me: "I've been telling my new boss all about you."

"You mean you're not ashamed any more that you worked for a woman?" I teased.

"Certainly not," she said indignantly. "I never stop talking about you, and my boss has a friend he wants to introduce you to. Can I give him your number?"

I said yes. This was so out of the pattern of Wall Street relationships that I was delighted Corrine wanted to do it. The man to whom she gave my name was Leonard Weinglass, also a lawyer. He called me and we arranged to meet. He turned out to be a warm, sensitive person, with a lovely sense of humor, who looked like a cuddly, vigorously sloppy teddy bear with flying hair. I learned with no surprise that one of his courtroom adversaries had once offered to pay for a hair stylist for him.

Almost a year later, I was looking at the eleven o'clock news, not paying attention, but watching out of the corner of my eye, when I saw a familiar face on the screen. It was Len Weinglass and he was talking about a trial in Chicago. I remembered that Len had once canceled a date because he had to go to Washington to appear with a client named Tom Hayden at a congressional committee hearing.

Hayden, who had been active in the Students for a Democratic Society, had been indicted, along with seven others, in connection with the demonstrations during the 1968 Democratic Convention in Chicago. Len was again representing him. In February 1970, Hayden and four of his co-defendants (Rennie Davis, Dave Dellinger, Abbie Hoffman, and Jerry Rubin) were convicted of crossing state lines with intent to incite a riot at the 1968 convention. All eight defendants and their trial lawyers (Len Weinglass and Bill Kunstler) had also been summarily convicted of contempt of court, allegedly for misconduct during the course of the trial. I hadn't read the trial transcript, and I was puzzled by Len's contempt conviction. He didn't strike me as the type who would be unnecessarily obstreperous in court.

Two months later, I called Len to ask about a book he had borrowed, and in the course of the conversation I politely asked about the Chicago case. "I almost called you," Len said. "We were desperate for help out there and I wondered what you were doing." Then he added, "You know, the women's movement has been on my back because we never had a woman in a decision-making position on this case. Is there any chance you could work with us now, on the appeal?"

I didn't know what he meant about the women's movement being "on his back," because I had no idea of the problems the women on the trial staff had faced. I later learned that they had done all the garbage work—Xeroxing, typing, filing, running around looking for exhibits—and for the most part had been excluded from policy meetings during the trial. As one of the women who had been on the trial staff told me, "You were either sleeping with a lawyer or a defendant, or you were nothing on this case."

Perhaps her comment was unfair, but there were indications that it might have been true, and it certainly typified the bitterness of the staff women, none of whom had been lawyers. The Chicago defendants and their trial lawyers had reputations as "unmitigated chauvinists." This was probably why Len asked me if I would play a visible role on the appeal, to make up for the way in which the women had been treated on the trial level.

I knew nothing about this when I thought about taking the case. I had left Wall Street nine months before, was in private practice, and was free to do as I pleased. The salary that the Conspiracy Defense Fund could pay me was much less than I had been making on Wall Street, but I could just about live on it. From what Len had told me, it seemed obvious that there had been a severe injustice. The legal issues in the case ran the constitutional gamut.

I agreed to meet with Len later that week to talk about my possible participation in the preparation of the appeal, and what I would be expected to do. When I met him, he assumed that the question of my participation had already been settled, so we never discussed it, and I found myself a member of the appellate team in the Chicago Eight case.

7

I Meet the Cast
of Characters

Unless you are in it from the very beginning, work on every major case seems to start off in the same way: wading through a morass of legal documents. The Chicago Eight case was no exception. Before I could make a detailed analysis of the legal issues and begin the research and writing of the appellate brief, I had to acquaint myself fully with what had gone on before I had joined the defense team. In terms of number of files, photographs, films, affidavits, motions, etc., the Pauling case, the most complex in my experience to date, paled in comparison with the disordered, unending stream of paper connected with the Chicago Eight case. Everything having to do with the trial was gargantuan: a 22,000-page trial transcript, hundreds of motions, a dozen pre-trial hearings, testimony by more than eighty witnesses, over four hundred trial exhibits—all of which had to be studied and digested.

My work for the next four months was an exercise in dedication to the onerous. I did nothing but read the trial transcript. Everywhere I went, I carried two or three hundred pages of transcript. I read it in the subway, in the bathtub, on the beach, all the while taking copious notes. The task was crucial but hardly inspiring. I developed a hostility toward the transcript, as though it were alive, and I never failed to refer to it without a string of profane adjectives.

Toward the end of April 1970, after I'd been on the case for about a month, Len Weinglass invited me to fly to Chicago with him, to attend a post-trial hearing which was to take place before Judge Julius Hoffman. The defense was making routine motions to overturn the guilty verdicts, with no expectation that they would be granted. I had no role to play at this hearing. Since these were the final motions to be made before the trial judge, and related to the trial itself (and were not part of the appeal), the hearing was being handled by Len and Bill Kunstler, the trial lawyers. However, Len understood that after a month of reading the trial transcript I was curious to see what Judge Hoffman looked like in the flesh. Since I was scheduled to write the section of the appeal brief dealing with his misconduct, I should see him in action in the context of this case at least once, and this appeared to be my only opportunity. In addition, there were some procedural matters about the appeal which I had to discuss with the United States Attorney, so this was a good excuse for me to go to Chicago.

"Meet me at the Center for Constitutional Rights at one o'clock and we'll go to the airport together from there," Len said. Before this time, I'd never heard of the Center, but I soon came to know and love it well. It is like a small law firm, though its atmosphere is far more relaxed and friendly than any office I've ever been in. It is a non-profit organization, supported by contributions (which also makes it slightly different from the average Wall Street firm), and was founded in the mid-sixties by lawyers who had been active in the civil-rights movement in the South. Center people have defended almost every major political case in the last decade—from the Chicago Eight to the Gainesville Eight to Wounded Knee—and the Center is affectionately known as the "Legal Aid arm of the movement." Although I've never been a part of the regular Center staff, I've worked closely with Center lawyers and have learned to respect the dedication and consistently high-grade work turned out by that office. It was a proud day in my life when I was later asked to be a member of the Center's board, but that was not until a couple of years after my first appearance at the Center.

When I arrived, I was told that Len was at a meeting and had left word that I should join him. I peeked into the conference room. Some of the faces hiding behind the beards and unruly hair seemed familiar, but I couldn't place them. Len saw me standing in the doorway and motioned me in. "This is Helene Schwartz," Len told the men sitting around the table. "She'll be working on the appeal." He didn't bother to introduce them to me. I guess he assumed I must have recognized them all. Actually, I hadn't at first and it was only just beginning to dawn on me that these were the seven defendants left in the case after Bobby Seale was mistried. (Seale was in jail in Connecticut, awaiting trial on charges of conspiracy to kidnap and murder, charges that were later dismissed.)

Eight defendants were originally indicted in United States versus Dellinger: David Dellinger, Rennie Davis, Tom Hayden, Abbie Hoffman, Jerry Rubin, John Froines, Lee Weiner, and Bobby Seale. They were christened the Chicago Eight. After six weeks of trial, co-defendant Seale was held in contempt and his case severed. The binding, gagging, and ultimate mistrial of Seale has been recognized by the courts and commentators as a prime cause of the disintegration of the Dellinger trial. Although the remaining defendants became popularly known as the Chicago Seven, no one associated with the case ever referred to it that way. To do so would show a lack of understanding of the impact of the Seale incident on the trial, which is why the case is referred to here

as Chicago Eight. It is also known as the Conspiracy case or
by its official name, the Dellinger case.

I think this was the first time that the remaining defendants had been together since the trial. The government's
original charges of conspiracy notwithstanding, many of
these men did not like each other personally. And as for their
political views, their divergence was best explained by Abbie
Hoffman in a line I always thought was one of the best in
the transcript. When asked whether he and the others had
agreed to come to Chicago to disrupt the convention, Abbie
testified: "We couldn't agree on lunch."

Len's introduction was barely acknowledged with a few
yawns and nods in my direction. I sat down next to Tom
Hayden, one of the few people I recognized, and was re-
warded with a smile and a friendly hello. On his right was
Rennie Davis, who leaned over and asked me: "What did
Len say your name was?"

"Helene E. Schwartz."

"Are you a lawyer?"

"Yes," I whispered, not wanting to disturb the others at
the meeting. I watched Rennie take out a piece of paper and
recognized his upside-down writing to be my name. "Are
you planning to investigate me?" I asked.

"Yes," he replied without the hint of a smile.

Rennie was obviously more sophisticated than I about
prosecutorial tactics in political cases. Now that I have been
educated and have myself experienced governmental invasions of the defense camp through the use of electronic and
personal surveillance, undercover agents, and informers, I
understand his caution. But at the time it bewildered me.
"Just like the right wing," I thought, unhappily reminded
of the mysterious lady with the political files. "You'll find that
I used to represent Bill Buckley," I said to Rennie. He
laughed at what he apparently thought was a joke. If he ever
did complete his "investigation" of me, he was in for a
surprise.

After the meeting, Len and I rushed to catch our plane, and to my regret, I didn't get an opportunity to talk with any of the strangers—to whom, unknowing at the time, I was to devote a substantial part of the next two years of my life. This was unfortunate, because among those who worked on the case there was a lot of bitterness at the lack of contact with the defendants, let alone assistance, financial or otherwise, from them. They seemed oblivious to the enormous amount of work being done on their behalf. When someone once complained about the defendants' lack of gratitude to those who worked on the trial, one of the defendants was alleged to have replied that the legal workers should be able to "'hack it' in the work of a revolution, without needing such support." * If he really believes that, then he is either a fool or a martyr. Most of us mortals need to be told constantly that we are loved and that what we are doing is important and appreciated.

A few months after we filed the main appeal brief, I met Tom Hayden in New York. He told me that he had just read the brief and thought it was "great." He was filled with enthusiasm for our work and told us so. He was the only defendant who ever gave so much as a thank you for the tears and effort that went into the appeal, something which deeply hurt me and the other legal workers. I like to think that he was a special enough person to have learned something important from the anger that infected the Conspiracy trial staff.

I spent my first night in Chicago with two people who had been on the Conspiracy staff during the trial. Len was staying with friends of his, so we arranged to meet for breakfast before argument the next morning. I arrived at the designated restaurant to find Len already there, seated in a booth with a tall man whose wild dark hair was streaked with

* From *Motion Will Be Denied: A New Report on the Chicago Conspiracy Trial*, by John Schultz (Morrow, 1972), p. 184.

distingué gray. The man saw me before Len did, and he watched me as I walked toward the table. His face lit up when he realized that I was coming to meet them. He rose and with a broad smile said: "Well, well, Len. Where have you been hiding this?"

It was Bill Kunstler. He seemed nice, not at all the flamboyant demon presented in the newspapers. This was an impression borne out by longer acquaintance with him. He is a warm, physically demanding person who is always grabbing his friends, men and women alike, hugging and kissing them with all the demonstrativeness of what he astutely describes as the "wet" person he is, as opposed to the "dry, dull types." In fact, he got a long sentence from Judge Hoffman for the alleged contempt of hugging Ralph Abernathy when the civil-rights leader appeared to testify at the trial. The judge was moved to say more than once that he had never seen so much kissing in a courtroom.

I liked Bill Kunstler at once, and although there were to be times when I was exasperated with him, I never stopped liking him. Bill has been subjected to a lot of criticism, from friends as well as political enemies. Overcoming his habitual chauvinism, elitism, and super-starism is not easy for him, but I have seen him try and even momentarily succeed. And for all of the criticism, it is hard for anyone to deny that Bill is a charming person and often a charismatic marvel before a jury.

After I had some chocolate milk, all I can ever manage to eat in the morning, we hurried over to court. As we got out of the elevator, Bill said: "Twenty-third floor. I feel like I'm home again." We were coming to Judge Hoffman's courtroom, scene of the trial. We entered the courtroom, and as Len and Bill were recognized by the judge's ancient clerk, they received the hearty welcome of returning heroes. An unexpected friend—but then, nothing ordinary ever happened in this courtroom, if past events were any indication. The clerk called the court to order and we all stood.

And in he walked. At least, I assumed it must be Judge Hoffman. I could barely see the top of his shiny pate as he approached the bench from a back entrance. As I looked at the diminutive figure sitting before me, I recalled the words of a Chicago lawyer about this man. "It's said that every time Julius goes on the bench, he proves that he is not small, not stupid, and not Jewish."

Some said that his rumored discomfort at his own Jewishness accounted for his animosity toward the defendants and their lawyers, a good half of whom were of Jewish background. I never believed this. His antagonism was more complex than that. He did not understand the defendants' life styles; their long hair, dungarees, colorful T-shirts, and beards infuriated him. He did not sympathize with their political activism; one could never imagine Julius Hoffman with a picket sign, chanting, "No More War!" He knew nothing about their music; defense witnesses Pete Seeger, Judy Collins, Phil Ochs, Arlo Guthrie, Country Joe McDonald were names to him, not famous singers ("I'm assuming Country is his Christian name," he said of McDonald). There was a chasm of understanding between him and the defendants that five months of trial exacerbated rather than bridged.

I was reminded also of the defendants' pet name for Judge Hoffman: Mr. Magoo. It was apt; he had a bald head and oversized glasses which covered his slightly bulging eyes. He spoke, and I was surprised to hear how slowly and deliberately the words came out in a barely audible voice.

Judge Hoffman was dissatisfied by what he insisted was the late filing of certain papers. He rescheduled argument for two o'clock that afternoon. We left the courtroom and went upstairs to the office of the United States Attorney, for a conference on technicalities having to do with the filing of the record on appeal. There I met one of the men who had prosecuted the defendants, the stocky, studious-looking Richard Schultz. To my surprise, there was an easy, friendly atmosphere, complete with laughs and jokes, between him and the two defense trial lawyers. As everyone knew, this trial had been unusually tumultuous and had been full of nasty exchanges between opposing counsel. The unwritten rule among lawyers that professional courtesy must be preserved at all costs was never illustrated better than in this astonishing rapprochement among the trial counsel of the Chicago Eight case.

When I voiced my amazement to Len, he laughed and whispered to me: "Wait until you see him in court. He becomes a dragon. He grows fangs, and hair comes out of his nose." I studied Schultz carefully. Like Bill and Len, he and the other government trial lawyer, Thomas Foran, were not working on the appeal and Schultz was here to clean up loose ends from the trial. I probably wouldn't see him again (I never did) and I was curious about him. He seemed like a nice enough fellow, though some of his outbursts during the trial struck me as less than professional. Still, I wondered whether Len wasn't exaggerating, his view of Schultz colored by the acrimony of the trial.

After what I hoped was a subtle perusal of Schultz, I turned my attention to the purpose of the meeting. At the rate at which I was reading the transcript, there was no way that we could have our brief ready by the due date at the end of June. I told Schultz that I intended to ask for an extension of the time for filing the brief. "I'll tell you now that I'm going to oppose it," he replied.

I was startled. It is customary not to oppose routine requests for adjournments, particularly in a case as complex as this one. The reason is a practical one: you never know when you're going to need an adjournment yourself (the government later asked for several), so there is no reason to antagonize your adversary. Anyway, the appellate court would probably grant us an adjournment in this case (a premise which later proved true), so the prosecutor's position was a strange one.

"Why are you going to oppose our request?" I asked.

Schultz looked me steadily in the eye and, in a serious, almost sermonizing voice, replied, "Your clients are out on bail. These men are dangerous and I want them off the streets. The longer the appeal is delayed, the longer they will be free. I will oppose all requests for extensions." At first I thought he was teasing me, but there was no smile on his face. I began to believe Len might be right, that Schultz was a dragon after all.

A quick lunch, then we returned to Judge Hoffman's courtroom for argument. Len and Bill did well, I thought, convinced of what my reading of the trial record to date had already told me: that in spite of the repeated slurs on their ability by the prosecutors, judge, and media, they were both competent lawyers. Then Schultz rose to make answering argument, and before my eyes, that nice man did indeed become a monster. Instead of making responsive legal argument, he launched into irrelevant rhetoric and an inexcusable personal attack on defense counsel. I looked expectantly toward the judge. Surely he would stop this unprofessional behavior. But he just sat there, condoning the attack by his silence. To me, for whom the turbulent trial was little more than the dry paper of the trial transcript, this incident was revealing of what the trial itself must have been like.

Motions were made to invalidate the verdicts on various legal grounds. Never having won a single motion before this judge, the defense didn't expect to be victorious at this late date. But the motions had to be made; otherwise, the issues would be considered waived on appeal. To no one's surprise, the motions were denied. We flew back to New York and I once again buried myself in the arduous task of reading the record.

8

Chicago Eight on Appeal

July 31, 1970, was a memorable date because I finally finished reading the transcript of the Chicago Eight trial. I had started in April, and with interruptions for various other duties on the case, it had taken me some four months of tedious work. I've often said that I probably have the dubious honor of being one of the few people in the whole world to have read the entire record of the Chicago Eight trial.

The next day, I began doing the legal research on which the argument in the appellate brief would be based. I hadn't been asked to take the responsibility for any particular issues, so I had an open field. I decided to work on the question of the deprivation of the defendants' right to a fair trial.

One thing most people know about criminal law is that the Constitution guarantees to every defendant the right to a fair trial. The Constitution itself, however, doesn't say it in so many words. The concept of a fair trial has been developed through case-law interpretation of several sections of the Constitution. The most important of these are the Fifth and Fourteenth Amendment guarantees that no person shall be deprived of life, liberty, or property "without due process of law." "Due process" requires that whenever the government seeks to deprive a person of "life, liberty or property" the government must supply procedures which guarantee at least a modicum of fairness. The courts have held that for the criminal defendant this means that due process requires a fair trial in a fair tribunal. In other words, the guarantee of the right to a fair trial has been read into the principle of due process.

(The Fifth Amendment requires that the federal government provide "due process." The Fourteenth Amendment guarantee relates to state proceedings. If you are interested in the reason for, implications of, and interpretations of the two "due process" clauses, consult your local lawyer. With the notable exception of the Pauling case, almost every case I've handled has been in the federal courts. My discussion of the law in the Chicago Eight and later cases is based on federal statutory and case law.)

What constitutes a fair trial? Some of the elements of a fair trial are set forth in the Constitution. Among these are the Sixth Amendment guarantees of the right to a speedy and public trial before an impartial jury; to notice of the charges against you; to confront witnesses against you and subpoena witnesses on your own behalf; to the assistance of counsel. Some of these explicit constitutional guarantees require further interpretation before they can meaningfully be applied. For example, precisely what is an "impartial jury"? The cases have held that this guarantee entitles a defendant to examine prospective jurors (voir dire) to see whether they may be biased; to challenge those who indicate bias; to have a jury that has not been infected by prejudicial pre-trial publicity. An "impartial jury" is also one which hears the case in an atmosphere conducive to judicious consideration of the evidence and conducts its deliberations free of outside interference.

Other aspects of the fair trial do not appear in the Constitution at all but have been read into the concept of "due process." Among these are the concept that a defendant can be deprived of the right to a fair trial because of the conduct of the judge or by improper actions by the prosecutor; that the defendant has the right to present a defense and may be deprived of that right by improper evidentiary rulings.

Of course, the right to a fair trial does not mean that every defendant is entitled to a perfect trial. There may be errors which are not substantial enough to have deprived a defendant of the right to due process. This concept is called the "harmless error" rule. Some errors, such as refusal to allow a defendant accused of a felony to consult a lawyer, may never be considered "harmless error." But suppose a prosecutor once refers to a defense lawyer (in the presence of the jury) as "an idiot." This is clearly unprofessional conduct. It may also be an error for the judge to refuse to chastise the prosecutor for his comment. But it is unlikely that either the comment or the judge's refusal to reprimand the prosecutor infects the fabric of the trial to such a degree as to deprive the defendant of the constitutional right to a fair trial. An appellate court would probably hold these errors "harmless beyond a reasonable doubt."

What made the Chicago Eight trial so incredible was that it was a case history of what to do in order to make absolutely certain that the defendant is deprived of the right to a fair trial. There was misconduct by the judge and prosecutors. There were dozens of improper evidentiary rulings. There was interference with the right to the effective assistance of counsel. There was a real question as to whether the jury was impartial: the voir dire was insufficient; there were no protections against prejudicial pre-trial publicity; there was a possibility that the jurors had been contaminated by improper influence during the trial. And so on. The record was riddled with error on the issue of the deprivation of the right to a fair trial. I hardly knew where to begin.

I was fascinated by the fact that in this most infamous of

cases it had taken less than a day to choose the jury. In major trials, choosing a jury takes days, weeks, and sometimes months. I had read the voir dire in this case and it seemed to me that it afforded the defendants no protection whatever against the massive publicity which had preceded the trial. I decided to begin my work by researching that issue.

My first task was to review and organize the evidence relating to the pre-trial publicity. A factual analysis of the material was a necessary foundation of my legal argument. As I already knew from what I had read and heard about the 1968 Democratic Convention, there had been extensive media coverage not only of the convention activities which were the basis of the indictment and the congressional and grand jury investigations that followed that chaotic week, but also of the trial itself and the pre-trial proceedings which had taken place prior to the selection of the jury. The Dellinger pre-trial publicity motions included over two hundred pages of newspaper cuttings, submitted as evidence of the depth of the press coverage. From them it appeared that the most damaging press stories had begun appearing in July of 1968, with news reports of preparation by local Chicago and national law-enforcement groups for anticipated violence at the convention. Newspaper articles harped on the theme that a violent invasion was being planned by various political groups, which necessitated the formation of "battle plans" by the authorities in order to "protect the public." Before, during, and after the convention, the five defendants who were ultimately convicted of the substantive charges of crossing state lines with intent to incite a riot (Dellinger, Davis, Hayden, Hoffman, and Rubin, sometimes referred to as the appellants) had been kept in the public eye. These five had repeatedly been named as the "leaders" of the groups which came to Chicago. They and the groups with which they worked were the continuous targets of a continuous campaign of vilification. They and their organizations were referred to in the Chicago press as "revolutionaries," "anarchists," "militants," "troublemakers," "agitators." Jerry Rubin and Abbie Hoffman were named as "potentially dangerous people" whose activities were "merely camouflage for organized violence." Tom Hayden was called "Hanoi's disciple," and it was implied that singlehandedly he had been responsible for the disruptions that had shaken Newark in 1967. Dave Dellinger was referred to as "the self-styled non-Soviet Communist" who "helped plan the disruptive protests." Rennie Davis was named as a leader of the "Communist-infiltrated" National Mobilization to End the War in Vietnam, which "has pledged to disrupt the August convention."

The success of this studied strategy of public arousal had been obvious. A public poll taken right before the convention reported that 48.3 percent of all Americans thought that the political demonstrations had been "organized to disrupt the convention and create riot conditions in Chicago." Even more frightening was a report in a Chicago newspaper on the day the convention opened; according to it, 90 percent of those polled supported the policy that authorities should "shoot to kill if agitators make trouble ."

The public outcry against Dellinger, Davis, Hayden, Hoffman, and Rubin escalated when the office of Chicago's Mayor Daley issued a self-expiating report entitled "The Strategy of Confrontation." The report endorsed the police action against the demonstrators and named all five appellants as the "fomenters of convention-week rioting." Headlines in the Chicago press screamed: "Blame Riot on 5; Ask U.S. to Act." Congressman Roman Pucinski announced his intention to present the report to Attorney General Ramsey Clark so that indictments could be sought against the five, whom Pucinski publicly denounced as part of a "conspiracy to destroy this nation." A week later, dramatic headlines in the Chicago papers reported: "HUAC to Hunt Subversion in Convention Disorders." Richard Ichord, who chaired the hearings, made further inflammatory statements, such as: "We know for a fact that some of the leaders of organizations that were at Chicago are self-admitted Communists." Front-page coverage escalated again as all five appellants were called upon to testify before the committee. Then, in March 1969, the recently indicted appellants were referred to in the Chicago newspapers as "revolutionaries," "notorious spreaders of disorder," "agitators," with "no scruples about abusing the law," "wild men."

The indictment itself was a study in public relations. It covered every angle and was meant to intimidate everyone. First, it named the five men Mayor Daley had already convicted as the "fomenters of convention week rioting." They represented the two most prominent groups at the convention protests. Dave Dellinger, Tom Hayden, and Rennie Davis were chairmen of the National Mobilization to End the War in Vietnam (known as "Mobe"); Abbie Hoffman and Jerry Rubin were the chief jesters of the Youth International Party (the "Yippies"). Defendants six and seven were John Froines and Lee Weiner, unknown before the trial and little heard of thereafter. Both were members of university faculties, and it was considered that their indictment was meant to warn academics to stay out of the political arena. The eighth defendant was Bobby Seale, chairman of the Black Panther Party. He had been in Chicago only one day during the convention, had made one speech (to a peaceful audience sitting on the grass), and had never met any of the other defendants before he walked into the courtroom. But the case needed its token black, so that other blacks would hesitate to demonstrate. To his own often-admitted bewilderment, Bobby Seale was it. The case against him was dismissed, and Froines and Weiner were acquitted of all charges against them. Only the five "wild men" were convicted, perhaps because they were the ones made most infamous by the media.

Most of the normal safeguards that would ensure an impartial jury in the typical case where there has been pre-trial publicity were ineffective in the Chicago Eight case. A change of venue, to another jurisdiction where there had been less publicity, was impossible because the publicity had been nationwide. Trial counsel had not even bothered to make such a motion. Instead, they attempted several times to get continuances of the trial date until publicity abated, but these motions had been denied. Anyway, continuances would have been relatively useless because the publicity was likely to flare up again whenever the trial was imminent.

Since the prospective jurors, all from the Chicago area, could not help but have been deluged by the massive publicity, the only protection against their possible prejudice was to screen them through careful questioning prior to their selection. To this end, the trial attorneys had requested that Judge Hoffman ask each of the prospective jurors what he or she had read about the case in the newspapers or heard about it on radio or television. Judge Hoffman refused to do this. The only question he asked which was even remotely connected (and remote it was) to the issue of possible prejudicial pre-trial publicity was a single general inquiry, directed to the entire panel, as to whether there was "any reason" that the jurors thought they "could not be fair and impartial in this case." This hardly met the well-settled judicial requirement that, in cases involving massive pre-trial publicity, there had to be penetrating voir dire of each individual juror to determine whether he or she knew of the publicity, had been influenced by it, or could still function as an independent, impartial trier of the facts.

The refusal of the trial judge to take even minimal steps to protect the defendants from the inherently prejudicial publicity that had saturated the Chicago community seemed to me to be strong ground on which to urge reversal of the convictions. I also felt that the danger that the jurors were not impartial had been compounded by the refusal of the trial judge to ask other questions submitted by the defendants, which had been designed to elicit other possible prejudices among the prospective jurors.

Questions to the prospective jurors afford counsel and the accused an opportunity to learn something about the jurors so that challenges can be intelligently exercised. The perfunctory voir dire conducted by Judge Hoffman told the Chicago Eight defendants almost nothing about the people who were to judge them. In most cases, they learned little more about a candidate for the jury than name, address, marital status, number of children, and occupation. The defendants had submitted questions which sought to determine whether the jurors might be prejudiced against people who demonstrated against the war and racism; how they felt about young people who wore long hair (as did many of the defendants), smoked pot, or listened to rock music; whether they held political beliefs or were members of associations which might indicate prejudice against the defendants because of their politics, race, or religion; whether the jurors had friends or relatives who were members of law-enforcement organizations or would give excess weight to the testimony of a police undercover agent. Judge Hoffman refused to ask any of these questions, with the result that the defendants' right to challenge possibly prejudiced jurors was thoroughly emasculated.

The impact of this interference with the right to an impartial jury was revealed after the trial, in an interview a Chicago reporter had with one of the jurors. All the voir dire had elicited about her was that she was a Chicago housewife with two children in school and a husband who had worked for General Motors for nineteen years, none of which was relevant to the question of her possible prejudice against the defendants. Yet, in her interview, she said "her one worry" was that her son might become friendly with "hippies" in his high school, and she admitted that she had been offended by Abbie Hoffman's long hair. Had her prejudices been brought out prior to her selection as a juror, she would have been dismissed from the panel. It was a good assumption that other jurors might have been similarly prejudiced and that the refusal of Judge Hoffman to ask the questions which would have revealed these prejudices forced the defendants to judgment before a jury that was not one of impartial peers, as guaranteed by the Constitution.

I also did a great deal of research into the standards for reversal of convictions on the grounds of misconduct by the trial judge and prosecutors. I was convinced that we would have solid grounds for reversal on these two issues, but I was afraid that the appellate court was likely to be predisposed against criticizing the judge and prosecutors in this case, because it had become a symbol, in the mind of the public, of the danger of courtroom disruption as a political weapon to destroy our system of justice. The media had kept the people advised of the activities of the defendants and their trial lawyers in the courtroom, but there had been less attention paid to the provocation they had suffered at the hands of the judge and prosecutors. The press did not gauge the impact on the defendants of the binding and gagging of co-defendant Bobby Seale and his ultimate mistrial and severance; the continued insults by the bench and prosecutors directed toward defense counsel; the repeated incomprehensible and often erroneous evidentiary rulings which interfered with the defendants' right to present a defense. I hoped that we might be able to convince the appellate court that the atmosphere at the trial made the actions of the defendants and their trial counsel both plausible and pardonable.

The legal issues were so interesting that the weeks flew by and it was a joy, for a change, to spend my days in the library doing research and analyzing the questions to be presented on appeal. During most of this time, I was on my own in determining where I should direct my energies and in making decisions about procedural matters on the appeal. Bill Kunstler was never available. He was always out of town making a speech or trying a case. I had looked forward to working with Len Weinglass, but I found that he was unable to focus his attention on the case. Of the people who had been involved with the trial, Len seemed to have suffered the most. Judge Hoffman's attacks on him, both personal and demeaning his legal talents, took their toll in his loss of confidence and spiritual exhaustion. He could not seem to clear his head and get to work on the appeal. Several times, when I asked for his input on crucial decisions, he admitted that he didn't want to think about the case. I tried to spare him from the everyday problems which arose in preparing the appeal, but I could not make all the decisions, even piddling ones, myself.

Ultimately, both Len and Bill withdrew from participation in the appeal and a law-school professor named Arthur Kinoy was brought into the case. He was an experienced lawyer with a long history of involvement in civil-rights activities and a reputation as a brilliant legal scholar. I met with Arthur briefly in August 1970, and we made a list of the issues that should be raised on appeal and assigned responsibility for the preparation of each part of the brief, I to continue with the fair trial points. But I did not see much of him for the first month or so that he was on the case, and I continued to work by myself.

In mid-August, I was joined in the library by another lawyer, a woman named Doris Peterson. She was a graduate of Yale Law School who had done commercial-law work for a few years and had then married. Her twenty-year retirement to raise four children had ended abruptly when she encountered Arthur (a personal friend) at a wedding and innocently asked if he knew where she could work for a few days a week, "just to get my feet wet in law again." Arthur grabbed her and threw her, head first, into the Chicago appeal. She was overwhelmed by her sudden immersion in this major case, but what she might have lacked in confidence because of the hiatus in her career, she more than made up in competence and dedication. She was and is, moreover, one of the sweetest, most unselfish people I have ever known. From the start, we took to each other and worked well together.

At about the same time Doris joined the appellate team, I received information about the jury deliberations which, if true, would be the basis of another strong argument for reversal of the convictions. John Schultz, a Chicago writer, had interviewed two of the jurors after the trial. They told him that during the course of their deliberations there had been communications with the trial judge. Supposedly, two messages had been sent to him saying that the jury was hung, unable to reach a verdict. A third note requested that certain evidence with respect to speeches allegedly made by the defendants be given to the jurors. None of the defendants knew anything about these communications; nor had their lawyers been notified of them—as of course they should have been.

Schultz also learned that one of the marshals in charge of the jury during its deliberations had made improper comments to the jurors, such as that they could be kept indefinitely; that the judge wanted them to reach a verdict; that it was their duty to reach a verdict. These comments were misleading and untrue. If they had in fact been made, they could have effectively deprived the defendants of their right to an impartial jury and might also be grounds for reversal.

Almost nothing is more sacrosanct in the law than the compulsion of independent jury deliberations free from the slightest tinge of bias or outside influence. This was especially important in the Chicago Eight case, where there were charges of personal embroilment on the part of the trial judge and the issues involved were politically volatile. Communications between the trial judge and a deliberating jury, without the knowledge, presence, or consent of the defendants or their counsel, are entirely improper and are grounds for reversal of a subsequent conviction. This rule of law is based upon two firm grounds. The first is that defendants have the right to be present at all stages of the proceedings against them. The communications were improper because they had taken place outside of the presence of the defendants. The second reason is that secret communications between a trial judge and a deliberating jury are violative of a defendant's Sixth Amendment right to the assistance of counsel. Had the trial lawyers been notified of the two hung-jury notes, they could have made motions for a mistrial or for additional instructions to aid the jurors in their deliberations. Had they been told of the request for transcript, they could have advised the Court as to whether to send the transcript, what portions to send, whether to read sections of the transcript to the jury; they could have objected to whatever decision the judge made, or requested the giving of additional instructions to the jury. In short, the right to the assistance of counsel means the right to the "effective" assistance of counsel, which in turn means that counsel must have the opportunity to act to protect a client's rights. The defendants had been deprived of this right if their counsel had not been notified of the communications from the jury.

The comments which the two jurors told John Schultz the marshal had made to the jury while it was deliberating posed yet another problem. If they were true, they might have coerced the jurors into reaching verdicts that violated their conscientious convictions. As in the case of the messages to and from the judge, the interference of the marshal with the deliberating jury raised a presumption that the integrity of the jury had been destroyed. The marshal's statements indicating that the jurors would be forced to deliberate for an indefinite period of time violated the judicial mandate that "no court shall require or threaten to require the jury to deliberate for an unreasonable length of time." The danger of coercion was particularly great in the Chicago Eight case because the jurors had been sequestered in a hotel, kept apart from their families and friends during the five months of trial; they had deliberated more than ninety-six hours and their notes to the judge indicated that they were deadlocked, delicately balanced between guilt and innocence. Under these circumstances, there was a real chance that the marshal's improper comments had coerced an exhausted jury into reaching compromise verdicts.

The problem was that we had only Schultz's word about the occurrence of these communications between the jury and the judge and marshal. Not that we didn't trust Schultz, but such evidence was unacceptable in court. We had to get sworn testimony by the jurors and marshals into the record, and we were precluded from interviewing the jurors ourselves by an order of Judge Hoffman's prohibiting post-trial interviews by counsel.

I thought that we should make a motion to the Court of Appeals asking that the case be remanded to Judge Hoffman for the purpose of supplementing the record. I wanted a reversal of his order prohibiting us from interviewing the jurors or, alternatively, a hearing at which the jurors and marshals would take the stand and be questioned under oath about the communications. I researched the law on the question of the right to interview jurors after a trial and the circumstances under which verdicts could be reversed where there had been interference with a jury's deliberations. I then broached the subject of a motion to the Court of Appeals to some of my co-workers. To my surprise, they opposed the idea. We never win anything, the theory was —so why bother? We've got plenty of work to do without it.

It was true that every motion the defense had made before

Judge Hoffman had been denied, but I hoped that the Appellate Court would be more receptive to us. Since I wasn't present at the trial, I was still able to be optimistic. Fortunately, by this time Arthur Kinoy and Doris Peterson had joined the appeal team. When I filled them in on the facts and the law, they too were enthusiastic about the idea of making a motion.

I spent the next couple of weeks drawing affidavits in support of the motion papers and a long memorandum of law setting forth the reasons why the Court should allow us to investigate further the possibility that there had been interference with the integrity of the jury deliberations. It was an odd time in my life because, all summer long, I had a recurrent virus and stomach upset. Labor Day weekend, when I put the finishing touches on the papers, I was feeling particularly queasy. In spite of the malaise, I was satisfied with the papers and was feeling confident about our chances for success on the motion. I dropped the papers off at the Center that Tuesday. Several of my colleagues called me within the next few days. They were generally pleased with the motion papers and had only minor suggestions to make, which I adopted.

The following Thursday, I was at the Center to do some more research, when I happened to wander into the room where the legal workers did their typing. I noticed that one of them was typing up the jury motion and that the copy from which she was working had been all marked up in a strange handwriting. I picked it up and began to read it. Numerous changes in grammar, style, and syntax had been made. This was annoying, because every lawyer has his or her own style, and my own was as good or bad as that of the changed version. Still, it was of no consequence and my pride wasn't hurt that my work had been changed. Any lawyer who works on teams had better be used to having suggestions made, and most take the "blue penciling" with relative ease, particularly when it comes from lawyers one respects. But you don't make major changes in a colleague's work without consulting him or her. It is a professional discourtesy and I had a sneaking suspicion that it would never have happened to papers written by one of the men.

What was even more extraordinary was that an entire section had been added to the brief and that the section was wrong as a matter of law. Whoever had written this new section had not done any homework. The legal argument was directly contravened by a case on point in the Seventh Circuit, the Court before which we were to make our appeal.

(Federal appellate jurisdiction is divided among eleven courts. Illinois, Indiana, and Wisconsin are within the jurisdiction of the United States Court of Appeals for the Seventh Circuit [sometimes referred to here as the Court of Appeals, the appellate court, or the Seventh Circuit]. As we were appealing from convictions in the United States District Court for the Northern District of Illinois [a federal court of first instance, or trial court], we were to be heard by the Seventh Circuit, and all previous decisions by it were binding on us.)

It was mere chance that I'd happened to be at the Center and caught this before it went out. What if the brief had gone to the Court of Appeals with the incorrect section? The public impression of the defense trial lawyers in this case, wrong though it was, was that they were "wild" and "incompetent." We appellate lawyers had an uphill struggle to show the Court that the defense lawyers associated with this case, both at trial and on appeal, were entirely professional. It would have damaged our reputations and our credibility if we had begun our work before the appellate court by submitting a brief that was wrong on the law. It was an intolerable situation, one which would never have occurred if we'd been better organized and if there had been some direction to the hordes of lawyers, legal workers, and law students associated with the appeal.

This near disaster brought about a change in the way our headless-chicken defense team had been operating. A meeting was held at which it was decided that Arthur Kinoy, Doris Peterson, and I would be the senior lawyers on the appeal. We would have prime responsibility for the case and no decisions would be made without consulting the three of us. It was a relief to get organized at last, and as Doris said, it was only fair that those of us who were actually doing the work should have the responsibility for directing the appeal.

Many other problems were worked out at that meeting. One decision which later had great importance concerned the jury motion. Everyone agreed that if the Court of Appeals acted favorably on our motion and either ordered a hearing or granted us the right to interview the jurors, I was to have the main responsibility for that. I think that this was readily agreed to because no one thought that the Court would grant us any relief. So it was no skin off anyone's back to accede to the idea that if we won, it would be my baby.

A few days later, that slippery virus returned with a vengeance and I found myself in the hospital, undergoing surgery. "We've been looking for grounds on which to apply for an extension on the due date of the brief," Arthur said when he heard about my illness. "Now we have them. One of our senior counsel is having emergency surgery."

"What I like about you best of all," Doris said when she came to visit me at the hospital, "is that you'll do anything for the good of the case."

9

Our Knight Errant

Arthur Kinoy is small of stature, but in the eyes of his colleagues and friends, his height is boundless. He combines a fine legal mind with a grasp of the political scene which makes it possible for him to quickly pinpoint the practical and political ramifications of even the most innocuous legal issues. But what truly makes Arthur beautiful is that he has a knack for getting people to sit down and talk out their problems. Even when he is at the center of a controversy, people are rarely angry at him. His counsel, both for his remarkable intellectual competence and his unusual peacemaking abilities, is often sought by other, more tempestuous personalities.

To keep Arthur from sounding like an unreal ministering angel, let me quickly point out that he has his faults. One is his inability or stubborn refusal to pronounce my name correctly. To Arthur, I am "Helaine," which he rhymes with "rain," in spite of my protests to the contrary. "Helene, my name is Helene. It rhymes with queen, bean, lean, soup tureen. It's Helene!"

I don't answer when he calls me Helaine. I threaten to call him Author instead of Arthur. I complain that he is

making me feel like a stranger he has just met. It is all to
no avail. On this one point, Arthur remains singularly
uneducable.

Arthur's second fault is that, in legal writing, his ver-
bosity and propensity for purple prose are unexcelled. It
took him 180 pages, almost forty percent of the Chicago
brief, to prove that the anti-riot statute was unconstitutional. The analysis was brilliant. But Doris and I agreed
that if we had written that section, it would have been
under seventy-five pages. After all, she and I ultimately
denounced the judge's misconduct in less than thirty pages,
and he, as we all knew, was as grievous an error as was
the statute.

The deep and sincere feeling which Arthur's friends have
for him was best shown in December 1970. Arthur had
been subpoenaed to appear before a federal grand jury in
New York to testify with respect to the whereabouts of his
daughter, Joanne. Actually, all that the grand jurors wanted
to ask her (the prosecutor claimed) was where they could
reach a former boyfriend of hers, so that they could subpoena him in order to ask him the whereabouts of a woman
who was a fugitive from justice. A bit convoluted, but that's
all it was.

Bringing Arthur before the grand jury was a clear abuse
of its subpoena power for a number of reasons, not the least
of which was that if the grand jurors wanted to know where
Joanne Kinoy was, they could look in the telephone book.
Not only wasn't she "underground," but only a few weeks
before, she had appeared with me in a federal courtroom in
Chicago and had been introduced by me to the U.S. Attorney, the U.S. marshals, and the press as Professor Kinoy's
daughter.

Everyone agreed that the real purpose of the subpoena
against Arthur was harassment. The government knew that
Arthur would never appear without a fight; to do so would

have been to admit the legitimacy of the government's abuse of process. The time we took off to quash the subpoena would interfere with our preparation of the Chicago appeal brief, which was then due in less than six weeks. That, we all felt, was the underlying reason why the grand jurors were suddenly interested in Arthur and his family.

We lost a motion to quash Arthur's subpoena, but we didn't pursue it further because we couldn't afford any more time on this question of principle. After all, our Chicago clients were facing an aggregate of fifty years in jail and $50,000 in fines; our primary responsibility was to them. Joanne Kinoy voluntarily appeared (that is, she flew in from Wisconsin, where she was a student at the university and had been living for the last few years), and accepted service of a subpoena. She went before the grand jury, where, instead of asking about her ex-boyfriend, the prosecutor asked all sorts of questions about her private life and political affiliations. She declined to answer on the ground that the questions violated the First Amendment and had a "chilling effect" on her exercise of her First Amendment rights. Her refusal to give a dissertation on her private life was upheld by the federal court. (Arthur and Joanne subsequently brought a suit against the government, alleging damages for harassment, abuse of process, and illegal wiretapping. That case is still [1975] pending.)

Arthur never did appear before the grand jury. However, during the proceedings we brought to quash his subpoena, the largest courtroom at Foley Square overflowed with his clients, friends, and fellow lawyers. They had assembled, on overnight notice, from all over the country, to show support for Arthur. It was an acknowledgment of his contribution to the civil-rights movement and the personal devotion he inspired in his colleagues.

Just a month before the grand jury contretemps, I had come to know what a special person Arthur was. In November 1970, I was forced into an uncomfortable confrontation over my role as a lawyer in the Chicago case, and Arthur made it clear how he felt about me and his other women colleagues at the bar. At the time, I was in New York recovering from the operation and had been restricted to the house for the past four weeks. The jury motion had finally been filed while I was in the hospital, and in the form in which it had originally been written. We expected that the Court of Appeals would soon act on our requests and I had been calling the clerk of the court every other day, to see whether a decision had come down (not because I was so curious, which I was, but because the mails were slow and we thought we might get only a day or two to respond after the order came down, which turned out to be what happened). The clerk and I had developed that sort of deep but impersonal friendship that comes from continued telephone conversations untouched by face-to-face association.

He knew that I had been ill, because, on the ground of my sudden hospitalization, we'd had to ask for an extension of time within which to file the brief. Now he was solicitous about my health. How was I feeling? Much better. When was I going back to working on the brief? I'd never stopped. I'd had conferences on the case even when in the hospital, and since I'd been home I'd been drafting legal points for the brief. How were things coming? Fine.

These conversations went on for about two weeks. Finally, the clerk took pity on me and my long-distance telephone bill. On Thursday afternoon, November 12, he said that it wouldn't be necessary for me to keep calling him, that he would call me when the decision came down. This was a bit irregular, but awfully nice, coming from a stranger.

Two hours later, at six o'clock our time, the phone rang. It was the clerk from Chicago. "Good news," he said. "The

decision has come down and the Court has granted a hearing." He read the Court's order to me over the phone. I
couldn't believe it. The Court had granted our request for
further investigation into "the contents of and the circumstances surrounding the communications, if any, between
the trial judge and the jury during its deliberations" and
"any communications by the marshals and other officers
in charge of the jury during its deliberations, which may
arguably have interfered with the jurors' exercise of impartial judgment." I could barely contain myself as I took
down the order in shorthand.

When I hung up the phone, I was so excited that I started
jumping up and down. My family was afraid I would have
a relapse.

I called Arthur Kinoy. No answer.

I called Doris Peterson. She wasn't home.

I called Len Weinglass. I had to leave a message with
his answering service.

I called Bill Kunstler. The phone rang incessantly.

How frustrating it was! I had to share this news with my
co-counsel. Every fifteen minutes, I repeated the four phone
calls. Two hours later, I reached Len Weinglass. "Len, it's
Helene. Guess what. The Court granted our jury motion.
They've sent the case back to Hoffman. We're going to have
a hearing!" I shouted jubilantly.

There was silence on the other end of the phone.

"Len, are you there?" I said. He answered softly, in an
unbelieving voice. "A hearing?" I could barely make out
what he was saying.

"A hearing!" I yowled with joy. "A hearing?" he asked
again, this time a little louder. "A hearing!" I replied.

"We're going to have a hearing!" he shouted. "They actually granted our motion? A hearing!" The rest of our
conversation consisted of little more than the repetition of
those two magic words, "a hearing."

An hour later, I finally reached Doris. "Where have you been?" I asked peevishly.

"I've been having dinner with Arthur," she replied. "What's the matter? You sound absolutely exhausted."

"Our motion's been granted. We're going to have a hearing on the jury questions."

Doris whooped with joy and began to recite the litany. "A hearing!" she said over and over again with disbelief. Then she made me read the Court's order to her twice, "because the words sound so nice."

"Call Arthur," she insisted. "He must be home by now." I called him, and this time he answered.

"Arthur, guess what. The jury motion has been granted."

"Wouldn't that be nice," he said with a low chuckle.

"No, no, for real," I said excitedly. "We're going to have a hearing."

"Whaaat?" It was a long, loud, exhaled, incredulous sound.

The next day, we received word that the United States Attorney had moved that the hearing be held the following Monday, only three days from then. We could never be prepared by that time. Saturday, we called an emergency session in New York. I was in no condition to travel on the subways, having been confined to hospital and house for the last six weeks, so my brother volunteered to drive me to the Center. When I arrived, the mood was exultant. Everyone who was working on the appeal, and several members of the trial staff came to share the moment of triumph.

After much hugging and excitement, the meeting got down to business. The first problem was to decide who would conduct the hearing. We'd had too many misunderstandings in the past because no one person had had ultimate responsibility for various projects. Arthur suggested that since I was the one most familiar with the jury problems and had drafted the successful motion papers, I should make the major decisions. Bill immediately concurred. "After all," he said, "we agreed at the meeting in September that if the Court gave us any relief on the jury motion, Helene would be the one to handle it."

I remembered how little chance we'd thought we had of winning the motion when we had that discussion. It was odd how things worked out. I gathered my papers together, thinking that I would now chair the meeting. As I was doing this, one of the men said, "I don't think that Helene should be in charge of this."

"Why not?" I asked. "After all, I did all the work on the motion and I've done all the research on the questions of law. I'll be writing the jury sections of the appeal brief."

He would not look at me while he was speaking. He directed his comments to the entire meeting. "The clients have no confidence in Helene," he said.

When I heard that, something inside me snapped. "Well, if they have no confidence in me, why have I been breaking my back on their behalf for the last eight months? If they have no confidence in me to conduct the hearing, why did they have enough confidence in me to draft the motion papers and work on the brief?"

I was beginning to match his anger. Doris was looking upset too. She, like me, didn't know any of the clients personally. The suggestion that they had no confidence in me was an indirect slap at her too.

"I won't agree to Helene's conducting this hearing," the man said.

"I suppose it's okay for me to do all the garbage work and then, when there is something that's fun to do, I have to sit back and watch you take over, is that it?" I was shouting, something I hadn't done for years, and I wasn't proud of myself, but I couldn't help it. "I worked hard on those papers and I think I have a right to play a major role in that hearing."

"We aren't talking about rewards, and you have no right to be so proprietary about this," he shouted back.

Who the man was didn't matter so much as why he was doing this, something Arthur finally put his finger on. "All right," Arthur interrupted in a rumbling voice that belied his size. "This has gone far enough. Why don't we just put the truth on the table. This is a women's-lib question, pure and simple. Admit it," he said to the man. "You would never be saying this if Helene wasn't a woman."

"That has nothing to do with it," the man said defensively, as others at the meeting murmured in agreement with Arthur.

"It not only has something to do with it," Arthur shot back. "It's the heart of the issue."

Heavy charges flew back and forth, but I neither listened nor responded. I was so tired physically and emotionally that I was not up to this continued in-fighting. I was just about to withdraw my name from consideration as a participant at the hearing, when something inside stopped me. "Helene," said the voice of the soul, "if you don't participate in this hearing, you will never forgive yourself. You will always regret it. You've worked much too hard on this to give up without a fight. Go outside and calm down."

I rose with difficulty and left the conference room. Everyone was so busy roaring that I don't think my departure was noticed. Or else they were too tactful to comment on it. I walked around outside the conference room and thought back over the months I'd been working on the case. All summer long, I'd been receiving phone calls from women active in the women's movement, strangers who'd heard I was working on the Chicago Eight case. "How can you work for those chauvinist pigs?" I was repeatedly asked. I was then told what I hadn't known when I'd taken on the case, which was how the women on the Chicago trial staff had been thanklessly used. I realized that, in a way, what was happening now was a repeat of what had gone on during the trial. I was a woman whose skills and time were being contributed to the "cause," and I too was going to get skunked.

The summer strangers had wanted me to quit the case, picket the trial lawyers, hold press conferences to denounce the defendants as "male chauvinist pigs." That wasn't my style. If I did anything negative, it would be quietly to quit.

But now I felt I owed something to the women who had worked before me, to the women I was currently working with, and to myself. So the phone calls, the urging, had accomplished something. They made me aware of the role I should be playing in this case. I had done the work of a litigator, both in and out of the courtroom, for the last five years. While on Wall Street, I had resented the fact that I was never given prime responsibility for important cases, but it had rarely occurred to me to question this, and when I did, I retired quickly in the face of the predictable resistance. But this was different. This was the "movement," and one of the things supposedly being struggled against was sexism. I couldn't duck out of this confrontation. I knew that Arthur was right. If it had been a man with my litigation experience who had drafted the jury motion, his role at the jury hearing would never have been challenged. Moreover, it had been decided at the September meeting that I was to be one of the three senior lawyers on the case (two of whom were women); if that was to be anything more than a mere title, then it was time for us women to get out of the traditional rut. No more would women remain in the background in this case, buried in the libraries and offices drafting legal documents, scurrying around doing Xeroxing and other scut work. If women did the paper work, women would make the presentations in court.

I went back into the conference room, knowing that I had reached a personal turning point. I don't think I would have been able to speak up on my own behalf under ordinary circumstances. To me, this was one of those "stand up and fight for yourself" situations at which my natural instinct is to gulp quietly and leave. But I knew without asking that I had the backing of the other women on the staff, and I knew that Arthur was with me. That gave me the courage I needed.

Everyone stopped talking and looked expectantly at me. It was up to me to take the first step toward reconciliation.

"You were right," I said apologetically, addressing myself to the meeting in general, but with words meant for the man who had opposed my having prime responsibility for the hearing. "I was being too proprietary about the jury motion. But you must understand that I've done nothing but work on jury questions for the past four months. Maybe they've become too important to me. I was wrong to regard it as a personal victory when we won the jury motion, but after all, I did draw the papers by myself and the motion was filed in the face of opposition from almost everyone but Doris and Arthur. If it was an ego trip for me, I'm sorry. But my ego *is* involved in this case. And more than that, my whole future as a lawyer is involved. I can't continue on this case if I'm not going to be an active participant in the courtroom work."

It was the longest speech I have ever made pressing my own cause. It was difficult for me to express how I felt and my voice was shaking with fatigue and emotion. There was silence in the room when I stopped speaking.

"Look," Arthur finally said, "I don't think this question over who should conduct the hearing would ever even have been raised if a woman hadn't been involved. If they are senior lawyers with as much experience as Helene has, the men who write the papers are always the ones who appear

in court. It shouldn't be different just because a woman
made the motion."

This time, there were no angry responses to Arthur's
assertions. I had expected a long and bitter confrontation,
but Arthur had obviously smoothed things out. I didn't
know what he had said in my absence, and I never asked,
because I didn't want to reopen old wounds. In a way, the
whole thing was anticlimactic, but I was relieved not to
have to fight about it. Moments later, it was agreed that I
would have prime responsibility for the hearing and that
Doris and I would leave for Chicago the next day. We then
began to discuss strategic problems about the types of
questions to be asked the jurors and marshals, the order in
which witnesses were to be called, and the like. I chaired
the rest of the meeting and it went well.

The confrontation over who was to have prime responsibility for conducting the jury hearing was far more than
a personal victory for me. It was a major breakthrough for
all of us women lawyers and staff members, who had long
been struggling for a greater role in the cases we worked
on. The fact that we had been progressing so slowly in our
battle was part of the vicious cycle. The men didn't respect
us, so they wouldn't let us appear in court; and it was also
because of their lack of respect for us that they would not
respond to our arguments that we should be allowed to
have a more prominent role in the courtroom.

We were fortunate that we had an advocate like Arthur
Kinoy, who was sensitive enough to appreciate that the
time was long overdue for women in law to come out of the
Xerox rooms and libraries and take their places in the court-
rooms. He could do what we could not: convince the other
men, all of whom respected him greatly, that they had to
recognize the new role of their sisters at the bar. That isn't
to say that we wouldn't have made it without Arthur, but
merely to acknowledge that he advanced our cause more
in a single hour than we had been able to do in years.

Word of what had happened at the meeting spread quickly. By the time I arrived in Chicago, there was a telegram waiting for me. It read: "DO YOUR THING," and it was signed "THE LAW CENTER WOMEN." With Arthur and the women behind me, I knew I couldn't fail.

10

The Jury Hearing

Doris and I flew to Chicago Sunday night, November 15.
Such was my determination to participate in the hearing and
such was her devotion to me that she took me to and from
the plane in a wheelchair and half carried me on and off
the plane. We both knew that I would get to Judge Hoffman's courtroom if I had to crawl on my hands and knees.

At ten the next morning, we were there. The May proceeding at which I had been a spectator did not really count.
This was my first formal appearance before Judge Hoffman
and the first time Doris had ever seen him. We were accompanied to court by our local counsel, Thomas Sullivan, a
partner of one of the largest establishment law firms in Chicago. Since neither Doris nor I were members of the Chicago
bar, it was necessary for Tom to introduce us to the Court
and to move for our admission to practice for the purpose of
this proceeding. So before our discussion of the substantive
issues, Tom said to Judge Hoffman, "May I first introduce
Miss Helene Schwartz of the New York bar to you. This is
Miss Schwartz."

"Good morning, your Honor," I said.

"Miss Schwartz," Judge Hoffman responded, with a nod
of his head in my direction.

"She is a member of the Bar of the Southern and Eastern Districts of New York and a graduate of Columbia University Law School and one of the attorneys in the Court of Appeals for the appellants here," Tom said. "She, with your permission, will appear at these hearings pursuant to the Court of Appeals mandate." This was the traditional introduction to the Court of a lawyer who is a member of the bar in another state or jurisdiction.

Judge Hoffman listened carefully, half smiled in my direction, and then turned toward the Assistant United States Attorney, James Thompson, and said to him, "Do you have any objection to a beautiful lady opposing you here, Mr. Thompson?"

"Not at all. If I had my way, I would ask that Miss Schwartz appear alone," Thompson said, as he waved toward my colleagues, as if to dismiss them.

"Maybe they could work it out in private," Tom suggested.

Standing beside him, I gasped with dismay at his comment. Later on, after we left the courtroom, I tried to explain why I was so offended by what he had said. It wasn't easy for me; talking about something important to me personally never is. But I had to try, even if what I said came out sounding stilted. I had already decided that I wanted Tom to play an important role at the jury hearing. If he was going to work with Doris and me, we would have to clear the air over these courtroom exchanges.

"Look, Tom," I said, "there is nothing I appreciate more than sincerely-meant compliments. But there is a place for that and the place isn't in court. At a social tea party it would be delightful, but not in court."

"What difference does it make?" he asked.

"It demeans my status as a lawyer," I replied. "And it isn't fair to my clients. If I am constantly teased about being a woman, it destroys my effectiveness as a lawyer. People won't take me seriously. And it's particularly hard in front of a jury. Women have enough difficulty in court without their friends, like you, making it harder by contributing to the teasing."

Tom admitted that he had never looked at it that way, that he had thought of it as the usual banter that goes on among lawyers and judges. He promised that he would watch himself and try not to make comments of that sort again. He thereafter referred to himself laughingly as "Helene's favorite male chauvinist pig," but I knew that he would make an effort to treat the women he worked with as fellow lawyers rather than objects for teasing.

Judge Hoffman admitted me to practice "for the purpose only of participating in the hearing" which the Court of Appeals had directed him to conduct. Tom introduced Doris to the bench and she was admitted without fuss. We then began to discuss the substantive issues before the Court, two of which were especially important: whether the defense or the government would call its witnesses first; and the date the hearing was to be held.

The first issue was a technical procedural question. Normally, whichever party has the burden of proof calls its witnesses first. Since we had the burden of proving that there had been communications with the jury, we should call the witnesses first. This would give us a strategic advantage, since we could determine the order witnesses would be called and control the manner in which the information we sought was elicited from them. On the other hand, if we called the witnesses first, we would not have the right to cross examine them. With few exceptions, when you call a witness to the stand, you vouch for that witness's credibility. This means you cannot impeach the witness through use of cross-examination techniques such as asking leading questions or referring to prior inconsistent statements by the witness. It was the same problem Pauling's lawyer had faced when he called the defendant Bill Rusher to the stand. The difficulty at this hearing was that the jurors and marshals were not "our" witnesses. This was not an adversarial proceeding. The witnesses were being called at the behest of the Court of Appeals and were technically "Court's witnesses." Although we wanted to examine them first, we also wanted the right to question them as though on cross examination. After hearing argument from both sides, Judge Hoffman was still unsure what to do, so he reserved decision.

We then turned to the question of when the hearing should be held. The government wanted to proceed immediately. Judge Hoffman was inclined to accept this request, as he was impressed by the language in the Court of Appeals order that "the hearing shall be held at the earliest possible date." On behalf of the defendants, Tom and I objected to the hearing's beginning on the next day. "I believe," I argued, "that the phrase 'the hearing shall be held at the earliest possible date' must be modified by the phrase which follows, 'to prevent any delays in the appeals.' Now I represent to the Court that if this hearing is held on Thursday [rather than the next day, Tuesday], there will be no delay in the filing of the brief. I think that is all the Court of Appeals is concerned with here. On the other hand, I cannot be prepared for a hearing tomorrow. It is too soon."

Tom then observed that we had not subpoenaed any of the jurors and did not know where the marshals could be located so they too could be served. We would need time to get this information. Thompson was prepared to proceed at once and was reluctant to give us any time to get ready for the hearing. We learned that he had already interviewed the marshals (who were Justice Department employees) and had contacted the jurors. We were at a distinct disadvantage.

Fortunately, Judge Hoffman seemed in an amiable mood. He set the hearing for Thursday, giving us two days to prepare for it. As we left the courtroom, Bill Kunstler hugged me and said, "Congratulations. That is the first motion the defense has ever won before Judge Hoffman. What kind of magic did you use on him?"

During the next two days, Doris and I worked feverishly to prepare for the hearing. We met with John Schultz, a delightful fellow with gorgeous sideburns and a treasure trove of notes from his interviews with jurors Seaholm and Fritz, which he generously shared with us. Schultz was almost as excited about the hearing as we were, because he knew that his interviews were the basis of our successful motion for a hearing. Using Schultz's notes as an outline of anticipated testimony, we spent hours formulating questions to be asked of the jurors and marshals, designed to elicit the information we needed to present this issue to the Court of Appeals.

> When you and the other jurors were deliberating, did
>   you ever send any messages to the judge?
> Which juror suggested that a message be sent?
> Did all the jurors agree that a message should be sent?
> [If the answer is no] Who disagreed?
> Was the message written or oral?
> Who wrote it down on the paper?
> Who decided what should go into the note?
> To the best of your recollection, what did the note say?
> How was the message sent to the judge?

And so on, for twelve pages. Ordinarily, a lawyer doesn't write down questions in advance in such depth. But we had a half dozen lawyers who might be participating in the hearing, each with a different technique in questioning witnesses. We couldn't take the chance that a personal quirk in cross-examination technique might result in failure to ask important questions. At the request of Tom and the other lawyers, Doris and I outlined the suggested procedure to be followed.

We also considered several tactical problems. The most important of these was whether Judge Hoffman should be asked to step down as governor of the proceeding, in order that we might call him as a witness. After all, if there had been messages sent by the deliberating jury to him, he was a central participant in the very circumstances into which the Court of Appeals had ordered this investigation. There was legal precedent for such a request, a Fourth Circuit case in which the judge had, on his own motion, stepped down from the bench at a post-trial hearing, so that he could testify as to his own knowledge of the events under scrutiny. We knew that Judge Hoffman would never step down of his own accord. Whether we should formally request that he recuse himself and subpoena him as a witness were sticky strategic problems.

We finally decided not to follow this course, as there was little hope that the judge would agree to step down and we would only antagonize him by asking. Besides, I had been aware of the Fourth Circuit case when I'd made the original jury motion and had suggested to the Seventh Circuit that it order Judge Hoffman to recuse himself. The Court hadn't taken my suggestion, which did not preclude us from remaking it before Judge Hoffman, but did make it even more likely that he would refuse to comply with our request.

During these harried two days, I also gave serious thought to the question of which lawyers should participate in the hearing and who should examine which witnesses. I knew that my own active participation, aside from a primary advisory capacity, would necessarily be limited by my convalescence, but I did want to examine at least a few of the witnesses. I also felt that, although they were not participating in the preparation of the appeal, Bill and Len should take part in this hearing. If they didn't, it might look as though they had been abandoned because of the contempt sentences that Judge Hoffman had meted out against them after the trial. These contempt convictions were being appealed by a team whose work paralleled ours, headed by Center lawyers James Reif and Morton Stavis. I thought that it was important for the contempt case that Bill and Len

actively participate in this hearing, a decision with which
everyone concurred.

I also wanted our two local counsel, Tom Sullivan and Bill
Brackett, to appear at the hearing. The rules of the Court
required that Chicago attorneys be associated with us out-
of-towners on the case. Although Tom and Bill Brackett
were not actively working on the case and had nothing to
do with the preparation of the appeal brief, they had been
doing a lot of uninspiring, though important things for us,
such as filing papers, talking to clerks, and straightening out
procedural problems that arose in connection with the appeal. In addition, I was impressed by Tom's performances
in court. He was a skilled litigator and Judge Hoffman
seemed more deferential toward him than toward the rest
of us. I was afraid that the judge might revert to the antagonistic and combative treatment of Bill and Len which had
typified the trial. If that happened, the participation of the
trial lawyers in this hearing would have to be limited. I
thought Tom might succeed in keeping the judge's eccen-
tricities within manageable limits, although Tom continually
assured me that no one could do that better than I could
myself. "He really likes you, Helene," he would say with a
puckish smile.

I wondered about the judge's "liking" me. I was concerned
about the possibility that he would continue to make comments about my being a woman. I was disappointed at my
failure to respond sharply when he had asked whether the
prosecutor had "any objection to a beautiful lady opposing"
him. In the years I had been practicing, I had never learned
how to deal with courtroom quips of this sort at my expense.
It wasn't a question of making a point with Judge Hoffman;
having read the transcript, I knew he was uneducable. In
addition, he had already exhibited a lamentable propensity
for citing lawyers for contempt when they irritated him and
I had no desire to languish in jail, especially at a time when I
was needed on the preparation of the appeal. There was no

sense in antagonizing Judge Hoffman, and that was all I could accomplish by making snippy answers to remarks I found offensive. Nevertheless, my conscience insisted I say something. I just had to be careful about what I said.

I was particularly sensitive to the problem at this hearing because everyone at the Center knew there had been opposition to my having prime responsibility and people were watching to see how I conducted myself. If I had previously been oblivious to or refused to face the truth about discrimination against me, after the confrontation over the jury hearing I could no longer ignore the problem. I felt I owed it both to myself and to those who had supported me to make a clear objection to the flippant treatment so often accorded women attorneys in the courtroom, of which this was typical. While preparing for the hearing, Doris and I talked about how I could handle this problem. We had to balance our personal needs against what was best for the case. After much thought, we decided that when the appropriate occasion arose, I would comment on the "charm" of one of the many men participating in the proceeding. A quiet remark of that sort would make the point without angering the judge or jeopardizing the appeal.

Late Wednesday afternoon, all the attorneys who had been asked to participate in the hearing met at Tom's office. We were five men and two women. I was apprehensive about the meeting, but I needn't have been; the decisions Doris and I had made met with approval and the meeting went smoothly. That night, we went out to eat, at a table covered with legal briefs and Chicago newspapers. Although I'm normally not a devotee of fortune telling, I took a peek at my horoscope. In the first paper, I read:

> You need to use good judgment in handling business problems now, so get on the beam. Gaining the good will of influential persons is most wise. Make your career what it really should be.

The second newspaper also contained an appropriate warning:

> Don't lean on anyone else's ability when your own is so potent, but accept proferred assistance from those who can help.

Dinner ended with a fortune cookie, which informed me: "Opportunity is rapping at your door." If the spirits were trying to send me a message, it was one I had already appreciated on my own. I was resolved that, not only for the good of the case, but for the sake of the people who had supported me, this hearing was going to be a resounding triumph.

The jury hearing opened that Thursday morning with a renewal of our motion that we be permitted to examine witnesses first. Again, the government opposed us on this point. On our behalf, Tom repeated the arguments we had made at the preliminary hearing as to why we should proceed first. When he finished his presentation, I rose and asked, "May I supplement what Mr. Sullivan has said?"

"I would hope you would say something, and not just decorate that table," Judge Hoffman responded.

I ignored his comment because I had an important substantive argument to make. "Mr. Thompson has just admitted that the government has no burden of proof," I said, alluding to Thompson's prior argument. "I think that is the crux of the matter here. The burden is on us. We are the ones who must come forward and verify these facts. I have never participated in a hearing where the person who has the burden goes second. It is like asking the government to negate the facts before we have a chance to prove the affirmative."

The point seemed obvious. If the defendants failed to prove that the hearsay set forth in the Schultz affidavit was the truth, we would have no basis for an issue in the main appeal relating to improper communications to the jury. We had the burden, so we should go first. It seemed an elementary point of procedure. Unfortunately, Judge Hoffman didn't see it that way. "I will permit the government to call witnesses first," he said, "but I shall also permit the defendants, of course, to cross examine those witnesses. It seems to me that, in the process, you get what you want."

We didn't agree, but there was no point in arguing further. The effect of the judge's ruling was that the government elicited through its own direct examination the information we needed. In most instances, all that was left for us to do when it was our turn to cross examine was to round out the testimony by seeking a few more details. Even the prosecutors seemed uncomfortable with the procedure.

During this colloquy, Tom and I had been standing at the podium in front of the bench, with Thompson on my left. As we started to turn toward the defense table, the judge suddenly said, "It's awfully hard when there is a man and a woman in front of me to address you. I am accustomed to saying 'Gentlemen.' I nearly made a slip that time."

"She is very active in the women's liberation movement, your Honor," Tom said. "I don't think she would stand on that formality."

I don't know where Tom got this idea. I'd never been active in the women's movement and always thought I'd make a pretty poor "gentleman." The only time Tom and I had ever discussed my role as a woman and an attorney was after the preliminary hearing, when I'd complained about his exchange with Judge Hoffman. Maybe he thought that any woman with a sensitivity to those kinds of remarks must be active in the women's movement. I wasn't, but I let the comment pass.

Judge Hoffman didn't. His brow shot up, his mouth opened soundlessly, and he leaned over the bench and said with disbelief, "She is active, did you say?"

"Your Honor," I said, "I don't see how any female attorney can fail to be active in the women's movement." For me, it was solidarity of consciousness that was important, not formal membership, a distinction I didn't bother to explain to the judge.

"Well," he said coyly, "if they all look like you do, I will give some consideration to applying for membership."

This was it. With a studied outward calm that hid a pounding heart, I addressed the judge. "I think Mr. Sullivan might be offended that you haven't complimented him on his good looks, your Honor," I said.

Tom's face turned bright red. I knew he had gotten the point. It went right over the head of Judge Hoffman, who continued to talk about the procedures we were to follow, as though I had said nothing at all. It might have been "nothing" to him, but it was the first time I had ever responded in kind to a courtroom remark about my being a woman, and I felt wonderful. The next day, *The New York Times* printed Judge Hoffman's comments to me, but not my answers to him. The Chicago papers ignored the incident altogether. The two papers ran the gamut of a typical media response to the issue of disrespectful treatment of women lawyers.

I had one more request to make of Judge Hoffman before the first witness was called. I had seen the Chicago Eight jury being shepherded into the witness room a few moments before I had entered the courtroom. The jurors looked nervous and I thought that they should be put at their ease.

"Your Honor," I said, "the appellants move that, as each juror is called to testify as a witness, the Court instruct her or him as to the nature of this proceeding. The reason for this is that the jurors are laymen and they may be very apprehensive if they don't understand what is going on here. They may feel that the thrust of this hearing is directed at them, for example. We therefore propose that the following statement be read to the jurors. This is, I might add, a very neutral statement:

> This hearing is being held at the direction of the Court of
> Appeals. This is not a new action but part of the same case
> in which you sat as a juror. You as a juror are not on trial
> here. I [meaning Judge Hoffman] will not make any decision
> or findings of fact in this matter. The sole purpose of this
> hearing is to provide information for the Court of Appeals.

The judge looked at the statement somewhat doubtfully
and indicated that he was not disposed to read it to the
jurors. "The danger, it seems to me, in making any explanation," he said, "is that there might be something in the tone
of my voice—you know, the tone of my voice has been criticized on occasion." I knew what he was referring to. When
the jurors were being selected at the original trial, Judge
Hoffman had read the indictment to them in a tone which,
some of the prospective jurors were later to say, indicated his
belief that the defendants were guilty of the crimes charged.

"Your Honor, we will trust you on this occasion," I said. I
was anxious that the jurors be reassured that they were not
the subjects of any punitive action.

The judge was still dubious. "It might make a juror understand one way and not another way and I am not disposed
to do it, but I will hear from the government."

"Your Honor," I continued, "witnesses are ordinarily interviewed beforehand and prepared, they know what is going
on, and I think we all—"

"Well, if they know, that is an additional reason for not
telling them," the judge interrupted.

"But these witnesses have not been interviewed and I think
that this is, as everyone agrees, an extraordinary proceeding,
and frankly, if I were one of these jurors, I would be scared,
and I would like to—"

"You would be what?" the judge interrupted again.

"I would be scared, frightened, apprehensive."

"Oh, no," said Judge Hoffman in a fatherly tone. "Not if
I was the judge."

It was hopeless. There I was, trying to argue on the law,

and instead of meaningful responses to the content of my argument, I was faced with patronizing remarks from the judge. I gave up and resumed my seat. Judge Hoffman sustained the government's objection to any instruction to the juror-witnesses.

The government then called the first witness. To our surprise, it was Shirley Seaholm, one of the two jurors who had been interviewed by John Schultz and who had told him of the communications between the jury and the judge and marshal. I turned to Tom and said, "All that fuss over who should determine the order the jurors would testify was for nothing. If we'd had our choice, we probably would have called Seaholm first."

Preliminary questions established the witness's name, address, the fact of her service on the Chicago Eight jury. Thompson then went into the chronology of the deliberations. Seaholm testified that the jury was sent out on Saturday, the fourteenth of February, and that it had deliberated until Wednesday, the eighteenth. Then came the crucial question. "During the course of your deliberations," Thompson asked, "did the jury ever send a written message to the trial judge?" We held our collective breaths. Would the juror hold up on the stand?

"Well, I believe it was a written message. I know we sent a message to the judge," said Mrs. Seaholm. Palpable relief flowed from the defense table.

"Was more than one message sent?" the prosecutor asked.

"I can't remember the second one," Mrs. Seaholm said.

John Schultz had warned us that Mrs. Seaholm couldn't remember the second hung-jury message, so we were not surprised. And it was not especially damaging. According to Schultz, juror Fritz remembered the second message and was willing to testify about it. And it was possible that other jurors would remember it too. Even if they didn't, we were home free on the issue of the communications between the judge and jury. The existence of at least one message which had not been revealed to the defendants or their attorneys had been verified under oath.

Juror Seaholm testified that she thought the first message had been sent on Sunday and that its contents were something to the effect of, "We cannot come to an agreement." Although she could not remember its exact contents, she was sure that the heart of the message was that the jury could not agree on a verdict. She could not remember whether the message was written or oral, but thought that it might have been written. She also recalled that the message had been given to one of the marshals for delivery to the judge.

"Did he communicate to you anything in response to your message?" Thompson asked.

"He said to keep deliberating, that the judge could keep us, you know; he wanted a verdict," juror Seaholm testified. Later she said, "He mentioned the Krebiozen trial had lasted for quite a while, their deliberations had lasted for two weeks." She also testified that the marshal told the jurors, "The judge can keep you here as long as he wants."

We relaxed completely. The factual basis of the second issue for our appeal, the improper comments by the marshal to the deliberating jury, had now been confirmed. Arthur Kinoy leaned over and said to me, "We can go back to New York right now."

Then Thompson asked, "Were any other communications sent by the jury to the trial judge during the period of deliberations which went after that first message and prior to the return of the verdict on Wednesday?"

"Well," Mrs. Seaholm answered, "I believe we asked for some speeches."

She was referring to what we had tentatively named the "third message," to distinguish it from the two hung-jury messages. Juror Seaholm could not remember when this message was sent. Again, she thought it was probably a

written message, but was not sure. She remembered that in
it the jurors had requested "some speeches by Jerry Rubin."
She was not certain of the response received through the
marshal. "I believe it was that the transcript was so large
that it could not be, you know, there was so much to it that
it would be impossible to give that portion to us."

This was incredible. The speeches given by the defendants
were the heart of the government's case against them. There
were transcripts of some of these speeches, given both before
and during the convention, which had been entered in evidence. Had the defense attorneys been consulted about the
jury's request, they could have advised the judge to send
these important pieces of evidence to the jury. As it was, the
jury conviction rested upon speeches which the jurors admittedly didn't remember.

Thompson examined juror Seaholm for a while longer,
about various details relating to the messages and the marshal's comments. Then he turned her over to us for cross
examination. We asked for a moment to consult, during
which we agreed that the cross examination of juror Seaholm
should be short. There was no reason to try to impeach
her, the normal purpose of cross examination, as she was
testifying to facts that we wanted to see verified.

I introduced myself to Mrs. Seaholm as one of the appellate
lawyers for the defendants. Even though Judge Hoffman had
denied our request that the jurors be told the purpose of
the hearing and that they had nothing to be afraid of, Len
wanted me to say something along those lines to Mrs. Seaholm. I refused to do it, and to this day I haven't figured out
whether I was being sensible or just lacked courage.

I began my cross examination, but didn't get very far. My
first question elicited an objection. "Mrs. Seaholm," I said
by way of review, "when you were testifying you mentioned
that somebody else took over in the deliberating room rather
than the foreman."

"Yes," she confirmed.

"Who was that person?" I asked.

"The government will object to that as not being relevant," Thompson interjected.

"I sustain the objection," the judge said.

"Your Honor, may I argue to that?" Hearing no dissent, I continued. "The Court of Appeals has indicated in its order that it wants to go into, not only the contents of these notes and unauthorized communications, but 'the circumstances surrounding' the communications. I believe the manner in which the jury decided to send these communications is definitely a 'circumstance surrounding' the communications." I convinced no one and the objection was again sustained.

"Mrs. Seaholm," I continued, "you said that these notes were written. Do you remember who wrote them?"

"I believe it was [juror] Kay Richards, but I am not sure," Mrs. Seaholm said.

"Your Honor," I said, turning to the judge, "at this point we have had a lot of discussion about the contents of certain messages."

"Oh, I am listening carefully," said Judge Hoffman, before I could make my argument. "I would never describe this witness's testimony as 'a lot of discussion.' Questions have been put to her and she has answered them. I don't generalize that way."

"Then let me say," I continued, "that questions have been put to the witness and answers have been given by the witness about the contents of certain written documents."

"You needn't review events of the last several minutes," Judge Hoffman said.

"I am laying a foundation, your Honor," I explained.

It was my intention to ask him at this point whether he still had the notes that the jurors had sent him. There is a rule of evidence called the "best evidence" rule, according to which it is improper to have testimony about the contents of a document unless it has been proven that the document itself is unavailable. There had been a lot of testimony about the contents of the messages from the jury, but no proof whatever that the messages themselves no longer existed.

"I know what has been asked. I will let my ruling stand with respect to the question you asked last. You may ask another."

I decided to try another tack. "Mrs. Seaholm," I asked the witness, "did you ever, after the message was given to the marshal, see the slip of paper again on which the message was written?"

"No," she answered.

"And it is your understanding that the message was given to the marshal to be delivered to the trial judge?"

"Yes."

I turned once again toward Judge Hoffman. "Your Honor, may I inquire whether you have that message? It is not in the record."

The government objected to my question and the judge again sustained the objection.

"Your Honor," I urged doggedly, "don't you think we are bucking the best-evidence rule? We are talking about a document—"

"I said," the judge repeated angrily, "I sustain the objection."

I stared at him for a moment. So this was what it had been like for Bill and Len for five months of trial. My admiration for them was growing. This ruling flew directly in the face of a basic rule of evidence. Nevertheless, I argued no further. We had made a tactical decision that under no circumstances would we antagonize Judge Hoffman. We knew that the Court of Appeals, having ordered this hearing, would closely examine the transcript of it. We were still conscious of the need to maintain our image as dispassionate appellate lawyers, because of the acrimonious atmosphere that had prevailed at the trial. Every instinct I had as a trial lawyer was stifled as I meekly returned to questioning the witness.

The rest of the cross examination was uneventful, though several details about the physical condition of some of the jurors who were ill during deliberations did come to light. These would be useful to buttress our argument that the jurors were anxious to go home and were improperly influenced by the marshal's comments about the length of time they would have to deliberate. When the examination of juror Seaholm was concluded, the judge told her she could step down. "It is my duty, Mrs. Seaholm, to order you not to talk with anybody about this case or let anybody speak with you about it and not to talk among your fellow jurors if you happen to see them."

"Excuse me, your Honor," I said to the judge as Mrs. Seaholm was leaving the stand, "has Mrs. Seaholm been instructed—"

"You are not listening to me," the judge said with annoyance.

"I was listening," I said.

"I did it very emphatically," he said.

"I know your Honor is emphatic," I said in a tired voice. "I just wondered if you made it clear to her, because of the subpoena which was served on her by the appellants, that it is possible that we will call her as a witness on direct, so that she shouldn't leave the courthouse."

He hadn't instructed her about the possibility of her being recalled as a defense witness, so he gave me permission to follow her into the hall and tell her that she might have to testify again.

When we broke for lunch, Jim Thompson came up to me as I was leaving the courtroom. "Julius loves you," he said.

"Yeah, sure," I said.

"I'm not kidding," Thompson said. "I've never seen him so calm in court. I think he's ready to marry you."

"Then what's he like when he's mad?" I asked.

Thompson laughed at my incredulity. "You're going to be famous in Chicago as the lawyer who charmed Julius Hoffman."

"Famous?" I muttered doubtfully. "More likely infamous."

11

Judge Hoffman
Seeks Combat

I watched with curiosity as the next witness approached the stand. Jean Fritz was rumored to have been one of the most intelligent and sensitive members of the jury. The defendants had counted on her to lead the deliberations. To her own later sorrow, she did not hold out against the jurors who wanted convictions. She had not realized that a hung jury would have been almost as much of a victory for the defendants as an acquittal. She told John Schultz that she had been afraid that a hung jury would result in a retrial and perhaps conviction on all counts, so she agreed to a compromise verdict of conviction on some counts, acquittal on others. It was a decision she now regretted and she was ridden with guilt over the part she had played in this trial.

More than any other member of the jury, this woman had suffered because of her participation in the Chicago Eight trial. The fact that she had been an "acquittal" juror had been published in the local newspapers. Because of this, I had been told, she had been subjected to bomb threats, obscene telephone calls, a barrage of uncomplimentary mail, and a loss of business at her family store. I later learned that after the jury hearing she had received more derogatory communications and another bomb threat as a result of the publicity attendant upon her appearance in court. I couldn't help admiring her courage as I watched her in the witness box.

After the usual introductory questions, Thompson asked Mrs. Fritz whether, during the course of the deliberations, any messages had been sent by the jury to the judge. She recalled that there were two, and that they had both been handwritten by juror Kay Richards.

"Do you know what the message said?" Thompson asked with respect to the first note.

"I don't remember," Mrs. Fritz responded. "It was supposed to have said that we couldn't come to an agreement."

"Did you see the actual words as they were written?"

"I don't remember that either. I have tried and tried, and I can't remember that," juror Fritz said. Listening to her testify, it occurred to me that the agonized tone of her responses was probably symptomatic of what she had gone through as a juror on this case.

Juror Fritz testified that in answer to the first message the marshal had said "that we had to keep on deliberating." He had told the jurors "that the trial had lasted a long time, you can't expect it to end in this much of a hurry." She verified juror Seaholm's testimony that there had been mention of the long period of time which the jury on another recent Chicago case, involving the cancer drug Krebiozen, had deliberated. She also said that the marshal told the jurors "that Judge Hoffman could keep us here as long as he saw fit." All this arguably gave the jurors the impression that they would be kept indefinitely until they reached a verdict.

Unlike Mrs. Seaholm, who didn't remember, Mrs. Fritz was able to testify that the marshal making these comments was Ron Dobroski. He was the one who had been sequestered with the jury during the five-month trial and had been in charge of the jury during its deliberations. Juror Fritz also remembered a second message to the judge, telling him "that we couldn't come to an agreement," which was written by juror Richards and sent to the judge, she believed, on Monday. We now had sworn testimony in the record of the two hung-jury messages.

During her interviews with John Schultz, Jean Fritz had expressed admiration for Len Weinglass, so I asked him if he would cross examine her, and he readily agreed. I thought there was something poetically fitting about the Fritz-Weinglass combination. They were probably the two most vulnerable people among those who had participated in the trial, and they were both still carrying its scars.

Len reminded juror Fritz that she had testified that there had been two written notes to the judge indicating that the jurors could not reach a verdict. He asked her whether, from the time the notes had been sent to the present day, she had ever seen those notes. She replied that she had not and that she didn't know what had become of them. Len then turned to the judge and repeated the question I had previously asked as to the whereabouts of the notes. "In light of the witness's answer," Len said, "I would request of the Court at this time that if the Court has knowledge or possession of these slips of paper to produce them to assist me in my further examination."

"I will again object," said Thompson, "on the grounds that, according to the order of the Court of Appeals, that is an improper request."

"I sustain the objection," said Judge Hoffman.

Len then asked Mrs. Fritz about her physical condition during the deliberations. We had information that she had been suffering from phlebitis and had been advised by a physician that to remain on the jury might endanger her life. The Court of Appeals had authorized us to investigate "the circumstances surrounding" the communications with the jury, and if Mrs. Fritz had been ill, her state of mind might have influenced her reaction to the marshal's comments about the indefinite length of time the jury could be kept deliberating. If we could get sworn testimony about her illness, we could argue that her illness might have made her anxious to go home and more amenable to compromise than she should have been.

"Now, Mrs. Fritz," Len asked, "as you were sitting there, is it not a fact that at that particular time you were suffering from an illness known as phlebitis?"

"The government will object to that question," Thompson said.

"I will sustain the objection," the judge said.

"If your Honor please," I said as I rose from my seat, "may I argue to this?"

"I will allow one lawyer to cross examine the witness, to participate in the cross examination," Judge Hoffman said. "Do you want to consult with your associate, Miss Schwartz? You may."

"I am sorry," I replied. "I understood I would be able to argue the substantive questions."

This was the procedure we had agreed upon among us: that while several lawyers would conduct the cross examinations, I would argue most of the questions of law as they came up. I had done the research on questions relating to interference with the integrity of the jury and was more familiar with the cases than the others were. We had told Judge Hoffman at the beginning of the hearing that we would follow this procedure, and he had voiced no objection. Now that the occasion had arisen when I wished to argue a substantive point, he refused to allow me to do so.

"If you want to make a suggestion to Mr. Weinglass," the judge said, "you may. I will wait."

I went up to the podium and discussed with Len a line of argument he could make in support of questions about the jurors' physical condition during the deliberations. I resumed my seat, Len made the argument, and the government's renewed objection was sustained. We couldn't help wondering whether the judge even bothered to listen to our argument or whether he automatically sustained all government objections. In spite of our suspicion that it was hopeless, we continued to make our legal arguments, for the purpose of preserving the questions in the Court of Appeals.

The prosecutor had neglected to question Mrs. Fritz about the third, or so-called transcript, message. I don't know whether it was intentional or he just forgot. Under Len's further cross examination, juror Fritz recalled that the jurors had "asked for certain speeches" by Jerry Rubin, Abbie Hoffman, and Rennie Davis. This request was also made in a written note, sent to the judge through the marshal. The response, as relayed by the marshal, was "something to the effect, 'you are not allowed to have the transcript.' "

Juror Frieda Robbins was then called to the witness box. During her direct examination, she corroborated the existence of all three messages and verified the substance of the comments that the marshal had made to the jurors. This was important; unlike jurors Seaholm and Fritz, she hadn't been interviewed by John Schultz. If the government had any plans to charge Fritz, Seaholm, and Schultz with collusion, Robbins's testimony made it clear that the two women were telling the truth.

The testimony of the first three witnesses differed as to the literal contents of the notes and when they had been sent. They also disagreed on their recollection of the exact comments that the marshal had made to the jurors. But the important thing was that they agreed that there *had* been messages and comments. Their inability to recall the incidents with precision was good for us, and would be an important factor in the presentation of this issue on appeal.

These three witnesses were known to have favored the acquittal of the defendants, as did the fourth witness, Mary

Butler, who claimed to remember nothing about any messages or comments and who was obviously terrified and anxious to leave the courtroom. The test would come when the "convict" jurors were called to the stand. The first of these was Edward Kratzke. Although one of only two men on the jury, and a blunt, truculent person who often misspoke, he had been elected foreman. He verified one of the hung-jury messages, the transcript message, and the improper comments by the marshal, so we knew that we would have no problem whatever convincing the Court of Appeals of the factual basis of our argument on these issues.

On cross examination of juror Kratzke, Tom Sullivan attempted to elicit information about the ailment Kratzke had complained of during the deliberations, which had necessitated his being examined by a physician. This went to the same point we planned to make about juror Fritz, that illness of jurors might have interfered with the deliberative process. The government again objected to this line of questioning. I asked for a moment to confer with Tom about another tack he might take on his argument of this question of law.

"Yes," replied Judge Hoffman, "provided you don't put your arm around Mr. Sullivan."

For a moment, I didn't understand what the judge was talking about. Then I realized that I had put my hand on Tom's shoulder as we whispered about our courtroom strategy. "He is an old friend," I said as I removed my hand.

"Hoffman is acting like a jealous lover," Tom whispered to me.

"No," Judge Hoffman suddenly said crossly. "I indicated that we would have one lawyer attend to the cross examination of each witness."

"I understood yesterday that you would permit me to consult with lawyers about substantive argument," I said.

"Well, you are taking a lot of time consulting here," he said peevishly.

"Well, if you would let me speak, I wouldn't have to consult," I replied.

"Perhaps if you would conduct the cross examination, we might save some time. I mean that as no reflection on Mr. Sullivan," said the judge with a nod toward my colleague.

"Your Honor, I am sorry," I said. "I am recovering from major surgery, and I am not able to conduct this hearing fully. That is why I have asked for help from my brother attorney."

I felt embarrassed to mention my illness in open court, but I didn't see how I could avoid it. The judge grumbled, but he let me consult with Tom. Kratzke then testified that he had suffered from a nervous stomach, a fact which might well have influenced his desire to get out of the jury room as quickly as possible.

Among the juror-witnesses, the next was particularly important. The other jurors had identified Kay Richards as the person who actually wrote the notes to the judge. She was a "convict on all counts" juror and was extremely hostile to the defense. At the time of the trial, she was engaged to a member of the Daley administration, whom she had since married. Because of the limitations that Judge Hoffman had imposed upon the voir dire, this information did not surface until after the trial. Had it been known prior to the trial, Kay Richards would most certainly have been challenged by the defense.

Brilliantly cross examined by Tom, juror Richards admitted that she had written three notes to the judge on behalf of her fellow jurors. She confirmed that two indicated that the jurors felt they could no longer deliberate, and the third "requested transcripts concerning some of the speeches that the defendants had given on certain occasions." She also recalled the substance of the comments made by the marshal, as testified to by the other juror-witnesses.

During the cross examination of juror Richards, Tom re-

newed our motion that the government or the judge produce
the three notes, if they had them. The government again
objected to the request, and in a flash of anger, one of the
prosecutors admitted, "We don't have any notes."

"I do not have any note," the judge added. So, at last, we
learned that the notes no longer existed.

It was soon after this important information surfaced that
our difficulties with Judge Hoffman over my right to consult
with the members of the defense team on questions of law
that came up while they were cross examining came to a
head. I walked over to Tom, who was standing at the
podium, to hand him a note suggesting a line of argument in
support of the questions he was attempting to ask. The judge
erupted in an angry tirade against me. "I hope I never have
a beautiful girl come in here and jump up so often while I
am talking," he barked.

Tom and I stood by the podium, startled into silence by
the suddenness and vehemence of his attack. New and often
complex questions of law were being raised at this unusual
proceeding. The judge himself had necessitated these con-
sultations by refusing to allow me to argue the questions of
law as they arose during the course of examination of the
juror-witnesses. He had justified his refusal by saying that
I could consult with my colleagues whenever necessary. Now
he seemed to be precluding consultation. It was a wearisome
business, for we never knew what would happen next.

"I am not accustomed to that, Miss Schwartz," the judge
said, continuing his harangue against me. "I don't mean to
offend," he said more calmly, "but I am not accustomed to
that here. We don't do that here. Maybe you do it in New
York."

At that last remark, I heard Doris give a muffled guffaw.
One of the ways in which the judge had denigrated the
defense trial counsel was by repeated references to the fact
that they were "foreigners" from New York. He was falling

into his old patterns in this case. I looked over at Len and saw him hunched over the table writing a note, trying hard to stifle his laughter. He passed me the note and I read, "Thirty days! Maybe twenty."

Then it was my turn to hide the giggles. I knew that Len was right. Had this been the trial, the judge might well have held me in contempt. I didn't think I was doing anything wrong. I was only trying to argue on behalf of my clients. And I was following the procedure which Judge Hoffman had himself approved at an earlier point in the hearing. If that merited a contempt citation, and it seemed from the record of this trial that there were times when it did, then I considered the remark by Len to be a backhand compliment, and I told him so.

Although their recollections varied, most of the rest of the juror-witnesses remembered at least one or two of the messages and the substance of the marshal's comments to the deliberating jury. Their testimony was elicited with a minimum of difficulty and no more confrontations between me and Judge Hoffman on the issue of my being allowed to argue or consult on questions of law. There was, however, one other small incident which was of no importance to the proceeding as a whole but which did have a personal impact on me.

One of Thompson's assistants had just concluded the direct examination of juror Lorraine Bernacki, and she was turned over to me for cross examination. It was late in the afternoon and I, struggling under the strain of the too-recent surgery, was on the verge of physical collapse. I looked at the courtroom clock. It was 4:29. The day before, Judge Hoffman had adjourned at 4:30. I rose and, again embarrassed by the need to mention my illness, I said: "Your Honor, I was prepared to cross examine this witness, but I really am not feeling very well and I would appreciate it if we could take our adjournment now."

The judge denied my motion. I was literally too weak to stand and I was sure that the judge would not grant me the courtesy of allowing me to sit during examination of a witness, so I asked Tom to examine her. Exactly thirteen minutes later, Judge Hoffman adjourned the proceedings for the day. And then something happened which had been my private nightmare ever since I had decided to go to law school. When I get angry, I sometimes cry. I have always been afraid that someday someone would say something nasty to me in court and I would burst into tears. Now my eyes were brimming with tears of rage and impotence. Thirteen minutes! He just wasn't a very nice man.

(In fairness to Judge Hoffman, he was probably thinking about the convenience of the witness. She was not an important witness and in those thirteen minutes her cross examination was finished, which meant that she wouldn't have to return to court the next day. But that didn't occur to me until months later. At the time, I just thought that the judge was being ornery.)

I blinked quickly to try to get rid of the tears. I've never understood why our society has such a thing against people crying in public, but I had the feeling that if anyone saw me it would be the end of my legal career.

Before this incident, I had been inexplicably reluctant to mount the diatribe against Judge Hoffman necessary to attack his conduct at the trial. I leaned over to Doris and with a vehemence that she understood, I said to her, "*Now* I can write the section of the brief on judicial misconduct!"

Doris reached across the defense table and hugged me. She knew exactly how I felt about what the judge had done. Together, we were to write the section of the appeal brief relating to the judge's misconduct during the trial, and it was one of the finest pieces of legal argument either of us has ever done. If he had accomplished nothing else, Judge Hoffman had succeeded this day in motivating us. And about those tears—well, I think Julius could probably make the Sphinx cry.

That night, Arthur insisted Doris and I join him in the hotel bar for a drink. Arthur wasn't actively participating in the hearing, as he was busy working on the section of the appeal brief attacking the constitutionality of the underlying statute. And although I didn't know it at the time, he had already been visited by the F.B.I., in the series of events that led to the grand jury proceedings I mentioned before. He had flown out to Chicago to satisfy his curiosity about the hearing, to give us encouragement, and to confer with his daughter Joanne about the F.B.I. interest in her whereabouts. I was glad to have him with us. Just seeing him sitting at the defense table made me feel good when Judge Hoffman was at his worst.

We had a lot to celebrate that night. On the whole, in spite of the problems with Judge Hoffman, the day had gone well. I thought that we had enough grounds for reversal of the convictions. And it was a safe, procedural issue, unlike the controversial ones, such as judicial and prosecutorial misconduct, or the questionable constitutionality of the statute.

I agreed to have a drink, which is rare for me. Three sips and I am under the table. Tonight was no exception. I have a vague recollection of sitting in a darkened room, a sort of mini-Playboy Club, with waitresses whose enormous breasts almost touched my nose whenever they leaned over to serve our table.

Someone brought in the evening papers and we looked to see what had been written about the hearing. The Chicago *Sun-Times* had a banner headline story that covered half of page 3. There was even a picture of Bill Kunstler. I sighed. No matter who else had been on the trial team, no matter who was now working on the case, no matter whose case it had become—to the newspapers and public, it would always be Bill's case. I looked back at the photo. Bill was standing next to a sickly-looking brunette. I peered closely at her. It was me.

"Look at that!" I shouted. People at other tables turned and stared. "Look, look!" I shouted again. "My picture is in the paper!" Media glamour! Instant glory! Helenie Superstar! I was overwhelmed.

I pushed the paper over to Doris and Arthur, but they were too busy laughing at my reaction to look at it. "I wonder who that is?" Doris finally said.

Hours later, when the gin and excitement wore off, I examined the news stories more closely. Glory was replaced by discontent. Every time my name was mentioned, it was preceded by a descriptive phrase such as "the attractive brunette," or "the mini-skirted lawyer from New York." There were no personal adjectives of that type preceding references to Tom Sullivan or the prosecutors.

Doris and I talked about whether we should hold a press conference, both to chastise the newspapers for the "offending adjectives" (as we dubbed them) and to discuss Judge Hoffman's comments and patronizing attitude toward me. Some of his actions exemplified his usual eccentric conduct in the courtroom, and could equally have been directed to a male lawyer. But many of his comments, his tone, and his attitude stemmed from the fact that I am a woman. The problems I was having with Judge Hoffman were typical of the difficulties women faced almost every time they went into a courtroom. Most of these incidents never come to the public's attention. But we had representatives of the networks, syndicates, and independent newspapers present every day in our courtroom. We had a ready-made audience before which to raise these issues.

Still, Doris and I were reluctant to have anything to do with the press. Part of this grew out of an essential shyness and dislike of calling attention to ourselves. We were also disturbed by the fact that the defense trial lawyers had been heavily criticized on the ground that they had catered too much to the press, held press conferences and issued press releases. We did not want the Court of Appeals to lose its respect for the appellate team, so we hesitated to bring the issue to the media's attention, although it was something that meant a great deal to both of us. Ultimately, we were influenced by our feeling that, irrespective of how much the issue meant to us personally, there was a limit to the degree to which a lawyer could indulge his or her own ego when the interests of a case might be at stake. We decided, regretfully, that we could not chance the adverse effects on the case as a whole.

Of course, the irony of the difficulties I was having with Judge Hoffman was the repeated assurances of both the prosecutors and our local counsel that never had the judge exhibited such control in the courtroom. "You've made a conquest," Tom kept saying to me. "He's letting you get away with murder." Tom pointed out that the judge let me ask questions that he precluded the men from asking when they cross examined, and that he was showing a very courtly demeanor toward me.

"You may be right," I admitted. "He probably does think that he's being chivalrous. But to me it seems as though he's being condescending. I wish he'd stop it and just treat me like a lawyer."

At the next session, we began hearing the testimony of the six marshals who'd had charge of the jury while it was deliberating. Four of them denied knowledge of any messages or comments. The fifth also denied knowing anything about the communications. But we had a little surprise.

A few days before, I had received a telephone call from Joanne Kinoy, who was then living in Wisconsin. She called to report an unusual coincidence. A friend of hers had just been at University Hospital in Madison for minor surgery.

His roommate at the hospital was a prisoner who was accused of having robbed a bank. The prisoner was guarded by a garrulous federal marshal who said, with great pride, that he had been a marshal at the Chicago Eight trial and he told the two patients that he was going down to Chicago in a few days to testify at a hearing. According to Joanne's friend, the marshal also said that twice the jury had sent notes that it was unable to come to a conclusion. He also told them that he had heard one of the other marshals tell the jurors that they had to keep deliberating indefinitely and that the judge could keep them there as long as he wished.

It was not important for us to get this marshal to make these admissions on the stand, because we had plenty of testimony from the jurors, who had no stake whatever in this matter (unlike the marshals, whose jobs might be at issue if they had done something improper) and whose credibility was not at issue. Still, if the marshal denied under oath knowing anything about the communications, it would be fun to try to rattle him. I asked Joanne to come to Chicago with her friend, so he could identify for us the marshal he had met.

As we expected, this marshal denied on direct examination that he had any knowledge of the messages or improper comments by any marshal during the deliberation. On cross examination, I got him to admit that earlier in the week he had been guarding a federal prisoner in a Madison hospital. He also admitted that he had told the prisoner he had been a marshal at the Chicago Eight trial, but he denied that he had said anything about notes or the marshal's comments.

The government fought this line of questioning all the way. I told the prosecutors that I had a witness who would have completed my impeachment of this marshal, had I been allowed to call him to the stand. "But I'm prevented from doing that by the order of the Court of Appeals," I said to them during a recess, when they privately reproached me.

"The order limits witnesses to marshals and jurors. My witness is neither. I can't call my impeachment witness, but I assure you I would if I could, because there's nothing I'd like better than to show that marshal up."

In his book about the Chicago Eight case, John Schultz wrote of this incident: "Appellant's Attorney Helene Schwartz made a startling attempt to impeach the testimony of one marshal . . ." Schultz noted that the marshal "grinned on the stand as he denied it." The marshal couldn't have grinned as broadly as I did when I read Schultz's description of my cross examination.

Marshal Ronald Dobroski was the last witness at the hearing. He was the marshal who had been identified by the jurors as the one to whom the messages had been given, and the one who had made the improper comments about the length of time the jury was to deliberate. He remembered two of the messages. The first was apparently one of the hung-jury messages, as Dobroski recalled that the judge's response when he delivered the message was to tell him to tell the jurors to "keep deliberating." The other was the third, or so-called transcript message, and Dobroski testified that the judge said to tell the jurors that they could not have any transcript. Dobroski confirmed that these were written messages and he testified that he had handed them to Judge Hoffman. Neither the government nor the judge now had these notes, it was claimed, and Dobroski was unable to shed any light on what might have become of them.

It was not surprising that Dobroski denied making any of the improper comments that the jurors attributed to him. After all, he was indirectly being accused of misconduct and it was possible that he might even lose his job as a result of the hearing. A tenacious cross examination could not shake his testimony.

The Court of Appeals order directing that this hearing be held had invited Judge Hoffman to add his recollections to

the record, if he desired to do so. We would have no opportunity to cross examine him, but we were still interested in
knowing what he would say in defense of what now seemed
to be an error of law on his part, his failure to inform trial
counsel and the defendants of the communications from
the jury. After the last witness testified, I asked him if and
when he intended to make a statement, but he was evasive.

That night, Doris, Arthur, and I left Chicago. We'd had
some difficulty getting flights, because it was just before
Thanksgiving, but we managed to get seats at the last
minute. I said a hurried and grateful goodbye to Tom, who
was going to cover for us the next morning, when some procedural issues remained to be discussed. The next day, Tom
called me after court had adjourned. He told me that Judge
Hoffman had decided to read a statement in open court. In
it, the judge said that he remembered two of the notes: one
hung-jury message and a request for transcript. He claimed
that the hung-jury message was sent "shortly after the jury
began its deliberations" on Saturday, which was why he told
the jury to "continue with its deliberations." He said that
on the following day (Sunday, the second of the four days of
deliberations) he had received another message. His recollection was of a note that telescoped the second hung-jury
message and the transcript message into one: a note "to the
effect that the jury was unable to agree on a verdict or
verdicts but that the jury was desirous of having me send to
the jury room a transcript or transcripts . . . of evidence admitted during the trial." He said that his practice "uniformly
has been to deny such requests," and that he told the marshal to so inform the jurors.

The judge also said that when he received the communications from the jury he had considered bringing the jury
back to the courtroom for further instructions. But then he
recalled that "from the outset of the trial there had been
repeated attempts by persons in the courtroom to influence

the jury by deliberately disrupting the trial with violence, disorder and confusion, and by directing improper and prejudicial statements to the jurors." This behavior, he claimed, had intensified on Saturday and Sunday (when he thought the notes had been sent), which was when he was sentencing the defendants and their trial lawyers for contempt of court. So he concluded

> that if the jury were returned to the courtroom during the deliberations, that there was a very substantial danger of their being exposed to prejudicial statements, courtroom disruption or violence. Therefore, as I recall it, to insure the integrity of the jury during its deliberations, I replied to the jury's requests through the deputy marshal rather than returning the jury to the courtroom.

"That still doesn't explain why he didn't tell the defendants and their trial lawyers about the messages," I said when Tom finished telling me about the judge's statement. "He didn't have to bring the jury back into the courtroom to do that. He could have heard argument in chambers, or something like that." We discussed the legal ramifications of the judge's statement, and then Tom said, "By the way, Helene, Judge Hoffman is very angry at you."

"Why?" I asked.

"You left without saying goodbye," Tom said. I began to laugh, but Tom interrupted to say, "I'm serious. You made your final appearance in court on Tuesday, and you didn't tell him that you weren't going to be there on Wednesday."

"But I didn't have to be there Wednesday. There weren't any witnesses. It was just procedural stuff. And you were covering for us."

"That's true. But you were one of the counsel of record at the hearing, and if you weren't going to be there, you should have told Judge Hoffman on Tuesday and asked that the hearing continue without you."

"Was he angry at all of us or just me?" I asked.

"Well, he was angry at all of you, but you were the only one he mentioned by name."

"Terrific."

"He said that you kept asking what he proposed to do about his 'recollections,' and he seemed hurt that you weren't interested enough to stay and hear them," Tom said.

"He never told us he was going to make a statement," I said. "I probably would have stayed if I'd known he was going to make a statement. But what the heck, when the man is right, he's right. I should have asked his permission to leave. I just forgot."

So ended the jury hearing. And, after all, Judge Hoffman had the last word.

12

Dayenu!

When I returned to New York after the jury hearing, work on the brief began in earnest. Arthur, Doris, and I went into hibernation, emerging occasionally for conferences, but generally working on our own. We surfaced for a week in December to help fight the subpoena ordering Arthur to appear before the federal grand jury. But the rest of our waking hours were devoted to the Chicago case.

We gave passing consideration to the possibility of taking a special appeal, solely on the issue of the improper communications the judge and marshal had had with the jury. I was pretty sure it was a winning issue and Arthur and Doris agreed. It would save us a great deal of work if we confined our argument to that one issue. Tempting as it was, we decided against it. The case had too many other issues of great import, not only legally, but for the political scene as well. How could we mount an appeal in the Chicago Eight case without attacking the constitutionality of the underlying statute, the notorious Rap Brown anti-riot act? How could there be an appeal in the case which was popularly known as the "Conspiracy case," without argument on the inherent unfairness of the prosecutorial use of conspiracy charges?

How could we ignore the issues of illegal electronic surveillance, the use of informers, the numerous improper evidentiary rulings? Most crucial, because it would affect the outcome of the contempt appeals, how could we not deal with the question of the misconduct of the judge and prosecutors during the course of the trial?

Although it meant an enormous amount of additional work, I was glad that we had decided to continue with the full appeal rather than restricting ourselves to the single issue of the communications with the jury. I had been working on the case since the previous April, and it would have meant that most of my work had been for nothing. In particular, there was no need to have read the inordinately long trial transcript if we were going to argue only the issue of the communications. More importantly, however confident I might be about the likelihood of our success on the jury-communication issue, there was no guarantee I was right. If we lost a special appeal on that issue alone, we would not be precluded from thereafter taking a regular appeal on the remaining issues. But we would be starting from a losing posture, which would hurt us.

The first thing we did upon returning to New York was to settle (at last!) on an outline of the major points of the brief. There were going to be fourteen sections to our argument. The first three points would deal with the constitutionality of the statute the defendants had been charged with violating. In these points, we would argue that the statute was unconstitutional on its face, as construed by Judge Hoffman and as applied to the defendants. The differences among these three points were subtle and complex, and the argument, which was to be written by Arthur, turned out to be an outstanding example of constitutional analysis.

The fourth point in the appeal brief would deal with the law of conspiracy. It was to be a technical exposition of the effect of the conspiracy count on the admissibility of evi-

dence and the consequences of the jury's having acquitted
all five appellants on the conspiracy count while convicting
them on the individual substantive counts.

The fifth point would be the one that prosecutors refer to
as the "guilt point" and defense lawyers as the "insufficiency-
of-the-evidence point"—itself an example of how lawyers can
play with words and say the same thing with a different impact. In this section, the trial-record evidence against each
appellant would be reviewed, in an effort to show that the
convictions were based upon a paucity of evidence and
should be reversed.

In the sixth point of the brief, we planned to argue that
the prosecution's case rested upon evidence illegally obtained
through use of government undercover agents and informers,
in violation of the First, Fourth, Fifth, and Sixth Amendments. Three witnesses whose testimony formed the heart
of the government's case were men who had been employed
by state and federal law-enforcement agencies to infiltrate
the political organizations of which the appellants were
members, to spy on their plans for and activities during the
convention. A fourth government witness was a reporter
who joined the appellants' political groups so that he could
report on their activities from the inside and who then turned
informer for the government. The danger of the use of undercover agents and informers in a case "in the shadow of the
First Amendment" was that it represented an encroachment
on the privacy of citizens which could well have a chilling
effect on the exercise of our political freedoms.

The seventh and eighth points in the brief were to deal
with illegal electronic surveillance conducted both before
and during the trial. At the time, we thought the wiretap
issues in the Chicago Eight case would be of great importance. As it turned out, another case on similar issues went
racing to the Supreme Court through an expeditious procedure known as mandamus, and beat us to the punch. The

Supreme Court's decision in that case came down before the Seventh Circuit's decision in our case and was binding on the Seventh Circuit,* so the wiretap issues were of diminished importance in our case.

In our ninth point, we planned to argue that the entire record of the case demonstrated that Judge Hoffman was not an impartial arbiter of the trial but was "an activist seeking combat," whose misconduct deprived the appellants of their right to a fair trial. More about that section later.

The tenth point would urge that the prosecutors were guilty of flagrant and purposeful misconduct, which deprived the appellants of their right to a fair trial.

In the eleventh point, we would deal with the numerous improper evidentiary rulings that effectively deprived the appellants of their right to present a defense. This point was to be divided into twelve sub-sections, each of which would relate to a different ruling or type of ruling. Among these were to be the refusal of the judge to allow Ramsey Clark to testify as a defense witness, the refusal to consider Mayor Daley a hostile witness, interference with the right to cross examine government witnesses, exclusion of defense evidence on the basis of a misinterpretation of the doctrine of self-serving statements, the refusal to allow Ralph Abernathy to testify as a defense witness, and the refusal to admit testimony of expert witnesses offered by the defense.

The twelfth point was to begin with a narration of the events that led to the binding and gagging of co-defendant Bobby Seale and his ultimate mistrial. It would then discuss the probable effect on the jury of the judge's mistreatment of Seale, and argue that since it irretrievably prejudiced the case of the other defendants, a mistrial should have been granted to all of them.

Point thirteen would urge reversal on the ground that the secret communications between the trial judge and the de-

* See page 212.

liberating jury, and the marshal's improper comments, interfered with the jury's free and unhampered determination of the verdicts and resulted in coerced verdicts.

In point fourteen, the remaining jury points were to be argued. These included improper selection of the grand and petit jury venires, the failure to protect the appellants from the barrage of prejudicial pre-trial publicity, the insufficient voir dire, and other improprieties in the trial which resulted in a deprivation of the appellants' right to trial by an impartial jury.

When we remembered that at our first meeting together, the previous August, Doris, Arthur, and I had come up with a list of seventy-five issues, just off the top of our heads, we were relieved to have organized our approach and narrowed down the issues. All that we had to do now was fill in the outline by writing the brief. That "all" was enough to make the three of us retire from the world for the next two months.

Arthur's major responsibility on the appeal was the attack on the constitutionality of the statute. He constructed sophisticated arguments, largely grounded in the statute's violation of First Amendment guarantees of freedom of speech, the right to peaceably assemble and to petition government for redress of grievances. To us, this attack on the constitutionality of the statute was the political heart of our case.

Most people think that the defendants in the Chicago Eight case were indicted for the crime of rioting at the Democratic Convention. That is not true. They were charged with crossing state lines with intent to incite a riot. The offense in the underlying statute is not "rioting" but improper "intent" while going from one state to another. All that the government must prove is this improper intent. No other criminal conduct of any kind need be shown. Pursuant to this statute, the Chicago Eight defendants had been

> charged, convicted and sentenced to five years imprisonment solely upon a finding by the jury as to what [they] *thought* while they were exercising their unchallenged constitutional

right to travel within the United States. The "intent" and the "intent" alone is the gravamen of this offense. This statute, unique in American jurisprudence, purports to punish men and women solely for their evil thoughts. This, the Constitution absolutely prohibits. [Appellants' Brief, pp. 45–46]

One of the main purposes of the First Amendment was to force the American government to keep its nose out of the realm of thought control. But this statute, which had come into effect only a few months prior to the 1968 convention, had been drafted in open disregard of First Amendment protections. As Representative Sikes, of Florida, bluntly stated during legislative debate on the statute, "Those who incite to violence should be punished whether or not freedom of speech is impaired."

The legislators who urged passage of this act made no secret of the fact that they viewed it as a means to stop or at least punish or intimidate the "rabble-rousing," "hate mongering" ideas of the "so-called leaders" of the black civil-rights movement, such as Martin Luther King, Stokely Carmichael, Rap Brown, and Floyd McKissick.

What infuriated the spokesmen for the legislation was that it was generally, if not universally, impossible to link directly or causally the expression or advocacy of these ideas contained in the many public speeches of the black leadership with any actual riots or disturbances. Thus they rejected consistently any efforts in the House or Senate to link in the statute the condemned "intention" of the actor, as evidenced by his advocacy, to any actual occurrence of riot or act of riot. Likewise, they rejected out-of-hand any effort to require as a basis for criminality a showing that the actor did in fact participate in any riot or act of riot or that his advocacy or expression of belief was related to in any way, to say nothing of being imminently related to, any actual riot or act of riot. [Our Brief, p. 43]

The legal basis of this part of our argument that the statute was unconstitutional was a Supreme Court decision which

had been handed down a little over a year after the effective
date of the statute. In Brandenburg versus Ohio, the Court
held that no legislature had the power to enact a statute
that by its own words purports to punish the mere advocacy
or belief in force, violence, or unlawful action, "except where
such advocacy is directed to inciting or producing imminent
lawless action and is likely to incite or produce such action."
We argued that both the wording of the statute and its legislative history made it clear that the statute was intended to
punish mere advocacy of ideas, in violation of the constitutional principles set forth in Brandenburg.

Sometimes I wondered whether Arthur had a mimeograph
machine and a computer in his office. I had never seen anyone do legal writing so well and so fast. Argument seemed to
pour from his pen. I had yet to begin writing any of the
sections that were my responsibility, as I had been busy at
the jury hearing. Still, I was determined not to be intimidated by either the length or the masterful reasoning of
Arthur's work. So I stopped reading the flood of material he
was sending over for my consideration and approval and
turned instead to my own work.

I decided to deal first with the issues raised by the jury
hearing, while it was still fresh in my mind. We had proven
through the testimony of the jurors, the marshal, and the
judge that the communications did exist. We also had affidavits in the record that the defendants and their trial
lawyers had not been informed of the messages. The law was
clear that it was error for the judge to have failed to inform
them of the notes. What we now faced was the legal doctrine
of "harmless error"—that although the judge had erred, no
harm had resulted, so reversal of the subsequent convictions
was not necessary.

Once we established the existence of the secret messages,
the burden shifted to the government to prove that the
judge's error was harmless. Our argument on the commu-

nications issue was therefore based on the premise that the government could not possibly meet this burden. First, the appellate court could not find that the communications were harmless "beyond a reasonable doubt" (which is the standard), because it could not possibly make findings as to the exact contents of the notes, since no two jurors, nor the marshal or judge, agreed on the contents of the notes or when they had been sent. Second, the judge had deprived the defendants of their right to a hung jury, a right which one jurist has characterized as just "as much a part of the jury system as a unanimous verdict." He did this by failing to inform trial counsel of the deadlock messages, thereby depriving them of the opportunity to urge that the jurors be instructed concerning their right to stand firm if they could not honestly come to an agreement. Finally, the defendants had been affirmatively prejudiced by the summary denial of the jury's request for transcripts relating to the speeches which were the heart of the charges against them. The subsequent convictions rested upon the contents of speeches that the jurors admittedly could not remember. This was a violation of the defendants' First Amendment rights, as the jurors could not have found from the character of the defendants' utterances that they intended to incite a riot, if the jurors could not remember the speeches.

Arthur, who had been deluging both Doris and me with samples of his own work, was getting increasingly twitchy on receiving nothing in return. The reason for this was that Doris and I both had different working and writing styles from his. We worked slowly, more meticulously, and our end products were far less lengthy. However, to assuage Arthur's feeling that nothing was being done, I agreed to send him a copy of my first draft of the judge-jury point. I then got so carried away with my other work on the brief that I forgot about that point. I didn't see it again until I got the galleys for the printed brief. To my horror, I realized that it was still in first draft and it was too late to change it. It was like all first drafts—a bit repetitive, slightly meandering, but passable. Fortunately, no one noticed.

My next project was to draft argument on the impropriety of the marshal's comments to the deliberating jury. First I reviewed the cases in which the courts held that deliberating jurors must be immunized from outside influences that might disturb their impartial consideration of the case. Then I summarized the testimony of the jurors about the nature of the marshal's comments, the thrust of which was to indicate to the jurors that they would be required to deliberate until they reached verdicts. I quoted from a recent Seventh Circuit case which ordered that the courts "shall not require or threaten to require the jury to deliberate for an unreasonable length of time." I argued that this deadlocked jury—which had been sequestered for five months during the trial, had been deliberating more than ninety-six hours, and several members of which were ill—was probably coerced into compromise verdicts by the specter, improperly raised by the marshal, of indefinite deliberations.

Soon after I completed the section on the marshal's conversations with the jury, I got a call from Arthur. "I've finished the sections on the statute and I'm working on the conspiracy point," he said.

"That's wonderful," I said.

"Have you spoken to Doris recently?" he asked.

"Yes, I have. As a matter of fact," I admitted, "I was going to call you about her. Is she all right? She sounded distraught."

"Wouldn't you be if you had to handle the issue of the judge's misconduct?" Arthur asked. "There is so much involved that she is going in circles."

No wonder Doris was troubled. Unlike the other issues in this case, the question of the misconduct of the trial judge was based on the entire 22,000-page trial transcript. Evidence

of his improper behavior riddled almost every page of the
minutes. It was a Herculean task to reduce to a manageable
level the factual material that would be the basis of the legal
argument on this point.

"I want you to go out to New Jersey and work with her,"
Arthur said.

"I can't," I replied. "I've got too much to do on the other
fair-trial issues. I haven't even touched the erroneous evidentiary rulings yet, and there are tons of them."

"You've got to go out there and work with Doris," Arthur
insisted. "This is more important."

I knew he was right. It wasn't that any of us dreamed that
Judge Hoffman's misconduct might be the ground upon
which the appellate court would decide to reverse the convictions. On the contrary, we had little hope that it would
condemn a brother judge's misconduct. This was not merely
because judges are reluctant to say anything bad about each
other but because this trial had become a symbol of contem-
porary attacks on the judicial system. We were afraid that
the Court would view its own reversal on the ground of
judicial misconduct as capitulation on the issue of courtroom
disruption as a defensive tactic in political cases. The best
we hoped for was a mild rebuke of the trial judge.

Irrespective of the fact that we didn't think we could win
on this issue, it was still a crucial part of our brief. If it were
done right, it could set the tone for reversal. That is, if they
were angered enough by Judge Hoffman's misconduct,
though they might not condemn it, the appellate judges
might be convinced that reversal was necessary and look
elsewhere for grounds. In addition, in our brief dealing with
the substantive issues (the issues relating to the jury convictions on the original indictment, as opposed to the contempt
convictions), we would set the framework for the contempt
case. If we had a powerful section on judicial misconduct in
the substantive brief, the contempt team would have an
easier time urging reversal of those convictions.

So I packed my bag and went out to New Jersey. I found Doris surrounded by paper. Working with students at Rutgers Law School, she had analyzed the transcript like a computer. The result was a large carton with thousands of index cards, each of which discussed a different page of the minutes as it related to the question of judicial misconduct. The amount of work that had been done was staggering.

Doris handed me several hundred pages of draft for the argument of the point on the judge's misconduct and left me to read. A few hours later, she came into the room and said, "What's wrong with it? I know it isn't working, but I can't figure out why."

I paused before I answered. I hesitated to criticize the approach Doris was taking, because I hadn't any idea what alternative there was. When I told her this, she insisted I was being silly. "If you tell me what's wrong, maybe together we can figure out what's right," she said.

"Well, you're taking each confrontation between the judge and the defendants or the trial lawyers and analyzing it. There are literally hundreds of these incidents, and some of them are tough to justify, particularly out of context, and they make the judge look good. It's too defensive. We have to take the offense." Doris agreed that might be what was wrong with the draft and asked me what I thought we should do instead. I hadn't the vaguest idea.

We looked at some of the cases, hoping they would give us a clue on how to proceed. In the recent Supreme Court case of Mayberry versus Pennsylvania, the Court had reaffirmed an earlier case, Offutt versus United States, in which it had said that a trial judge must not be "an activist seeking combat" but must represent "the impersonal authority of the law." And our own Seventh Circuit had just handed down an opinion in which it said:

> Beyond question the neutrality of the trial judge is of critical importance to the fairness of a criminal trial. His influence upon the jury is great and he must carefully guard against

prejudicial comments which might create even the appearance of partiality. . . . This principle extends to the relations
between the court and counsel.

These cases contained our theme: that Judge Hoffman was
"an activist seeking combat," and that he had made "prejudicial comments" galore, both within and outside of the
presence of the jury. The problem was how to prove this by
best utilizing the massive amounts of material available from
the transcript. On the issue of judicial misconduct, knowing
the law didn't make it any easier to organize the facts.

"Maybe if I look through some of these index cards, I'll
get an idea," I said hopefully. And for the next hour I sat
on the floor beside the carton that represented months of
hard work. I read card after card, but I didn't get anywhere.
I couldn't seem to work with other people's encapsulations
and analyses of the transcript. "Doris," I said, "I'm going to
go through the three pads of notes I made when I read the
transcript. Maybe I'll come up with something."

My notes had been made some six months before and
were mostly in shorthand. As usually happens to me with my
own shorthand, I found it almost impossible to read. Working slowly, I pulled out references to judicial misconduct
and typed them up. I ended up with dozens of pages that I
still found it difficult to work with. So I decided to organize
my notes further into categories of misconduct. I picked one
type of incident and put together all the examples of it I
could find in my notes. When I finished, it looked like this
(with the transcript references omitted):

The judge denigrated defense witnesses.

He threatened defense witnesses with contempt. [Ann Kerr
(Member of Parliament), Mark Lane, appellant Rennie Davis
(who was sentenced to contempt arising from his testimony
on the stand)]. He was openly hostile and disrespectful to
defense witnesses. Snappy to M. P. Kerr: "Don't make it easy
for me. That is not your responsibility." To witness [Fred-

erick] Gardner: "I didn't ask you to come," after which defense counsel complained of abusive treatment of defense witnesses. He laughed at witness [Allen] Ginsberg. To witness [Angus] MacKenzie, "You don't have a good memory, do you?" To witness [Donald] Kalish: "This is not a lecture program, you're on the witness stand"; and "You haven't been worried about my time up to now, so don't begin now." To witness [Caroline] Mugar: "The lawyer who brought you here wants you to speak up louder." To witness [Ronald] Young: "If you are unhappy about being here, maybe you can make an arrangement with the lawyer who called you to withdraw." He was extraordinarily impolite and bigoted toward witness [Arthur] Waskow, a practicing Jew, at first refusing to let him take the witness stand because he was wearing a skullcap. Sarcastically to witness [Charles] Kissinger: "Will you try? Will it be a great effort for you?" To witness [Donald] Peterson, after he was precluded from testifying: "That didn't hurt a bit, did it?"

I began to read the material I had gathered, trying to think of a way to present it in the brief. As I read it, I realized that it was powerful just the way it was. "Doris, come here," I said. "There is something I want you to look at."

She took the summary from my hand and began to read. "This is great stuff," she said.

"Doris, I have a suggestion," I said. "Why do we have to delve deeply into every incident between the participants at the trial? Why can't we outline the judge's misbehavior in the body of the brief and use long footnotes, heavily laced with transcript references, just like this? If the appellate judges want more information about a particular type of misbehavior, they can go to the places we've directed them to in the record. After all, we've always said that the transcript itself was one of our best defenses on this point, and if the judges would only read it, we'd win. What do you think?"

"It might work," she said.

"Let's try it on some other aspects of judicial misconduct,"

I said. "I'll do a footnote on how he denigrated defense
counsel by casting aspersions on their veracity."

"I'll do one on his use of his discretionary powers with
respect to time," Doris said. "This might work, it really might
work."

We did the next two long footnotes and were pleased with
them. Then we decided to call Arthur, to see how he felt
about this approach. I explained what we planned to do and
read the first footnote to him, the one about the judge's mistreatment of defense witnesses. For a moment, he was silent.
Then he said, "You've done it! Congratulations!"

After we hung up, I looked at Doris, she looked at me, and
we began to shout with happiness and hug each other.
"Yahooo!" I cried as we danced in the middle of the room
like two drunk children. What a relief!

When we calmed down, we returned to work on a draft of
the point. First, we outlined the various areas of the judge's
misconduct.

> He actively interfered with the presentation of the defense
> and precluded admission of whole sections of essential de-
> fense testimony.
>
> He was deferential to government witnesses and took steps
> to protect them from searching cross examination and im-
> peachment, but he was openly hostile and disrespectful to
> defense witnesses, refused to protect them from heavy badg-
> ering by the prosecutors, and threatened several of them
> with contempt.
>
> He condoned personal attacks by the prosecutors on de-
> fense attorneys by refusing to admonish the prosecutors or
> otherwise prevent their repeated and blatant professional
> discourtesy.
>
> He often overstepped the traditional bounds of courtroom
> conduct by his outrageous characterizations of defense coun-
> sel, undermining the appellants' right to the effective assist-
> ance of counsel, as guaranteed by the Sixth Amendment.
>
> He denigrated defense counsel by casting aspersions on
> their veracity.

He made repeated adverse comments about defense counsels' legal ability, often coupled with a stubborn refusal to give the basis for his rulings.

He persisted throughout the trial in charging that counsel had failed in his duty as an officer of the Court when he [Kunstler] withdrew as attorney for co-defendant Seale after Mr. Seale stated in no uncertain terms that he did not wish his services.

The trial judge further manifested his antipathy to defense counsel by his repeated insistence upon taking literally the colloquialisms and legal terms of art which would pass unnoticed in any courtroom (and in this courtroom, but only when used by a prosecutor) and his pedantic devotion to semantic distinctions.

He used his discretionary powers respecting time as a weapon against the defense.

He denigrated defense counsel for being from out of town and referred to them as "foreigners."

He unnecessarily abused the defense staff.

He took things personally and improperly injected himself into the proceedings.

He applied a double standard, ruling differently for the prosecution and for the defense.

He turned the courtroom into an armed camp.

We ended our outline of these various types of misconduct, each accompanied by a long, detailed footnote similar to the first one I had done, with the following argument:

It may be that any one of the episodes discussed here might not necessarily in and of itself require reversal. However . . . the cumulative prejudicial effect of the trial judge's behavior requires reversal of appellants' convictions.

"You may laugh," I said to Doris, "but this part of the brief reminds me of a section of the Passover Seder."

"What are you talking about?" asked my friend, whose Scandinavian background precluded acquaintance with such esoterica.

"There's a part of the Passover service called *Dayenu,*

which is Hebrew for 'It is sufficient,' " I explained. "It outlines all the things that God did for the children of Israel.
After a short description of each deed, everyone sings
Dayenu. It begins, 'Had He brought us out of Egypt and
not split the sea for us, *Dayenu*. Had He split the sea for us
and not brought us through dry-shod, *Dayenu*. Had He
brought us through dry-shod and not sustained us in the
wilderness for forty years, *Dayenu*.' And so on. Then at the
end it says something to the effect of, 'But He did all this for
us and more, and isn't the Lord terrific?' "

Doris was beginning to catch on. "It's just like the section
with the judge," I continued. "If he had only interfered with
the presentation of the defense, it would have been sufficient
for reversal. If he had only been deferential to government
witnesses and hostile to defense witnesses, it would have
been sufficient. But he did all these terrible things, and surely
there must be reversal."

"*Dayenu!*" Doris concluded in an emphatic Midwestern
accent. From then on, that part of the brief was affectionately known as the "*dayenu* section." Doris added quotations
from relevant cases at the beginning and end of the discussion of the record. We drafted a narrative of the judge's
misconduct during the pre-trial hearings (which showed
that his attacks on defense counsel started as early as the
arraignment), and the point was finished.

We brought the draft to New York. The contempt team
liked it so much that, without telling us, they reproduced it
verbatim in the contempt brief. That section of the brief had
been a real struggle, but it was worth it.

I returned home to finish the sections on the jury, and
Doris began work on the chapter on prosecutorial misconduct. She used the same type of structure we had used in
the section on the judge: argument interspersed with long
footnotes with detailed references to the transcript. Her section on the prosecutors greatly interested the appellate

judges, so a few words on the argument might be in order.

The interest of the prosecutor in a criminal prosecution "is not that it shall win a case, but that justice shall be done." As Mr. Justice Fortas has said, "There is no place in our system of criminal justice for prosecutorial misconduct." In our case, the attorneys for the government had persistently attacked defense counsel, defense witnesses, and the defendants themselves. For example, with the jury present, the prosecution had accused defense counsel of "playing Perry Mason," of "gross impropriety," of asking a "trick question," of making things up "out of whole cloth," of "playing fast and loose," of making statements he "knows" are false, "instead of watching yourself on TV, you can study evidence," and so on. Doris argued:

> This barrage of attacks against defense attorneys which continued throughout the trial could well have made the jury view with suspicion everything which defense counsel said. These improper statements were being made by the representatives of the government, whose "improper suggestions" and "insinuations" are "apt to carry much weight against the accused." [Berger versus United States]

In addition, in the presence of the jury, the prosecutors said that defendants Rennie Davis and Abbie Hoffman had perjured themselves on the stand. They also improperly attacked the credibility of defense witnesses by implying that they had been coached and were saying what defense counsel had told them to say. And in his summation, one of the prosecutors told the jurors that they were not "supposed to ignore how these people look or act" (grossly improper, as jurors are supposed to decide the case on the merits, not on their prejudices against the defendants). He also called the defendants "evil men," "profligate extremists," "haters, violent anarchists," "liars, obscene haters."

As with the judge, there was a pattern of prosecutorial improprieties. It was made even more prejudicial because of

Judge Hoffman's refusal to reprimand the prosecutors for
their misconduct. By his repeated inaction, the judge seemed
to condone the prosecutors' excesses, and further diminished
the defendants, their trial counsel, and their case in the eyes
of the jurors.

By the time the sections on judicial and prosecutorial misconduct were finished, we were getting close to our deadline.
We began meeting every day and working in each other's
offices, because constant consultation was necessary. The
tension was sometimes unbearable, and it was a tribute to
our stamina and our basic love and respect for each other
that we managed to finish the brief and remain friends.

How many legal issues are there now? The master list has
over seventy-six. But I have twenty more that aren't even on
that list. Impossible. We've got to cut down. The brief is too
long already. If anything is that important, put it in a footnote. No, we can't get a copy of that case to you today. The
Xerox machine is broken. We haven't been paid for nine
weeks. What do those defendants think we are living on? As
it is, we only get subsistence salaries; the least they can do is
pay them. So the Chicago lawyers think the attack on the
constitutionality of the statute is too long. It's easy for them
to criticize, sitting on their fannies. Why don't they help us
with some of this work? What? Arthur has broken his foot?
I don't want to hear about it. The Xerox machine is broken
again? Well, when am I going to get a copy of the pre-trial
motion on publicity? How can I write an appeal from its
denial if I don't know what was in the original motion? I
can't believe it. The ACLU *amicus* brief looks like it was
written by the enemy. Why doesn't it attack the statute? I
thought they were supposed to be on our side. Who wrote the
damned thing? An ex-Department of Justice lawyer. Are you
kidding? He's probably John Mitchell's nephew. No, we
can't schedule any meetings between six and seven at night.

Helene won't come. She's busy watching Star Trek reruns.
When did our researcher fall off the sled? Is she badly hurt?
The second jury section is almost finished. There was a blackout last night and I had difficulty reading by candlelight.
Arthur is getting a little paranoid. He said the blackout was
probably part of a government plot to keep us from finishing
the brief. I must be getting paranoid too: I'm not sure he
isn't right. The typists refuse to work unless they get paid.
I don't blame them. I haven't gotten a cent in twelve weeks.
Tom Sullivan likes the section on the jury hearing. Thank
goodness for something. The brief is over a thousand typed
pages. According to the rules of the Court of Appeals, the
page limit is seventy-five. But that's insane for this case. Our
record alone is over thirty thousand pages. The Court will
have to give us an extension. We hope. What do you mean,
you want a section about jury nullification. For heaven's
sake, the brief is due tomorrow. I don't know anything at all
about jury nullification. Here's a student memo. Rely on that.
All right, all right, I'll do it. God willing, this agony will
soon be over.

We were sleeping on our feet. A typewritten copy of the
brief had to be served on the government, after which we
had two weeks to get the brief printed. We had been up
until four o'clock in the morning, helping to Xerox and collate the brief. Then we were too excited and overtired to rest.
By ten that morning, Doris and I were on the plane to
Chicago, on our way to serve the brief on the government.
    I had great plans for this brief, which had been the bane
of my recent existence. But because I was lacking some
essential materials to carry out my idea, it was necessary to
let Doris in on it. She was appalled. She was adamant. She
would not let me do this. It was undignified. Arthur would
kill us. She wouldn't have any part of it.
    But she was sleepy and I was feeling silly and very per-

suasive, and to give Doris credit, once she was won over, she was an enthusiastic co-conspirator. We rushed around the Chicago stores, making our purchases and giggling like schoolgirls. We took pictures of ourselves, holding the brief in front of us. And in we marched to the federal building, laughing all the way. In the hall, we bumped into Jim Thompson, the Assistant U.S. Attorney who had participated in the jury hearing. He saw us coming and playfully shouted down the hall: "Here come those Commie nuts with the Chicago Eight brief."

I handed him the brief. He took one look at it and insisted on taking it and us to the U.S. Attorney.

"Guess what brief this is," he said to Bauer as we entered.

Bauer looked, chuckled, and then said with a deep, self-pitying sigh, "It *must* be the Conspiracy brief."

In respectful tribute to our Yippie clients and friends, the brief was wrapped in a huge, velvet magenta ribbon.

13

The Issues Are Met

Ten months and several extensions later, we received the government's answering brief. Our one-volume, 547-page printed brief elicited a six-volume, almost 2,000-page response. If quality was to be judged by quantity, then it was truly a magnum opus. The government urged that the statute was constitutional, the judge's demeanor exemplary, the use of warrantless wiretapping legal, the secret communications with the jury harmless, and the like. None of this was exactly unexpected.

What surprised us was the attack on us, the appellate counsel. The brief was riddled with statements that went beyond the bounds of normal adversarial assault. If most of what the government said about us had been true, we probably deserved to be disbarred. At first, we thought we might do something about the tone of the government's brief, such as making a motion to strike some of the more abusive statements. So I went through the brief and pulled out some of the best one-liners.

> . . . with the latitudinarian attitude of Alice in Wonderland towards language, the defendants pretend. . . .*

* "The defendants" referred to by the government did not actually write their brief; what the phrase means is the arguments presented on behalf of the defendants by us, their appellate counsel.

> When the record is examined, the dishonesty of the allega-
> tions surfaces, and the contrast between the morality pro-
> fessed by the defendants and the immorality practiced on
> their behalf is seen in bold relief.

> Perhaps it was their belief that the impudence of their fraud
> would screen it from detection that prompted the defendants
> to make these allegations.

> With considerable emotion but little adherence to the law
> and the facts, the defendants urge. . . .

> The above-quoted legal generalizations, which the defend-
> ants regurgitate as a substitute for legal analysis. . . .

> It would be euphemistic to call defendants' claim . . . a mis-
> statement. . . . Candor compels the labelling of that statement
> as a blatant lie. . . .

Never in my professional career had I been on the receiving end of such a brief. Even my brother, a veteran of some
years' service in a state prosecutor's office, was surprised at
the tone of the government's brief. "It's the sort of hysterical
rhetoric you expect in a defendant's brief," he said. "The
government's briefs are always cold and impersonal, and
that's why courts are more likely to believe what they read
in a prosecutor's brief than in a defendant's. But in the
Chicago case the defendants have the cold, reasoned brief
and the government has the emotional one. I've never seen
anything like it."

Upon reflection, we felt that nothing would be gained by
countering the government's personal attack in its own
terms. Instead, we decided that the brief's style would do
more to destroy the Court's faith in the substance of the
government's legal arguments than anything we could say.
With the exception of a little irresistible teasing here and
there, (Arthur's response on the issue of the constitutionality
of the statute is the best example of this; see page 190), we
confined our reply to the legal issues.

Even there, we had some surprises. On the issue of judicial

misconduct, the government attorneys had fallen into the
same trap that had originally enticed us. They had attempted
to deal with each confrontation between the judge and the
defense camp. The result was a separate volume, a 400-page
rewrite of the trial, a sort of Revised Standard Version of
the Gospel According to the Government. How to reply to
this caused us almost as much trouble as writing our original
argument on the point. Because we had written the section
on judicial misconduct in the main brief, Doris and I under-
took to respond to the government's answering brief on that
point. For two days, we sat in my apartment in New York,
trying to figure out how to handle it. In the time we agonized
together, we came up with little that satisfied us. I thought
that there was only one good paragraph:

> We agree with the government that the issue of prejudicial
> misconduct by the trial judge "must be resolved in an environ-
> ment supplied by the full record." (Gov. Br. 416, citing
> United States versus Thayer.) But the "full record" means
> the transcript of the trial on file with this court, not a "study"
> which the government has put together as a *substitute for*
> the full record. In the face of this attempt to give the impres-
> sion that Volume II [of the government's brief] can replace
> the full record, we can only conclude that the government
> is afraid to have this court read the trial transcript. We are
> not. We stand on the record of this case. It is the best evi-
> dence that can be offered on the extraordinary misconduct
> of the trial judge.

Our other efforts were fruitless. Tired and disappointed, we
told Arthur that we were getting nowhere. He advised us to
drop the judicial-misconduct section for the moment and go
on to something else. When the rest of our reply brief was
finished, the three of us met and I showed Arthur what had
been written. He took the paragraph I had liked, made it the
focus of argument, and in fifteen minutes wrote a wonderful
response. We added some long footnotes in the style of our
main brief, which gave examples of where the government's

version of the trial left out important occurrences and dis-
torted others. The section concluded:

> We are confident that the Court will ignore this contrived
> account and base its consideration of the arguments we have
> advanced in Point IX upon an examination of the actual
> record of the trial.

The whole thing was less than five pages, and what I liked
best was that it was simple. Simplicity was the approach
Doris and I had stumbled upon when we were doing the
main brief. But we had played ourselves out, and on this
rerun we were too tired to take our own advice. Arthur was
still flying high, however. The government had characterized
our argument on the issue of the constitutionality of the
statute as "panegeryzing [sic] the first amendment." Arthur
pounced on this:

> The act we are "guilty" of [Arthur wrote in reply], "pan-
> egyrizing," the dictionary tells us is to "praise highly; extol
> in public; write or deliver a panegyric on; eulogize." And a
> "eulogy," we are informed, is a "public speech or written
> tribute extolling the virtues or achievements of a person or
> thing; especially an oration honoring one recently deceased."
> The slip in language reveals much. Appellee's brief in fact
> proceeds on the unstated premise that the First Amendment
> is dead.

While Arthur was moving along with his usual zest, I
found that I couldn't get started. I felt as though I was
suffering from the same sort of shell shock that had im-
mobilized so many members of the defense staff after the
trial. This case had absorbed almost two years of my life and
I was sick of it.

I've found that when I'm stymied in a case, it sometimes
helps to do mechanical organization work. So I decided to
analyze the over eighty pages in the government's brief
which dealt with the communications by the judge and marshal to the deliberating jury. I looked for distortions of the

facts which were the basis of the argument, because if you can show that an opponent is sloppy on the facts, the Court will be more likely to believe that he or she is also sloppy on the law.

I was especially interested in mistakes the government had made in discussing the testimony as to when the notes had been sent. The deliberations had lasted from Saturday to Wednesday. It was important to know precisely when the notes had been sent, because if they were sent early in the deliberations, the judge might have been justified in telling the jurors to "keep deliberating," since they hadn't been at it long enough. If they were sent later in the deliberations (Monday or Tuesday, as some of the jurors testified), the judge was wrong in not giving the jurors further specific instructions. In a leading case in the Seventh Circuit, the Court had held that a judge should instruct deadlocked jurors (as ours obviously were) that they do not have to surrender their honest convictions as to guilt or innocence. Had this instruction been given by Judge Hoffman, the Chicago Eight jury might have been hung.

In addition, our overall point was that the testimony was so contradictory that the exact time and date of delivery of the notes could not be determined with certainty. The presumptions had to be resolved in our favor, because the procedure followed by Judge Hoffman could not be held harmless beyond a reasonable doubt. So discrepancies in testimony about when the notes were sent were crucial, and any factual errors I could find in the government's discussion of the testimony would be useful. Some samples from the list I made:

They say: Jurors Kratzke, Bernaki, Burns, and Seaholm remembered one hung-jury message.

Truth: So did jurors Hill and Nelson.

They say: Jurors Seaholm, Fritz, Robbins, and Stevens said first message was Sunday.

Truth:	Juror Kratzke said Sunday or Monday. Juror Bernacki said Saturday or Sunday. In effect, six jurors testified that the first hung-jury note either was definitely (4) or might have been (2) on Sunday.
They say:	Jurors Kratzke and Burns "concur with Fritz, Robbins, and Stevens that on Monday . . ." the jury "informed the judge of its stagnation. . . ."
Truth:	Jurors Fritz, Robbins, and Stevens said this was the *second* hung-jury message.
They say:	Juror Robbins said transcript message "was on Monday."
Truth:	Juror Robbins gave no date on the transcript message. She testified that the second hung-jury message was on Monday.
They say:	Marshal [Dobroski] and judge's testimony "differ only slightly."
Truth:	Marshal said transcript message was Monday; judge said it was Sunday. Note: In the rest of their argument, they assume *arguendo* that the judge was correct in his recollection that the notes were sent Saturday and Sunday.
They say:	Notes were "the only two major events in which they [marshal and judge] were involved during the jury's deliberations," intimating that their recollections should be better than the "busy" jurors'.
Truth:	On Saturday and Sunday, when the judge recalls receiving the messages, he was in court all day, handing out contempt citations to the defendants and their lawyers. These were among the most emotion-packed days of the entire trial.

After I picked out the holes in the government's legal argument, I began to write my reply. I called Arthur and Doris and read them the outline I had drafted. "This is the first point-heading," I said:

The jury hearing did nothing more than establish the existence of the communications. Their content, number, and time of transmission to the judge cannot be conclusively established from the "vacillating and contrary" [citation to the government's brief] testimony of the participants. Therefore, this Court cannot determine that the secret communications were "harmless beyond a reasonable doubt."

Before I could read any further, I was interrupted. "That's much too defensive," they said. "Try again." I went back to my typewriter and ten minutes later I had revised the whole outline. I called them again. "How does this strike you?" I asked, as I read the new initial point-heading:

The government's contradictory presentation of the testimony at the jury hearing is the most convincing proof of the impossibility of determining harmlessness "beyond a reasonable doubt" when a judge fails to make a record of communications from and to a deliberating jury.

"Great!" And thank goodness for that. At last I was on the right track.

I finished the reply on the secret-communications issue and brought it to the Center for Constitutional Rights, where Doris and Arthur were working. They liked the argument, so I turned my attention to some of the evidentiary questions. These issues had been dealt with in a cursory way in the main brief (because we had run out of time) and we had to go into them in more depth than is usual for a reply brief. Of special importance were the issues of the refusal of the judge to allow the jury to hear testimony by Ramsey Clark and the exclusion of articles written by the defendants which showed that they did not intend to come to Chicago in order to incite a riot. As we had done when writing the main brief, all three of us worked on various sections of the reply brief, read what each had written, criticized, and approved. Being together again was like a repeat of the preparation of the main brief. Only, this time, we were more relaxed and confident.

Without a doubt, the highlight of our work on the reply brief was the sensational discovery we made about the section of the government's brief dealing with the wiretap issues.

"What do you think about the government's answer on wiretapping?" Arthur asked me one morning.

"Well argued," I said, "although I don't agree with a word of it."

"Did you notice anything funny about it?"

"Now that you mention it, I did. There were a few words and phrases here and there that didn't make sense."

"Like what?"

"Well, once they referred to us as 'the respondent' rather than 'the defendants' or 'the appellants,'" I said. "And in another place they talked about 'the defendant' being overheard. All five of the defendants were tapped. And then there was this whole business about an order being in excess of jurisdiction that I didn't understand at all."

"Take another look at that paragraph about the order again," Arthur said.

I opened the government's brief and read:

> For all the foregoing reasons, we submit that the order of any court which limits the power of the President to authorize the use of electronic surveillance in cases where he has determined that such surveillance is necessary to preserve the national security is in excess of its jurisdiction.

"It doesn't make sense," I said. "What order are they talking about?"

"Yes. What order?"

It was obvious that he wasn't going to tell me. He wanted me to figure it out for myself. I looked at the exotic paragraph again. And suddenly it hit me. "It's the Keith case," I shouted. "They lifted this brief from the Keith case and they didn't even bother to change the mandamus wording!"

Let me explain. The Keith case was the wiretap case I mentioned earlier, the one which had issues similar to ours and which was on its way up to the Supreme Court. Judge Damon Keith had handed down a decision in which he ordered the government to turn over certain wiretap logs relating to one of the defendants. The government claimed that the surveillance involved could not be revealed because it would endanger national security. Were it to follow the judge's order, the government argued, the nation would suffer irreparable harm. So the government took an expedited appeal by way of a procedure known as mandamus, which (among other things) pushed its case to the head of the appellate calendar and allowed for an immediate hearing.

In its mandamus petition to the Court of Appeals for the Sixth Circuit, the government ("the petitioner") "sued" Judge Keith ("the respondent"), claiming that he had acted outside his jurisdiction in issuing the order. So "the defendant" and "the respondent" mentioned in the Dellinger brief referred to the parties in the Keith case, not ours. Even the mysterious concluding paragraph now made sense. It was the prayer for relief which ended the government's mandamus petition. (The Keith case is one of the most important constitutional law cases in our nation's history. I discuss it more fully in the next chapter.)

We had heard rumors that the wiretap section of our brief had been written, not by the U.S. Attorney's office in Chicago, but by someone in the Justice Department in Washington. The word was that it had been written by William Rehnquist (who was then John Mitchell's right-hand man in the Justice Department, and had not yet been appointed to the Supreme Court). We never did learn for sure whether Rehnquist was the author of that section, but we heard that the same person who had structured the government's argument in Keith was responsible for the wiretap section in the Dellinger brief, which made a lot of sense now that we knew the two briefs were exactly the same; either their author was the same, or the Dellinger argument had been "borrowed" from the Keith brief. What was more, nowhere in its brief in Dellinger did the government tell the Seventh Circuit that the precise arguments it was making had already been rejected by the Sixth Circuit.

Having made this fascinating discovery, there wasn't much we had to say by way of reply.

> We do not feel that it is proper for appellee [the government] to reproduce verbatim its brief to the Sixth Circuit as its argument in this case without acknowledging to the Court the source of this material, and without informing the Court that these *precise arguments, word for word,* were the arguments made before the Sixth Circuit and rejected by the Sixth Circuit in a long and thoughtful opinion. . . .

We noted that the Sixth Circuit's decision was presently under review in the Supreme Court, and would be argued there two weeks after our own case. We rested on the briefs filed before the Supreme Court and, with that final stroke, finished the reply brief and sent it off to Chicago.

Oral argument before the Seventh Circuit had been set for February 8 and 9. One week before argument, an emergency meeting was called in New York. There it was urged that Bill Kunstler and Len Weinglass participate in the oral argument. The reasoning was the same that had motivated me to ask them to participate in the jury hearing: it was important that the appellate judges see the trial lawyers in action, that they see that Bill and Len were not "wild men" but competent lawyers. This, it was felt, would have an impact on the judges' consideration of the trial lawyers' contempt convictions.

I was furious when I heard this, and it was over the issue of the trial lawyers' participation in oral argument that Arthur and I had our only contretemps in the two years that we worked together on the appeal. My resentment centered on Bill. People had been telling me all along that he would

never let go of this case and that, even though he hadn't
worked on the appeal, he would find some way to participate
in oral argument. I felt naïve because I hadn't believed this,
and now that it was happening, I reacted badly. It was
childish of me, and I knew it. But much as I liked Bill personally, I couldn't help feeling that the case was being
"stolen" from Arthur, Doris, and me.

In addition to my somewhat irrational private pique
(which I kept to myself), there was another reason why I
was disturbed by the suggestion that the trial lawyers participate in oral argument, and this one I voiced loudly. We
had assumed that, as is customary, only two lawyers could
argue for each side. Arthur and I were to argue the substantive case, urging reversal of the jury convictions. Center
lawyers Jim Reif and Morty Stavis planned to argue the contempt convictions of the trial attorneys and the defendants
other than Bobby Seale (who had his own lawyers from
California). Now it was urged that Bill share the respon-
sibilities with Arthur and me, while Len would argue with
Jim and Morty.

I felt strongly that if there was to be a third lawyer arguing the substantive case, it should be Doris, who was the
other senior lawyer on the appeal. I objected to the sudden
intrusion of lawyers who had done no work on the appeal
brief and who, except for their participation at the jury
hearing, had not been actively associated with the case
for the past two years. "It's a woman's issue again," I said.
"It's always the women who do the backroom work and the
men who argue. If we have a third person arguing, it has to
be Doris. This isn't fair." The problem was solved by Doris,
who stifled whatever personal feelings she might have had
about arguing the case, while she tried to convince me how
important it was that the trial lawyers participate in the oral
argument. I knew that she was right. Reluctantly, I gave up
the struggle.

It was decided that Bill and Len would argue for ten minutes each on the ramifications of the wiretap issues in the
substantive and contempt cases respectively. Even if the
judges were unreceptive to their participation, the overall
cases would not be hurt, because the issue of warrantless
wiretapping would not be decided in the context of our case
but by the Supreme Court's action in Keith.

Two days before argument, we received a notice that four
attorneys would argue the substantive case on behalf of the
government. That seemed to me to be the final blow, and I
was very disappointed on Doris's behalf. But it was too late
for her to participate, as she could never prepare in time.
She has since appeared numerous times in court and has
done brilliantly, but I have always regretted that she didn't
participate in the Chicago argument.

(In 1974, after a re-trial of the contempt citations, Doris
participated in the argument of that appeal. "I finally felt
like part of the Chicago case," she told me. It was an odd
comment coming from someone who was a senior lawyer
on the substantive case and whose role in its preparation for
appeal had been so crucial. Still, I knew exactly what she
meant.)

Arthur prepared for argument by putting together what he
called his "argument book." It was a loose-leaf notebook
with sections on every aspect of the case for which he was
responsible. I never read it, so I didn't know exactly what
was in it. During the two weeks prior to argument, I never
saw Arthur without it. I usually stood up for argument holding no more than an index card or two with a few notes. But
I was so intimidated by Arthur's attachment to his argument
book that I decided I needed one too. I got a loose-leaf,
paper, and page dividers and made a section for each of the
important fair-trial issues I would be arguing. Into these
sections I put quotations from leading cases, Xerox copies
of the crucial parts of our brief and the government's answer,

and an outline for my argument. It was the nicest art work
I had done since the plaster-of-Paris map of Chile I made for
a ninth-grade social-studies project. When I argued the case,
the loose-leaf was open before me. I occasionally turned its
pages, but never once looked at it.

The closer the day of argument got, the more nervous
I became. I kept thinking of what the demonstrators had
shouted when the police rioted in Chicago: "The whole
world is watching, the whole world is watching." That was
the way I felt about my argument. Every litigator gets tense
before a court appearance, but this was different. I was beginning to lose confidence, which is the worst thing that can
happen to a lawyer. If you don't have confidence in yourself,
it shows, and can only reflect badly on your confidence in
your case. It had never happened to me before and I hope it
never happens again, because it was an awful experience.
I guess the historic magnitude of the Chicago case finally
got to me.

In an effort to restore my faith in myself, I began to argue
the case aloud. I've always been a good talker and I made
some of my finest arguments to the walls of my apartment.
(If that apartment was bugged—and everyone kept assuring
me that it must be—then the F.B.I. has long since certified
me a lunatic.) The fluency of my arguments with the walls,
which, unlike judges, always asked me questions I could
answer brilliantly, made me feel much better. Then I put a
sign over my desk: "The Court Knows Nothing. Helenie is
the World's Leading Expert on the Chicago Case and She is
Going to Chicago to Enlighten the Court." After a while, I
began to believe it. By the day of argument, I was completely calm, though I've an idea that it was the sort of calm
one experiences before surgery—a defense mechanism that
says: "There is nothing to worry about, because this simply
isn't happening to me."

We had one last meeting before argument, at which we

discussed our strategy. There were to be three judges on the panel hearing both the substantive and the contempt cases. Judge Cummings was known to be a liberal and we thought we had a good chance to convince him that the statute was unconstitutional and that the defendants had been deprived of their right to a fair trial. Judge Pell, on the other hand, was rumored to be extremely conservative. We gave him up as a lost cause and decided to concentrate instead on Judge Fairchild, a middle-of-the-roader who we assumed would be the swing vote.

The day of argument was distinguished by a Chicago winter temperature of three below zero, embellished by the Arctic winds that stream across Lake Michigan. The weather reflected the cool atmosphere in the courtroom. Argument was low-key, perhaps because everyone unconsciously wanted to counteract the explosive nature of the trial.

Arthur argued first. He began by repeating his response to the government's characterization of our argument on the statute as "panegyrizing the First Amendment," that according to the government "the First Amendment is dead." As the three judges laughed, I leaned over to Tom Sullivan, who had joined us at the defense table, and whispered, "Laughing judges never convict." He smiled and nodded his hopeful agreement.

Arthur continued in a more serious vein, urging that the thrust of the government's reasoning was to "wipe out the First Amendment" guarantees of freedom of speech, the right peaceably to assemble and to petition for redress of grievances. He reviewed the legislative history of the statute, touching upon the more salient aspects of the congressional debates, which showed that the statute had hastily been passed to curb the black civil-rights movement in the South. He argued that the haste resulted in a poorly drafted statute that violated the First Amendment by penalizing "mere advocacy" of violence when there was no "clear and present danger" that a riot might occur. Arthur concluded his presentation with a technical discussion of the impact of the use of a conspiracy charge in a case such as this one, "in the shadow of the First Amendment."

Bill's brief argument on the wiretap issues included a discussion of the interrelationship of the Dellinger and Keith cases. With just the right amount of indignation, Bill told the Court of our discovery that the argument from the memorandum in support of the Keith mandamus petition had been reproduced verbatim in our brief, but that the government hadn't bothered to tell the Court that it had lost these arguments before the Sixth Circuit. The judges listened and made few comments. They seemed to be favorably impressed with Bill's pleasant demeanor, something we all hoped they would remember when they considered his contempt convictions.

Then it was my turn. I rose and began the traditional opening statement. "May it please the Court," I said. "My name is Helene E. Schwartz."

Before I could get any further, I was interrupted by a question from the bench. "I'm sorry to interrupt you at this early stage of your argument, but should we call you Miss, Mrs., or Ms.?" It was Judge Pell, the one who we had been told was so conservative. Considering his political proclivities, I thought he was trying to be funny. In the second before I answered, it occurred to me that the only reason I was in this courtroom was because I was a lawyer. Did it matter whether I was married or not? I looked back at Judge Pell and impulsively said, "Why don't you just call me counselor?" He smiled, and for the rest of argument the judges addressed the other lawyers as "Mr." and called me "counselor."

The substance of my argument was premised on our contention that the trial judge had displayed "blatant antagonism toward the defendants." I did not go into any of the specifics, relying on the *dayenu* section of our brief to convince the appellate court that Judge Hoffman's conduct had been improper. Instead, I concentrated on the effect of this antagonism, pinpointing evidentiary rulings where judicial discretion had erroneously been exercised against the defendants. My theory was that the net result of the judge's bias was to deprive the defendants of their right to a fair trial.

Other than in the broadest outlines, I have to confess that I remember very little about argument—mine or anyone else's that day. When you're standing up there at the podium, everything is a blur. Time rushes so fast that you barely know what is happening. Any plans you might have had about what you wanted to tell the judges disappear when they start asking you questions. You then begin to focus, not on what you intended to say, but on what they want to hear. Sometimes they ask questions you can't answer. I know that they asked me about the "guilt points" and I had to pass, saying that they were Arthur's responsibility. They asked him about the voir dire, which was in my bailiwick. He asked me what the leading cases were, and after I handed him a paper with the information he wanted, he gave a better answer than I would have given myself.

The one thing that stands out in my mind about that day was that during my argument Doris kept handing me notes written on sheets of yellow legal-size paper. "Ten minutes gone," said the first one. (How can that be? I just finished saying, "May it please the Court.") "Twenty minutes gone." "Thirty minutes gone." (That's impossible. I haven't reached the heart of my argument yet.) "Forty minutes gone—get to Ramsey Clark and the jury communications." At this last, I turned to Doris, dear friend, confidante, source of encouragement, devotion, and love, and snarled at her (yes, snarled): "Stop giving me those damn things!" I think I got to Ramsey Clark and the jury hearing, but I'm not sure.

The government's answering arguments, which consumed

most of that afternoon, were for the most part predictable. Again, I recall little more than the broadest outlines, but I do remember being impressed with Jeff Cole, the fellow who presented the arguments in favor of upholding the statute. The one aspect of the government's presentation I remember clearly stands out because it was so unexpected. One of the members of the prosecution team admitted that he would "not characterize Judge Hoffman's conduct as totally neutral by any means." Had this concession been made by a senior lawyer, it might have constituted grounds for summary reversal. As it was, we all knew that this young man's inexperience had led to what amounted to a slip of the tongue. And, in spite of any haphazard admissions by the government, we realized that the Court would make its own determination of the propriety of the trial judge's conduct.

The next day, argument was heard on the appeal of the contempt convictions. I thought they were beautifully done and I was proud of my colleagues. Everyone said that argument had gone well for us, but as a participant it was hard for me to tell. It all went too fast and was exceedingly anticlimactic. There was no way that two years of work could be condensed into two hours of argument. I felt I hadn't told the Court anything I knew about the case. But we had done our best, and now all we could do was wait. The burden had passed to the Court of Appeals.

14

Decisions, Decisions

February 1972. It was sleeting that cold, ugly day in Washington, and I shuddered as I made my way to the Supreme Court to hear argument in the Keith case. Arthur was going to argue on behalf of the defendants. I wondered how he could do it. It was only a couple of weeks after our argument in Chicago and I felt as though I needed several years of vacation from lawyering. But Arthur jumped from Dellinger to Keith with barely a moment's respite.

The decision in Keith was going to have far-reaching effects for us all and I didn't want to miss the argument. I knew that there were going to be hordes of people trying to get into the courtroom, so I arrived at the bottom of the steps of the courthouse at 6:30 in the morning. People were already milling around outside, huddled together under blankets and army jackets in a futile attempt to keep warm. A self-appointed marshal from the ranks added my name to a list on a clipboard and told me that I was number 27. "Why won't they let us in?" I asked through chattering teeth.

"They said not until nine o'clock," he answered. So we froze together for two and a half hours, as buses arrived and hundreds of people lined the steps of the courthouse, waiting to get in.

A little after nine o'clock, a guard opened the front doors of the courthouse, but he still refused to let us in. A few minutes later I saw an old gentleman slowly climbing the stairs. He was wearing striped pants, and when his coat flapped open in the wind, I saw that he had on a morning jacket. He approached the guard and announced heartily, "Member of the bar!"

"Right this way, sir," said the guard, with a slight bow and a sweep of his hand, and the old fellow disappeared into the warm confines of the court.

"Excuse me, sir," I said to the guard. "How come that man got in ahead of us?"

"Well, dear," he replied, "he's a member of the bar. There's a reserved section for members of the bar."

"Well, I'm a member too," I said.

"You are?"

"Yes, I am. Does that mean I get to go inside too?" I asked this question with hesitation because it struck me as unfair that members of the bar should have precedence over people who had been standing outside in the freezing rain for almost three hours. But if I sat in the reserved section, there would be one more free seat in the spectator section and someone else could get inside.

"Well, that isn't good enough, dear," the guard told me. "You have to be a member of the bar of the Supreme Court."

"I am," I said. I started to walk past him into the courthouse, but he stopped me. "Just a minute, dear. Do you have any proof of that?"

"You didn't ask that old guy for proof. How come you're asking me?"

"My dear," he replied, "we don't have many women who are members of the bar of this Court."

"Well, you'd better get used to us, because there are hundreds more of us coming," I said with a wave of my hand toward the students standing behind me, many of whom were women.

He still didn't believe me. Since the only proof of membership in the Court is a large, ornate scroll that doesn't exactly fit in one's pocket, he wouldn't let me in. I argued a bit, and finally he went to the marshal's office to see if my name was listed on the roll of attorneys. It was, so he had to let me in.

Then it occurred to me that some of the other attorneys standing outside might also be members of the bar of the Court and, like me, might not know of the special section for members. I found a shivering Nancy Stearns near the middle of the line and told her to come forward. She was reluctant to take advantage of her professional privilege until I reminded her that someone else would be able to get in if she sat in that special section.

I left Nancy to cope with the guard while I wandered through the crowd looking for more lawyers. When I went inside again, I expected to find Nancy there, but she didn't join me for another ten minutes. "What happened?" I asked.

"That idiot," she said. "He wouldn't believe that I was a member, so he went to check the roll. He told me that there weren't many women who were members of the bar of this Court."

"The same thing happened to me," I said.

"I told him he'd better change his attitude," Nancy said dryly. "There will be more of us coming all the time."

The wiretap issues in the Keith case arose out of the indictment of three men—John Sinclair, Lawrence "Pun" Plamondon, and John Forrest—who were accused of involvement in the bombing of C.I.A. offices in Ann Arbor, Michigan. Prior to their trial, their lawyers had filed a motion for disclosure of electronic surveillance (commonly known as a "wiretap motion"). In answer to the motion, the government admitted that it had overheard conversations by the defendant Plamondon. He himself had not been tapped, but was a "stumble tap"; that is, he had called a telephone number which was under surveillance. No one knew for sure, but we thought Plamondon had been overheard during conversations with members of the Black Panther Party.

The government argued that the surveillances were lawful even though they were conducted without prior judicial approval (i.e., they were warrantless), because they were a reasonable exercise of the power of the President, acting through the Attorney General, to gather intelligence information in order to protect the national security. In support of its assertion that the surveillances were lawful, the government filed an affidavit by the then-Attorney General John Mitchell. In his affidavit, Mitchell said that the wiretaps in question were being used to "gather intelligence information deemed necessary to protect the nation from attempts of domestic organizations to attack and subvert the existing structure of the government," and that the Attorney General had "expressly approved" installation of the taps. Mitchell also certified that "it would prejudice the national interest to disclose the particular facts concerning these surveillances other than to the Court *in camera*."

Judge Damon Keith rejected the government's contention that the taps were lawful. He held that since there had been no prior judicial sanction, the surveillance violated the Fourth Amendment proscription against unreasonable searches and seizures. He ordered the government to give Plamondon the wiretap logs of the overheard conversations, so that a hearing could be held to determine whether the government's evidence in the case had been tainted by the illegal surveillance.

Since the government claimed that the national security would be irreparably harmed if it turned over the logs, it took an immediate appeal to the Court of Appeals for the Sixth Circuit, by way of a petition for a writ of mandamus,*

* See page 194ff.

to set aside Judge Keith's order. The Court of Appeals denied the petition. By a two-to-one vote, it found that the defendant's conversations had been illegally intercepted and that Judge Keith had not abused his discretion in ordering disclosure of the logs.

The government then filed a petition for a writ of certiorari in the Supreme Court. There was little doubt that it would be granted. The question involved was of national importance and there was disagreement among the lower courts as to how to answer it. Judge Keith, the Sixth Circuit, and a California district court had ruled that warrantless surveillances under these conditions were unlawful. But in the Dellinger case and a case in the Kansas district court, similar surveillances had been held lawful.

Interestingly enough, it was in response to a pre-trial wiretap motion in the Dellinger case that the government had first put forward its contention that it could lawfully tap members of domestic organizations which were "suspected" of trying to use unlawful means to subvert the existing structure of government. The government admitted tapping all five of the defendants who were ultimately convicted (Dellinger, Davis, Hayden, Hoffman, and Rubin), but refused to turn over most of the logs, claiming that to do so would prejudice the national interest. Judge Hoffman read the John Mitchell affidavit in support of the government's contention and concluded that the surveillances were lawful. He declined to order the government to disclose the wiretap logs, a ruling which was now being appealed in the Seventh Circuit. But although this question had initially been raised in Dellinger, it reached the Supreme Court first in the Keith case, because of the expedited mandamus procedure which allowed for hearing of the issue prior to trial and the ordinary appellate procedure thereafter.

To no one's surprise, the Supreme Court granted cert in the Keith case. The problem was now to convince five of the nine justices that the executive branch of government was exceeding its powers by ordering warrantless surveillances. Justices Brennan, Marshall, and Douglas were known to be liberal and would probably vote with us. The Nixon appointees—Justices Burger, Blackmun, Powell, and Rehnquist —could be counted on to support their man. Justices Stewart and White would be the swing votes. If we were to win, both of them had to vote for affirmance.

I couldn't understand why no one had made a motion to recuse Mr. Justice Rehnquist. Although we had no proof, we were sure that while he was a member of the Justice Department he had been instrumental in shaping the Nixon Administration's wiretap policies. And we were equally certain that, prior to his appointment to the bench, he had been responsible for structuring the government's wiretap arguments in Keith, the ones that had been appropriated in the Dellinger brief. Under these circumstances, it would be natural to ask him to step down from hearing the Keith case. When I asked Arthur whether he planned to make a motion to recuse Mr. Justice Rehnquist, he said it "just wasn't done" in the Supreme Court. It was left to the justices, without prompting from the parties, to decide whether they would step down in a particular case. You wouldn't know who would hear a case until the moment it was called, when a recusing justice would leave the courtroom. If Mr. Justice Rehnquist left, there would be only eight justices on the bench, and we would have to convince only four of them. A four-four decision meant that the Sixth Circuit's opinion would be affirmed. We would need only one of the "swing" votes instead of both.

Most of the morning was consumed by a case which had something to do with airport taxes and whether the airlines could pass them on to the consumer. Like almost everyone else in the courtroom, I was there because of the Keith case.

Airport taxes, even if I might end up paying them myself, were exceedingly unimportant today.

After what seemed like endless argument in the airport-tax case, the Keith case was called. Mr. Justice Rehnquist rose from his seat at the far right of the bench and walked from the courtroom. As is customary, he gave no reason for stepping down. But I was convinced more than ever that he was the author of the arguments in the Keith and Dellinger briefs.

Assistant Attorney General Robert Mardian* opened argument on behalf of the government. He claimed that the executive was not contending that the President was exempt from the Fourth Amendment or was above the Constitution. "The question is whether electronic surveillance is a permissible government tool; the question is whether in the narrow area of counter-intelligence activities the President of the United States may authorize electronic surveillance without a warrant under the Constitution," he said. He also said that federal judges are "not necessarily qualified to decide" when national security necessitated wiretapping, and furthermore, to put all the necessary information before a sitting federal judge might involve a security risk.

Mr. Justice Marshall interrupted to ask a question that was bothering all of us. "Isn't it possible that the President could authorize an unreasonable invasion of the rights of the citizens of this country?" What was the guarantee that just because the President authorized a tap, it was inherently reasonable? The government had argued in the Dellinger brief that the fact that the discretion was being exercised by the office of the President raised a presumption that it was reasonable.

William Gosset, who was representing Judge Keith, hit home on this point. He argued that the Fourth Amendment

---

* In January 1975, Mardian was convicted on charges arising out of his role in the Watergate cover-up conspiracy.

contemplated a judicial process when it spoke of the "reason-ableness" of searches. "The President is a political man," Gosset said, "and the Attorney General and all those who work for him are politicians." The intervention of a neutral judiciary was thus necessary to ensure that searches and seizures were reasonable.

On behalf of the defendants, Arthur began his argument by characterizing the government's theory in this case as "a totally unprecedented outrage of tremendous historical significance." "The government is attempting to obtain the imprimatur of this Court for a program of intimidation of political opponents unprecedented in the history of this country," he said. If the government's arguments were accepted by the Court, he urged, the result "would be the stifling of political freedom guarded by the First Amendment."

Arthur's argument came down hard on the political aspects of the case. The judges didn't ask him a single question, which is a rare occurrence during oral argument. Were they alienated by what he was saying? We watched with apprehension as Chief Justice Burger's face turned to stone, as he sat silently, staring ahead of him. We didn't know what the silence meant, but it was unnerving.

In his rebuttal, Mardian stressed that the Court "must rely on the integrity of the Executive Branch" to ensure that surveillances were reasonable. I thought that he was asking for a rather large leap of faith, one which was antithetical to the theory behind the entire system of checks and balances. But I had no clue as to how the justices of the Supreme Court would vote.

In May there was tremendous excitement when the contempt convictions of the eight original defendants and their trial lawyers were unanimously reversed on procedural grounds. But still no word on the substantive case.

In June, Arthur got a call from the clerk of the Supreme Court. The decision in Keith had come down.

"How did they vote?" Arthur asked.

"It was eight to nothing," the clerk told him.

"You mean we didn't even get a single vote?" Arthur asked.

"No, no," said the clerk. "You got all eight votes. You won."

We couldn't have asked for a much better opinion if we had written it ourselves. Speaking for the Court, Mr. Justice Powell (Nixon appointee!) firmly rejected the government's argument that the President, acting through the Attorney General, had the power to authorize electronic surveillance in internal-security matters without prior judicial approval.

> The Fourth Amendment [he wrote] contemplates a prior judicial judgment, not the risk that executive discretion may be reasonably exercised. This judicial role accords with our basic constitutional doctrine that individual freedoms will best be preserved through a separation of powers and division of functions among the different branches and levels of Government. . . . Prior review by a neutral and detached magistrate is the time tested means of effectuating Fourth Amendment rights.

The clue to the fervency of the Court's opinion and the unexpected unity among eight justices with disparate political leanings was this discussion of the "judicial role" and the constitutional doctrine of separation of powers. We had been so concerned about the politics of the various justices that we hadn't appreciated the enormity of the one issue that could unite them. It was obvious that the Supreme Court, as head of the judicial branch of government, regarded the executive wiretap practices as an attack on the powers of the judiciary. Acceptance of the arguments made on behalf of the executive branch would have meant surrender of one of the strongest checks the judiciary exercises over the executive, the warrant power.

Nor were the justices happy about the suggestion that members of the judiciary were not competent to question a determination by the executive branch that a surveillance was necessary for internal security reasons which were "too subtle and complex for judicial evaluation."

> There is no reason to believe [Powell wrote] that federal judges will be insensitive to or uncomprehending of the issues involved in domestic security cases. . . . If the threat is too subtle or complex for our senior law enforcement officers to convey its significance to a court, one may question whether there is probable cause for surveillance.

The justices recognized that they were being asked to relinquish judicial scrutiny over the executive branch in an area where the executive has the greatest potential for excess and abuse of power.

> Security surveillances are especially sensitive because of the inherent vagueness of the domestic security concept, the necessarily broad and continuing nature of intelligence gathering and the temptation to utilize such surveillances to oversee political dissent.

As Mr. Justice Douglas wrote in his concurring opinion:

> If the Warrant Clause were held inapplicable here, then the federal intelligence machine would literally enjoy unchecked discretion.

According to Mr. Justice Powell, the theory of government asserted by the executive in this case was a "danger to political dissent."

> History abundantly documents the tendency of Government —however benevolent and benign its motives—to view with suspicion those who most fervently dispute its policies. Fourth Amendment protections become the more necessary when the targets of official surveillance may be those suspected of unorthodoxy in their political beliefs.

In cases involving prosecution of domestic political dissidents, the Keith decision forced the government either to disclose wiretap logs (where there had been illegal surveillance) or to dismiss the case. In Sinclair, the underlying case in Keith, the government decided to dismiss the charges rather than turn over the logs.

The effect of the Keith decision on Dellinger wasn't as clear as we had hoped it would be, because in Dellinger there was an additional problem that wasn't present in Keith. In its original wiretap affidavits in Dellinger, the government had claimed that it was gathering "foreign intelligence information" as well as information about suspected domestic subversives. In Keith, the original affidavit from John Mitchell had referred only to domestic intelligence gathering. At the last minute, the government claimed that foreign intelligence problems were involved in Keith too, but the Supreme Court refused to consider this radical change in the government's position. As a result, the holding in Keith related solely to domestic intelligence gathering. The Court expressly refrained from ruling on the power of the President to order (warrantless) wiretapping in cases involving suspected foreign subversion. Nor did the Court give guidance as to what was to be done in cases involving mixed questions of domestic and foreign subversion, or give any indication as to how the two, which may often be related, were to be disentangled. Since Dellinger involved mixed questions of domestic and foreign intelligence gathering (or so the government claimed), we didn't know how the Seventh Circuit would apply Keith to our case, if at all.

The decision in Keith was handed down two days after the Watergate break-in. One of the most fascinating things about it was the way in which the Court's opinion intuitively predicted so much of what the people were to learn in the next two years about the Nixon Administration. Those of us who represented political dissidents had known for years that, to the Nixon Administration, anyone who disputed government policies was "viewed with suspicion" (in the words of the Keith decision). The public learned this with the release of the White House "enemies list." And in the broadest sense the revelations of Watergate made it clear that the mere fact that the discretionary powers which Mardian had sought on behalf of his client were to be exercised by the President did not raise a presumption that the powers would be exercised without abuse. Indeed, Mardian's argument that the Court should trust in "the integrity of the executive" was particularly ironic. The office of the Presidency is only as trustworthy as the person who occupies it. And that servant of the people, no matter who it might be, must continue to be subjected to the constitutional restraints of the other branches of government. If Watergate taught us anything, it was that the runaway powers of the executive branch need more than ever to be curbed.

In light of the Supreme Court's unanimous and firm resolve to protect its own power, as evidenced by the Keith case, its later decision in the Nixon tape case was not surprising. The President's argument that the judicial branch lacked the power to compel production of executive records was another attempt by the executive to erode the constitutional duty of the judiciary to check the actions of the executive branch. It was a power play which was doomed to failure (another unanimous decision by the Supreme Court against the executive), as the Court's reaction to the government's arguments in Keith might have foretold.

15

Convention '72

In the summer of 1972, I went to Miami Beach to work with
the people planning the demonstrations around the national
political conventions. I found the atmosphere completely
different from what my work on the Dellinger case had
taught me about Chicago in 1968. Led by Miami Beach
police chief Rocky Pomerance, Beach authorities were co-
operating with the "non-delegates" (as the demonstrators
were euphemistically called), determined to avoid the mistakes that had led to the confrontations in Chicago. Parade
and rally permits, which had been delayed and finally denied
in Chicago, were granted in Miami Beach. Permission to use
the Chicago parks for outdoor housing for the young people
had been refused in 1968. Four years later, Flamingo Park,
not too far from the Miami Beach convention hall, was set
aside for use as a campsite for the non-delegates.

I was equally impressed by the coalition of demonstration
representatives, who were working with local authorities and
coordinating the activities of the non-delegates. An efficient
communication system had been set up through the office of
the Miami Conventions Coalition. Press releases, manuals,
and daily communiqués kept the media and authorities informed of demonstration plans and also served to advise the

flood of young people coming to the Miami area about living conditions and demonstration schedules.

The groups planning activities during the conventions publicly pledged themselves to a four-point program: no disruption of the senior-citizen community; no provocation of the police or military; no attacks on delegates or their families; no trashing or street violence. Behind these guidelines was a practical political strategy. As the ubiquitous "Manual for the Republican Convention" made clear: "Indiscriminate disruption, rock throwing, trashing and setting fires only plays into Nixon's hands—it will allow him to harp on law and order issues." For this reason, the organizers of the demonstrations were determined to keep the activities non-violent.

A low profile was planned for the Democratic Convention in July. A few demonstrations were scheduled, but the major focus of activity was to be the Republican Convention in August. I attended a few July meetings of legal personnel, to plan for potential mass arrests later that summer. A bail fund was incorporated, a legal collective office set up, and it was agreed that, wherever possible, there would be full cooperation with local authorities to ensure the most expeditious legal proceedings in the event of mass arrests.

The heart of the plans for August was the non-violent civil disobedience scheduled for Wednesday, the twenty-third of August, the night President Nixon was to make his acceptance speech. The plan was to prevent the delegates from reaching the convention hall by disrupting traffic, so that Nixon would address an empty hall. In addition, the demonstrators had been given a permit to conduct a rally in front of the convention hall. No problems were expected to arise from this rally. But the sit-ins and other actions designed to create major traffic jams were likely to result in mass arrests, and it was for this contingency that the legal collective office had to plan.

The legal office staff was divided into two parts. Some

people were to remain in the office to answer the phones and take down information about those who had been arrested. The others were to act as legal observers, patroling the streets in teams of two. We hoped the presence of legal observers would deter acts of brutality by law-enforcement officers. If that did not work, the teams were to take down the badge numbers of the officers and details of the misconduct, for later use at judicial proceedings.

Nixon's speech was scheduled for eight o'clock that evening, so the traffic disruptions were to begin at six. I started for the legal office a little after three o'clock, but did not get there until almost five-thirty, although the normal bus ride was about twenty minutes. Some of the demonstrators had started early. Collins Avenue, the main Miami Beach thoroughfare, was already blocked by four o'clock.

When I arrived at the office, I was asked to work on a street team. I was given a man's T-shirt with the words "GET TOUGH! LEGAL" and the telephone number of the office stenciled on both sides of the shirt in bold red letters. I also had a homemade laminated badge with my picture on it, which said that I was a member of the bar. We were acting as observers, and we wanted to be clearly identified. In truth, I was a little frightened about going out into the street, and I was glad to have both the shirt and a sturdy partner.

Center staff member Rick Wagner and I went out together. As we walked toward Collins Avenue, we could see that the non-violent civil disobedience was in full swing. People were dragging garbage containers to the middle of the street and setting them afire, driving cars to the main streets and stalling them, or sitting in front of vehicles so that traffic could not move. On Collins Avenue, a bus carrying delegates from a Midwestern state was stopped near Twenty-first Street. The air had been let out of all four tires. The delegates peered fretfully through the windows. Although they were only a few blocks from the convention hall, they were afraid to leave the bus, and I didn't blame them. Eventually, police arrived to escort them by foot to the hall.

As legal observers, we were not supposed to participate in the street activities. But it was difficult not to get caught up in what was going on around us. At one point, I saw a young woman reach up for the windshield wipers on the stalled bus and begin to bend them. I ran up to her, grabbed her arm, and shouted, "Stop that. No trashing."

Others saw what she was trying to do and began to yell at her. "You're playing into Nixon's hands. Cut it out." "Stop escalating things. What are you? A police provocateur?"

That last comment measured the extent of the demonstrators' paranoia. Everyone knew that police undercover agents had infiltrated the movement, and it was feared that they would escalate demonstration activities toward violence, for which the non-delegates would be blamed. People were especially sensitive about this, because members of the Vietnam Veterans Against the War had already been indicted, charged with crossing state lines with intent to disrupt the Republican Convention. It seemed like a rerun of what had happened in Chicago in 1968. Violence at the convention would only hurt the Vets. So anyone seen trashing or wantonly destroying property was suspected of being either a crazy or a police undercover agent, and was stopped.

I kept bumping into old friends and colleagues. Len Weinglass was there, as were most of the Chicago Eight defendants. So was Bob Lamb, who had been active in organizing the Chicago demonstrations and was also involved in this summer's activities. He introduced me to some of the women who were part of the Miami Conventions Coalition. "This is our lawyer," he said to them. Then he turned to me and said, "These women have played a major role in planning the demonstrations, and if the government doesn't indict them, it isn't our fault."

Bob was referring to the fact that although women had been among the organizers of the Chicago '68 convention demonstrations, none of them had been indicted. Several, including Kathy Boudin and Donna Gripe, had been named as unindicted co-conspirators, but none had been charged as defendants. It never occurred to the authorities that women were important members of the demonstrating organizations, so only men were indicted, some of them only minor participants in the convention-week activities.

"Talk about sensitivity to charges of chauvinism," I said, laughing. Bob grinned and replied, "I just wanted you to know where I stood."

Rick and I continued to wander up and down the streets. Police were riding around in patrol cars, indiscriminately shooting Mace at anyone who happened to be standing close by. Several times we were forced to scramble out of range or protect ourselves with the wet scarves we had around our necks. There is always danger of gassing at a demonstration, but I had thought that the police wouldn't use gas in an area populated largely by senior citizens. When the use of Mace and pepper gas increased around Collins Avenue, I begged the old people lining the porches adjacent to the streets to go inside. But the demonstration was the best entertainment since Lawrence Welk, and nothing I or anyone else said could convince them that the gas might be deleterious to their health.

The police were beginning to arrest demonstrators. I knew that the legal office would be swamped with calls, so I went back to help. For a while I answered phones, taking down information on who was arrested, what the charges were (mostly disorderly conduct or obstructing traffic), where the arrest took place, whether bail had been set, and any details of police brutality. Of this last, there was little, no doubt thanks to police chief Pomerance's special training sessions for his men.

It was tedious work answering the phones, but we did have our lively moments. "Leslie Bacon's been arrested," one of the volunteers said, reporting an incoming call. We all looked up. Leslie Bacon had achieved media notoriety in 1971, when the government had spirited her away to Seattle to appear as a material witness before a grand jury investigating the bombing of the Capitol.

"What are the charges?" I asked.

"Stealing sand from a public beach."

There were whoops of laughter. "What kind of freaky charge is that?" "The beaches belong to the people. How can you steal what already belongs to you?"

"Her bail's been set at five thousand dollars," said the woman holding the phone.

"That's what she gets for being a media super-star," someone said.

The phones continued to ring. Over eleven hundred people were arrested that day. After an hour of answering calls, I turned my phone over to another volunteer and again went out on the streets, this time with a woman partner, Jackie Friedrich. We walked over to Washington Avenue, near the convention hall, where Chicago Eight defendant Dave Dellinger was chairing the rally for which the permit had been issued earlier in the week. "What are you doing here?" he asked when he saw me.

"Getting defense witnesses for your next anti-riot indictment," I said.

Jackie and I joined the several hundred people who were sitting in the street opposite the convention hall, listening to the anti-war speeches. After half an hour, Dave announced that the rally was at an end; the next action would be a parade to the Doral Hotel, the White House headquarters, where there would be a sit-in. We wandered over to where the demonstrators were lining up for the parade. Suddenly, without warning, we were heavily sprayed with pepper gas.

The crowd reacted with predictable panic; people began pushing each other to try to avoid the gas. I lost sight of Jackie. Everyone was choking and coughing; tears were streaming down my face and my eyes were burning.

"Don't rub your eyes," someone yelled. "That will only make it worse. Get water. Wash out your eyes. Whatever you do, don't rub them. The Vet medics have hoses. Get to the hoses."

I stumbled toward one of the senior-citizen hotels on Washington Avenue. I could barely see and my eyes felt as though they were filled with fire. I made my way into the lobby of a hotel and was embraced by a small lady with a large bosom. "Come here, dear," she said, as she led me to a fountain and splashed water on my eyes. "She looks just like my granddaughter," the woman announced to her astonished friends. "How could they do such a thing to a nice girl like her?"

When the worst effects of the gas wore off and the air became clearer, I went back outside. There was something I had to find out. Police procedure requires that before an area is gassed, the people there should be asked to leave. I hadn't heard any announcement asking the people to leave. Nor had I seen any provocation for the gassing. Maybe I'd missed something.

I approached several policemen, all of whom were wearing gas masks, and I asked why the demonstrators had been gassed. They refused to talk to me, but one of them directed me to a man he said was in charge of the area, who might answer my questions. "Excuse me, sir," I said to the gas-masked officer, who had no badge or identification. "I am here as a legal observer and I would like to know why the people were gassed. What happened to provoke the attack?"

"There was no provocation," he said. "We just got word from inside the convention hall that they wanted this place cleared before the delegates came out."

"But the people had a permit to demonstrate. They had a

right to be here," I said. "There's been no civil disobedience
here. These people have been sitting on the ground listening
to speeches. I didn't hear any order for them to disperse.
Was there a police request for clearance of the area?"

"No," he said.

"Why not?" I asked.

"I got my orders from inside the hall, ma'm. I just followed
my orders."

A few minutes later, I found Jackie and we decided to go
to the Doral Hotel where the sit-in was planned. It was a
long walk, and at the end of it I was carrying my sandals in
my hand, hoping that the bandages applied by the Vet
medics would protect my blistered feet. When we arrived
at the Doral, the entire area was cordoned off by police.
Hundreds of people sitting on the ground in front of the
hotel were being carried from the site, photographed with
Polaroid cameras, and unceremoniously deposited into large
vans. The police were obviously well organized. The procedures being used were the result of a lesson learned from
the Mayday demonstrations in Washington, D.C., in the
spring of 1971. Charges against thousands of mass arrestees
had been dropped because the D.C. police had been unable
to identify the people whom they had arrested. Coordinated
field-arrest forms and on-the-spot photos were designed to
prevent this from happening in Miami Beach.

It occurred to me that, in spite of the attempt to educate
the demonstrators about legal services, they might not know
where to reach us. I wanted to make sure that they knew
the telephone number of the legal collective office, so I approached a police officer who was standing in front of the
cordon and looked as though he had some authority. "Excuse me, officer," I said. "I'm an attorney for the non-delegates. I'd be grateful if you would let me through the police
line so that I can tell the people the telephone number of the
legal defense office."

"Sure," he said. "That's a good idea."

He led me through the police cordon and directed me toward the trucks that had already been filled with arrestees. As he walked back to the perimeter, he waved in my direction and said, "Let me know if you have any trouble. Tell the officers near the trucks that Captain Smith [as I shall call him] said it's okay for you to be there."

I thanked him and continued toward the trucks. From the voices that floated from the first one, I knew it was filled with men. "Come to the window," I shouted.

Curious faces appeared at the small barred window. "Who are you?" someone asked.

"I'm working with the legal collective. I just want to make sure that you have our telephone number." One of them shouted that he had it inked on his hand—standard procedure for an experienced demonstrator. After he repeated it for me, to make certain he had it right, I said, "Make sure that the others all have it. And don't forget to call us as soon as you can, to give us your names and the charges against you." As I moved away from the truck, there were cries of "Right on," "Thanks, sister," "Keep the faith." I had to laugh. It seemed more like a class outing than a political action.

I was walking toward another truck when a young policeman stopped me. "What are you doing here?" he asked angrily.

"I'm a lawyer and . . ."

"I don't care who you are," he interrupted. "Get the hell out of here."

"But Captain Smith said . . ."

"I don't give a damn what he said. Get moving, or I'll move you myself. Get behind that cordon where you belong, or you'll join your friends in the wagon."

He continued to scream at me, every sentence laced with obscenities. I had no desire to become a mass-arrest statistic, so I moved toward the outer perimeter of police officers. He followed me, still cursing. Then he poked me with his night stick. "I'm going, I'm going," I said as I half ran from the paddy wagons.

"Well, you're not going fast enough for me." Cursing again, he pushed me with his shoulder.

"Stop pushing me," I cried. "I'm going as fast as I can."

"I'll do more than that if you don't get the hell out of here," he said.

I ran the rest of the way, and as I reached the line of policemen, I saw Captain Smith. "What happened to you?" he asked. I told him. "There's something the matter with that guy," I concluded with a shudder. "He seemed like a psycho."

"Well, these officers have been subjected to a lot of abuse today," Captain Smith said. "It's been hectic. That guy probably was young and inexperienced and he's had a hard day. He's just overreacting to the pressure."

Captain Smith volunteered to escort me back to the paddy wagons so that I could talk to the rest of the demonstrators. But then he was summoned to another area, so I said good night and thanked him for his help. Not anxious to venture inside the cordon unprotected and risk another confrontation, I decided there was nothing more I could do. It was already early Thursday morning, and I was tired.

The morning newspapers made no mention of the fact that the attack on the demonstrators in front of the convention hall had been unprovoked. Apparently, the network coverage had been equally obtuse. A friend who had been watching Walter Cronkite said that he had reported that the demonstrators had been gassed "while they were pushing toward the hall." Actually, when the gassing took place, the demonstrators were lining up for the march to the Doral, and they had their backs to the convention hall.

The newspapers also reported that there had been excitement in the courtroom when two of the women arrested the night before had identified themselves as Leslie Bacon and Bernadine Dohrn, a member of the Weather Underground who was on the F.B.I.'s "ten most wanted" list. Hearing the names, F.B.I. agents rushed over to question the women. "Dohrn" turned out to be a woman named Sue Vanderveer. "Bacon" insisted that was her real name. Because of her media-grown star qualities, "Bacon's" bail had been set at five thousand dollars. Later the authorities decided that even if her name was Leslie Bacon, she was not the Leslie Bacon, and her bail was lowered, the newspapers said.

According to the stories in the press, most of the demonstrators had been released on bail the night before. My call to the legal collective proved that this was not true. Some six hundred demonstrators remained in jail. "Listen, Helene," Jeffrey Fogel said to me, "there are over a hundred women who are in prison. They've heard that there is a woman lawyer in town working with us, and they want you to represent them."

Before going to the jails, Jeff, Daniel Alterman, Gustin Reichbach, and I met at the office to discuss our strategy. Since most of the demonstrators had been charged with misdemeanors, their bail was low: ten dollars per man and five per woman. "Typical chauvinism," one of the female legal workers muttered.

There was enough money in the bail fund, and among those arrested, to bail out most of the people. The problem was that thirteen of the arrestees either had been charged with more serious crimes, such as resisting arrest, or had in some manner irritated the judges before whom they had been taken. One fellow told the judge that his name was "Typical Youth"; he had been held on $2,500 bail. For the thirteen, bail totaled over $13,000. We could not raise so much money, and the feeling was that none of the demonstrators should leave the jails until all of them were released. It would be the final political action of the 1972 convention summer.

The refusal of some six hundred people to post bail and leave the jails could put enormous pressure on the authorities. There was a rumor, which I never confirmed, that within the last year a suit had been brought alleging that the Miami area jails were overcrowded and conditions in them were unhealthy. Prison administrators were said to be under a court order to restrict the number of people in the jails and to improve prison life. Undoubtedly, the number of people now in jail far exceeded the court's order. Because of the extenuating circumstances of the convention, the court was probably looking the other way, temporarily. But the longer the demonstrators remained in jail, the greater the risk that prison officials would be held in contempt of court. In addition, the demonstrators had to be fed three times a day and that was costing the city a lot of money. In all, the authorities were probably anxious to get the demonstrators out of jail and on their way home. If the people refused to leave unless they were all released together, we might succeed in convincing the authorities that bail on the thirteen should be reduced.

Later that afternoon, we had a conference with a representative of the Miami area prisons. We explained that we did not have enough money to bail out all the demonstrators and that a decision had been made that all would leave, or stay, together. He was cooperative and agreed to relay this information to those in a position to influence the question of bail.

Then, together with legal worker Helen Horn, I went over to the City of Miami jail, where the women arrestees were being held. "Thank God you're here," the director said. "I've never seen anything like this group of women. They've been singing all night long. For the last two hours they've been yelling that they want their lawyer. I'm so glad you've finally come!" As we walked toward the cells, I could hear voices chanting, "We want our lawyer, we want our lawyer."

"Here she is, girls," the director shouted.

The main cell door was opened for me, and when I entered, I was embraced by dozens of women. There were one hundred and twelve women still in jail. They had been divided into two large cells, about eighty in the cell I was in and thirty in the cell to which Helen had gone. I could see that each cell was filled to capacity with double-decker beds, and had open toilets and showers near the doors. I was told that the male guards and trustees stood outside the cells and watched as the women used the facilities. Aside from this—which I complained about to the director—the women were being well treated.

I was hoisted to the top of a double-decker bed, so everyone could see me. I introduced myself and at their request told them something about my previous legal experience. "Aren't you the one who argued the Chicago Eight appeal?" one of the women asked. When I said yes, there was excited murmuring. Then I explained about the thirteen arrestees whose bail had been set so high, and someone shouted, "We already know about that. We're not leaving."

"Either everyone leaves or no one leaves."

"We'll stay forever."

"Power to the sisters!"

"I have to make sure I have all of your names and addresses," I said. "Answer when I read your name, and tell me if the information is right."

I called the name Leslie Bacon and a woman pushed through the crowd. I had done some legal work in New York in connection with one of the grand jury proceedings involving the Leslie Bacon. When I saw the woman who answered to this name, I said, "But you *are* the Leslie Bacon."

"I know, I know," she replied. "I kept telling the F.B.I. men that I was *the* Leslie Bacon, but they wouldn't believe me. At least it got my bail lowered."

"Sometimes I think the only thing that saves us is the incompetence of the F.B.I.," I said.

When I finished checking the names, I asked the women to collect the money they had with them, to be used for bail.

While this was going on, I was approached by Shari White-head, one of the organizers of the convention-week activities. She was leading a plump, slightly older woman by the hand. "This is Madge Zietlow. She is one of the thirteen. She was charged with contributing to the delinquency of a minor and her bail was set at one hundred dollars."

"What was the basis of the charge?"

"I was demonstrating on Collins Avenue," the woman told me. "When I was arrested for blocking traffic, my two teen-age daughters were with me, so I was charged with contributing to their delinquency."

"Are you serious?" I asked, staring at her in disbelief.

"That's all it was."

I gaped open-mouthed at Shari, looked back at Madge, and then we began to laugh. "Of all the things I've heard that went on last night, that has to be the craziest," I said. "Don't worry, Madge, we'll get you out."

I circulated among the women for a while, taking personal messages and promising to try to communicate with friends and families. Madge Zietlow, for instance, was worried about her daughters. When last seen, they were being herded off to a home for wayward juveniles. I attempted to contact her husband but was unsuccessful. I learned from the newspapers that the family had been reunited the next day.

Then I went to the other cell to join Helen and to collate the information we had gathered. Spirits were lower there. The women appeared much younger, and several were close to tears. I told them there was no reason for them to stay if they didn't want to; enough women were staying to provide a presence. I offered to bail them out, but at the last moment they all decided to remain. I arranged for medical attention for two of them and then went back to the larger cell, to say goodbye to the women there. I told them I would confer with the lawyers who had talked to the men and get back to them about what was going on.

As I turned to leave, several of the women lifted me on top of a table and the room began to rock with lively voices shouting in discordant singsong, "We love our lawyer, hurray for Helene." "And Helen too," I cried, lifting my co-worker up on the table beside me. The women sang and cheered as Helen and I hugged each other.

I reported back to Dan, Jeff, and Gus that the women were determined to stand firm. They told me that the men were equally solid and would not leave without the thirteen. Several hours later, a compromise was reached. With the exception of a few people who had been picked up on serious drug charges, all the demonstrators were released the next morning, without any payment of bail and with no record that they had been arrested.

A lot of people worked hard setting up the legal collective and preparing for the possibility of mass arrest. My contribution may have been small, but my participation in the convention-week activities had an enormous impact on me. When I stood on top of that small table in the jail cell, embarrassed and close to tears, while the women serenaded me, the spirit and togetherness in that room made for one of the most beautiful experiences of my career.

16

"The Judgments Appealed from Are Reversed"

The following November, I decided to fly to Florida to spend Thanksgiving with my family. A friend picked me up at Rutgers-Camden, where I was teaching, and drove me to the Philadelphia airport. Thick rush-hour traffic made the normally twenty-minute drive almost two hours. While our small car was sitting, dwarfed, behind a belching truck, my friend casually said, "By the way, I think I heard something on the radio about the Chicago case." I swerved in her direction and asked excitedly, "What did you hear? What happened?"

"There was a lot of static," she said. "I just heard a passing reference to something about the Chicago case."

"The decision must have come down," I said as I began turning the dials on the car radio. Rock music, a news story about police corruption, the weather, sports, Dylan, more rock music. "Are you sure you don't remember anything?" I said. "Did we win or did we lose?"

"I didn't hear anything specific," she said.

The ride to the airport seemed endless. It was highway all the way and I couldn't stop to telephone New York to find out what, if anything, had happened. I later learned that Doris and Arthur had been trying to reach me all afternoon.

Somehow, their frantic messages had gone astray. When we finally reached the airport, I grabbed my bag, mumbled a barely polite "goodbye and thanks," and ran to the nearest newsstand. And there it was, in bold black headlines: CHICAGO CONVICTIONS REVERSED. I looked at the words without understanding what I was seeing. I ought to have felt elated. Instead, I felt alone and isolated in the Philadelphia airport. What I wanted more than anything was to be in New York with Doris and Arthur. The papers were sketchy about the reason for reversal, so I walked to a pay phone and called the Center in New York. There, excitement was so great that everyone I spoke to was incoherent. People kept grabbing the phone and yelling, "Congratulations!" "Great job!" "We're proud of you!"

"What were the grounds?" I kept asking. "Where are Doris and Arthur?" Finally, Doris was located and she came on the line. "Did you hear? Did you hear?" she repeated excitedly.

"I haven't heard a thing," I said. "Everyone is too excited to talk. What were the grounds?" I asked again.

"They really came down on Judge Hoffman," Doris said. "I haven't seen the opinion yet, but Tom Sullivan called and he read me parts of it and they really gave it to Hoffman and the prosecutors. And the jury communications, and the self-serving statements, and the voir dire . . ." She turned away from the phone. "What?" I heard her say. Then she was back to me. "I have to go," she said. "The Canadian Broadcasting Company is calling and I have to talk to them."

"Wait, wait," I cried. "What about the statute? Did they hold it unconstitutional?" But she was gone and I was holding a dead phone. I had the sudden feeling that I was going to be the last person in the world to learn the contents of the Chicago Eight opinion. Then I decided to call Tom Sullivan and I learned at last the grounds on which the convictions had been reversed.

In some respects, the decision was an incredible victory for us. Almost every point relating to the question of the deprivation of the defendants' right to a fair trial had been decided in our favor. On the issue of the improper questioning of prospective jurors, the Court held that Judge Hoffman's "severe restriction of the voir dire may well have curtailed defendants' challenges for cause and failed to provide them with reasonable guidance in exercising peremptory challenges." On the question of the impact of the pre-trial publicity, the Court concluded that the judge's "failure to inquire into the effect of pre-trial publicity upon the jurors was error." The appellate court also held that the defendants had been effectively deprived of the right to present a defense through wrongful evidentiary rulings which went to the heart of their case, such as the judge's refusal to allow the jury to hear the testimony of Ramsey Clark; the exclusion of documents written by the defendants which showed that their intent in coming to Chicago was to peacefully demonstrate, which directly refuted the heart of the charges against them, that they had crossed state lines with intent to incite a riot; the rejection of expert witnesses who were to testify on crowd or riot control, to show that the Chicago police utilized improper crowd-control techniques and may themselves have been responsible for the ensuing disturbances.

The Court was also persuaded by our arguments on the issues related to the jury hearing. The Court noted that the testimony at the hearing proved there had been "at least one, and probably two, notes to the judge that the jurors were unable to agree on a verdict and one note asking for 'transcripts,' apparently speeches made by one or more defendants." After reviewing the testimony about the notes and the comments by the marshal, the appellate judges said they were "not prepared to resolve the conflict in testimony" among the various witnesses. Bearing in mind the presumption that communications with a deliberating jury are prejudicial, the Court concluded:

> Under the circumstances related, we are unable to find with certainty that these out of court communications were harmless and therefore conclude they are grounds for reversal.

"What did they say about conspiracy?" I asked Tom.

"Not a word."

"That's weird," I said. "This is the case known as the Conspiracy case, and they don't discuss conspiracy. What about the constitutionality of the statute?"

"They upheld the statute," Tom said.

"Oh, no!"

"The section of the opinion dealing with the statute is really strange," Tom continued. "All through it, the judges keep repeating that 'the case is close,' that the statute 'creates a serious problem,' and language like that. Listen to this," he said as he began to read from the opinion. " 'We do not pretend to minimize the First Amendment problems presented on the face of this statute.' Then they go on to uphold it."

"It's really too bad. They gave us so much, but they just wouldn't go all the way. Well, at least the convictions were reversed."

"Pell dissented."

"The stinker. Well, we never thought we had a chance with him."

"No, no, you don't understand," Tom said. "Pell was with you on the fair-trial issues. It was three to nothing for reversal. He dissented on the question of the statute. He thought it should have been declared unconstitutional. He was with you all the way."

"Pell!?" I bellowed with disbelief.

"We were all wrong about the judges on this case," Tom continued. "We never expected to lose Cummings on the statutory issue and we thought there was no hope of getting Pell. But Pell's dissent is just beautiful. He agreed that the statute was badly drafted and he cited a lot of the legislative history that was in our brief, to show why it was pushed through Congress. He said that the statute punished 'mere advocacy' of violence without 'clear and present danger of imminent violence,' and that in view of the Supreme Court's holding in Brandenburg, he thought the statute was 'clearly violative of the First Amendment right of freedom of speech.' "

My mind leaped back to the time of argument, when Judge Pell had asked me whether I wished to be called Miss, Mrs., or Ms., and I had assumed that he was making fun of the women's movement. "I think maybe I owe Judge Pell an apology," I said. "You just never know."

A few days later, I received a copy of the opinion. If imitation is the sincerest form of flattery, then the judges had really liked the part of our brief dealing with the misconduct of the trial judge, because they had adopted the same form we used in the *dayenu* section: short discourses in the body of their opinion, followed by long footnotes detailing specifics of judicial misconduct during the course of the trial. The appellate court recognized that Judge Hoffman's "deprecatory and often antagonistic attitude toward the defense" was evident in the record from the beginning of the proceedings. The opinion noted that "the judge was more likely to exercise his discretion against the defense than against the government" in making evidentiary rulings.

> Most significant, however, were remarks in the presence of the jury, deprecatory of defense counsel and their case. These comments were often touched with sarcasm, implying rather than saying outright that defense counsel were inept, bumptious, or untrustworthy, or that this case lacked merit. . . . Taken individually any one was not very significant and might be disregarded as a harmless attempt at humor. But cumulatively, they must have telegraphed the judge's contempt for the defense.

Dayenu!

The Court also said that numerous remarks made by the prosecutors "were not called for by their duties" and "fell below the standards applicable to a representative of the United States." In particular, the Court held that in his final argument the prosecutor whose remarks had been objected to "went at least up to, and probably beyond, the outermost boundary of permissible inferences from the evidence in his characterizations of defendants." The Court concluded that "the demeanor of the judge and prosecutors would require reversal if other errors did not."

The outright disapproval of Judge Hoffman's conduct was the most unexpected part of the decision, and in some respects the most welcome. We felt that it did much to justify, if not vindicate, the behavior of the defendants and their trial counsel and we suspected that it would be helpful to the contempt team when that case was retried. This proved to be true. The judge before whom the contempt case was heard ruled that "the contumacious conduct of the defendants and their lawyers cannot be considered apart from the conduct of the trial judge and prosecutors" which had been decried by the appellate court. With this in mind, he found the members of the defense camp innocent of most of the charges against them and gave no sentences on the remaining few convictions.

On the wiretap issue, the Seventh Circuit noted that it was unclear from Attorney General Mitchell's affidavit in this case whether the surveillance was being done for purposes connected with foreign or domestic intelligence operations or both. The decision in Keith applied only to warrantless wiretaps connected with domestic intelligence gathering. The Court declined to reach the wiretap issue in Dellinger,

> since the record does not unequivocally show that some of the overheard conversations stemmed from surveillance of activities of foreign powers or their agents nor segregate those logs, if any, from the ones disclosure of which is required by [Keith].

The Court's decision on wiretapping was somewhat disappointing and its statutory ruling was a disaster. We planned to appeal the statutory question by applying to the Supreme Court for a writ of certiorari. But two months after the appellate decision, the government announced that it would not retry the defendants on the original charges against them. The Supreme Court dismissed our cert petition as moot and the case vanished into the law books.

The relationship between the Keith and the Dellinger cases is more subtle than the surface correspondence of the wiretap issues would indicate. What is more important is that both cases involve a recognition by the courts of the possibilities for abuse when government toys with legal rights in order to intimidate dissent. In Keith, the judiciary imposed limits on procedural excesses by the executive branch in its treatment of political dissidents. In Dellinger, the judiciary assessed its own procedures in its treatment of political dissidents who were on trial, and found itself wanting.

Only a few months after the Chicago Eight trial had ended, Mr. Justice Douglas warned that the problems of political indictments "raise profound questions going to the heart of the social compact." He urged that majorities "undertake to press their grievances within limits of the Constitution and in accord with its procedures." The decision in Dellinger was an attempt by the judiciary to outline the "limits of the Constitution" in a political trial. If the underlying trial itself was a textbook on how to ensure abuse of due process, the decision was a lesson on how to avoid it.

When people ask me about the grounds for the reversal of the convictions in the Chicago Eight case, I talk about the numerous violations of the First, Fourth, Fifth, and Sixth Amendments. Sooner or later, while I am deep into an explanation of due process, someone is bound to interrupt me to say, "Oh, it was just a bunch of legal technicalities."

Which makes me wonder. In the minds of too many Americans, the Constitution itself is nothing more than a "legal technicality." If that is the way people think, then maybe the old cliché should be rewritten, for it is the legal technicalities which shall keep us free.

17

Of Fire Bombs and Presidents, of Rock Groups and Things

Soon after the Chicago Eight decision came down, I got involved in another case which in some ways seemed a repeat of Dellinger. It was also based on charges arising out of the demonstrations at a national political convention: this time the Republican Convention in Miami Beach in the summer of 1972. Of course, in terms of its notoriety and impact, not every case is in a league with the Chicago Eight proceedings. Still, the nice thing about the "Keiser-Birdsell" case* is that it illustrates in miniature some of the problems common to the major political trials of the last decade.

With the exception of a few drug cases, most of the misdemeanor charges against the 1,100 people arrested during the demonstrations coinciding with the 1972 Republican Convention had been dropped. There were two major felony cases that remained. The first was the proceedings involving the Vietnam Veterans Against the War, eight of whom had been indicted for conspiring to cross state lines with intent to incite riots in Miami Beach (the same statute involved in the Chicago Eight case) and for violations of the National

---

* The names of the defendants and the people associated with the rock group I call "The Cowboys" have been changed.

Firearms Act. This case was being handled by lawyers from
the Center for Constitutional Rights, in cooperation with
attorneys from Florida and Texas. I was later to find myself
peripherally involved in the Vet proceedings. But for the
moment I had been asked to undertake prime responsibility
for the trial of the second case, in which Tim Keiser and
Sandy Birdsell had been indicted for violations of the National Firearms Act: possession of unregistered and illegally
made fire bombs on the night of President Nixon's acceptance speech.

Since I had been in Miami Beach during the national
political conventions in 1972, the Keiser-Birdsell case seemed
a natural continuation of the scenario. I had learned so much
while working on the Chicago Eight appeal that it would be
fun to see if I could handle a "convention case" from the
beginning, and possibly avoid some of the difficulties that
had plagued the Chicago Eight trial lawyers.

Tim Keiser and Sandy Birdsell had been in the Miami
area from May through August 1972. They were there to
cover the activities of the demonstrators on behalf of the
Underground Press Syndicate, a network of some four hundred counter-culture newspapers. In addition, they were
prominent members of the Zippies, a splinter group of the
Youth International Party, and had worked on plans for
several Zippie demonstrations. While living in Miami, they
became acquainted with Randolph Piper, the leader of a rock
group called "The Cowboys." The group was in Miami Beach
hoping to get publicity by entertaining the non-delegates.
Bushy-haired, bearded Randy had rented a flatbed truck for
use as a stage for the rock group's performances. On the
afternoon of August 23, the truck was in Flamingo Park,
where members of the group and its stage managers were
working on the sound equipment on the flatbed. The large
rally, coinciding with President Nixon's acceptance speech,
was planned for that evening. The Cowboys intended to

park their truck near the convention site, where they hoped to get media attention while they sang anti-war songs for the demonstrators.

At approximately three-thirty that afternoon, the truck left Flamingo Park, destined for the convention hall. Tim Keiser had volunteered to drive the truck, so that Piper could ride on the flatbed with the rest of the Cowboys, who planned to sing while the truck was en route to the convention site. Sandy hitched a ride in the cabin of the truck, with Tim and Brett Hotchkiss, the rock group's equipment manager. Some thirty other non-delegates were riding on the flatbed along with the rock group.

Tim drove the truck down Meridian Avenue toward the convention hall, but progress was slow because there was a lot of traffic. Suddenly a corps of motorcycle policemen approached the truck from the opposite direction. Tim attempted to back the truck up but only succeeded in further blocking traffic. The police stopped the truck and asked to see Tim's license. He said that it was in the glove compartment, but was pulled out of the cab without being given an opportunity to get it, and was arrested for reckless driving and driving without a license. The police also arrested Brett Hotchkiss for driving without a license, something which interested me, since I wondered how two people could drive a truck at once.

When they saw the police, the thirty or so hitchhikers on the flatbed jumped off and ran away. The police searched the back of the truck and impounded a can of gasoline that the rock group used to fuel the generator which powered the sound equipment.

When the truck was stopped, Sandy was holding a tin can with wax in it. She had found it on the floor of the truck and had been using it as an ashtray. It looked like one of the many homemade candles that the demonstrators who were camping in Flamingo Park had used to light the tents at the campsite. When one of the police officers asked her what she was holding, she replied, "It's a candle." The policeman took it from her and she did not see it again until her trial.

A few minutes later, the police identified Piper as the rental owner of the truck and allowed him to drive it to the convention hall. Sandy was still in the cab of the truck, but Brett and Tim remained in police custody. The truck was parked on the grass, on the Lincoln Road side of the convention hall, and the rock group began its program of entertainment. Sandy remained with the truck until eight-thirty or nine o'clock, when the whole area was gassed and everyone was forced to leave. (As Sandy was telling me this, I realized with a chill that I was there at the convention hall on the night in question, and couldn't have been far from where the truck was parked.)

We ultimately learned that the police claimed to have taken from the cab of the truck a total of three tin cans filled with waxy substances. Sandy said that she had seen only the one candle that she had been using as an ashtray. Tim had never even noticed that. Neither of them had seen the police remove the second and third cans.

The federal grand jury for the Southern District of Florida handed down a sealed indictment against Tim and Sandy on February 8, 1973. They were arrested in New York on the tenth. On February 12, Roger Lowenstein and I appeared for them before a federal magistrate in New York, and they were released after they posted bonds. On February 15, I represented them before a federal magistrate in Miami, where they entered pleas of not guilty. "Am I going to jail because I was holding a candle?" Sandy asked fearfully. "It wasn't even mine. I just found it on the floor of the truck." It was hard to answer her question, since I did not actually know the basis of the charges against her. The indictment merely alleged the statutory violations and did not go into detail about when and where the "fire bombs" had allegedly been possessed. In an effort to ease her nervousness, I replied that I knew of no jurisdiction in which it was illegal to possess a candle. What I did not tell her was that I was sure there must be something more to the government's case.

Before I go any further, I think it only fair to explain what I mean when I refer to this as a "political" trial. The commentators have written articles and books on the meaning of that phrase, and it is not my intention to compete with their more extensive work. For my purposes here, the phrase has a simple meaning. As the outcome of the Keiser-Birdsell trial will make clear, the charges against these two defendants should never have been brought in the first place. So one must ask why the defendants were indicted, and it is in the answer to that question, in the government's motivation in seeking indictment of these defendants, that this trial becomes "political."

The ostensible political motivation for indicting Keiser and Birdsell was that they were activists, leaders of the politically and culturally dissident Zippies. Indictment of the leaders of political action groups as a means of intimidating activism among their followers was a common weapon of the Nixon Administration, which feared dissent and seemed to equate it with lack of patriotism and even subversion. Anti-war activists had been forced into the legal arena in the Spock, Chicago Eight, Harrisburg Seven, Flower City Conspiracy, and a legion of other trials of the late sixties and early seventies, of which the Keiser-Birdsell case was the most recent example.

The more subtle political motivation for indicting the two Zippies was apparent from the timing of the Justice Department in presenting the case to the grand jury. The alleged fire bombs were seized in August. This was a possession case, pure and simple. Either the defendants had the devices or they did not. Either the devices were legally made and reg-

istered or they were not. Either they were fire bombs or
they were not. From the government's point of view, there
was nothing complicated about the substance of this case. In
spite of the fact that no lengthy preparation and gathering
of evidence could possibly be involved, it took the government over six months (from the time of seizure in August
to the time of indictment in February) to bring this case.
Why?

To the defendants and their supporters, the answer was
simple. One only had to read the newspapers. At the time of
the Keiser-Birdsell indictment, the current big story was the
conviction of the Watergate burglars, who were then awaiting sentencing. In justification of their crime and in an
attempt to mitigate punishment, the Watergate burglars
were publicly claiming that their deed was done in order to
prevent violence at the Republican Convention. Their aim,
they alleged, was to thwart the riots by which dissidents
planned to disrupt the convention.

All very well and good. Except those of us who were
working with the dissidents that summer of 1972 knew that
no violence whatever was planned by any of the groups
participating in the convention demonstrations. Unfortunately, this strategy did not fit in with the Nixon Administration's public-relations plans for the convention. If the demonstrations were to be orderly, then violence would have to be
provoked. I realize that this is a serious charge, but I was
an eyewitness to the effectuation of the plan. I saw the
gassing at the convention hall and I know that the demonstrators did nothing to warrant it.

But even gassing a few hundred demonstrators and senior
citizens had apparently not been graphic enough to fulfill
the Administration's "game plan." The more serious the
Watergate mess became, the more important it was to justify
the covert steps taken to ensure Nixon's reelection. The
American public was becoming more sophisticated and skep-
tical. One could not mitigate the burglary without proof that

there had actually been plans for violence at the convention. The indictment of the Vietnam Vets was intended to provide this proof; but by February 1973 the Vet case was bogged down in pre-trial hearings. A short trial and a quick conviction were necessary. Enter the Internal Security Division of the Justice Department in Washington, which had somehow gotten hold of those tins seized by the Miami police. The Department sent an attorney to the Southern District of Florida to present evidence of nefarious plans by Zippie leaders. There followed the indictment of Keiser and Birdsell. These two may have been guilty of many anti-social acts, but they were not bombers. Violent mouthers, perhaps, but not violent activists. In fact, the most "violent" act Keiser had ever publicly performed was to throw a pie in the face of a member of an obscenity commission. Both Keiser and Birdsell were self-proclaimed members of the drug culture. They were not much admired by the serious left-wing political dissidents and were unlikely candidates for the martyrdom that often accompanies indictment in a political case. But political expediency demanded their indictment.

"I'd like you to represent me," Sandy said after the Florida arraignment. "But before I make a final decision, you have to tell me when your birthday is."

"October 25th," I replied. "Why do you want to know?"

"You're a Scorpio on the cusp of Libra," she said thoughtfully. "That means you're on the borderline between Scorpio and Libra and you're influenced by both. I'll have to ask my astrologer whether you'd be a good lawyer for me." She then asked me the year and time of my birth and where I'd been born.

The next morning, she called to retain me as her lawyer, saying that her astrologer had said I would be an excellent choice. "There's one problem," she continued. "On the day the trial is supposed to start, Mercury is retrograde."

"What in the world does that mean?" I asked.

"It's terrible," she said. "It means we're going to lose. I might as well bring my toothbrush to the courtroom, all prepared to go to jail. You've got to ask the judge for an adjournment. The trial can't start that day."

"Now look, Sandy, I can't ask for an adjournment on the ground that Mercury is retrograde. I'd be laughed out of court."

She was deadly serious, and I was equally adamant. Fortunately for us both, there was a last-minute change in the trial date because of the unavailability of a witness. Mercury was no longer retrograde and I had a calmer, more confident client.

Sandy's parents also needed to be soothed. Understandably upset over their daughter's indictment, they were appalled when they heard about the political activists whom I'd represented in the recent past. They were conservative Republicans, so I sent them a copy of the photograph of me with Bill Buckley taken on the courthouse steps on the day of our victory at the Pauling trial. In their pantheon, Buckley was a hero of only slightly less magnitude than Moses. Sandy told me that the photo reposed in a place of honor in their den. "My mother says to tell you that you're not getting it back unless you win this case," Sandy said.

Trial had been set for March 26 before Judge Peter T. Fay. "What do you know about Fay?" I asked Bruce Rogow, a Miami attorney who had agreed to appear as our local counsel.

"He's conservative, but he's supposed to be fair," Bruce replied.

"How conservative?" I asked.

"Well," Bruce said, "he was Nixon's campaign manager down here in 1968, and I guess that's one reason why he was appointed to the bench."

"Nixon's campaign manager?" I repeated dully. I relayed this information to the clients.

"Can't we get another judge?" Sandy asked.

"We might as well go back to court and plead guilty," Tim said.

I was equally disturbed by news of the judge's background. As a Nixon partisan, he would not be delighted by defendants who were alleged to have plotted to fire-bomb the convention-hall area on the night of his man's acceptance speech. We could always ask him to step down by making a motion to recuse. The problem was that the grounds for such a motion related to actual bias, such as kinship, financial interest, etc. The fact that the judge might have different political views from the defendants was not considered a ground for recusal, even in a political case. I told Tim and Sandy that I doubted that a motion to recuse would be granted, and it would only anger the judge. Then, to cheer them up, I told them the story of Judge Pell, the conservative judge who had surprised us all by a decision for our side in the Chicago Eight case. "Conservative doesn't necessarily mean unfair," I said. "And Bruce did tell us that Judge Fay was reputed to be fair. We'll just have to take our chances with him."

My first encounter with Judge Fay, however, did not seem to warrant any optimism. As soon as I returned to New York, I filed a motion for an adjournment of the trial. Roger Lowenstein, who had agreed to represent Tim, was engaged on another case that was taking almost all his time. The burden of trial preparation would fall largely on me and I knew that there was an enormous amount of work to be done in the way of legal research and drafting of pre-trial motions. Then, too, we were going to have problems locating witnesses. The crime charged was alleged to have taken place during the convention, when thousands of people had converged on the Miami area. Now they had all returned to the fifty states from which they had come. All the prosecutor had to do was ask an F.B.I. agent from any one of the dozens of local F.B.I. offices to interview potential witnesses. For us, finding the

witnesses and running around the country to interview them
seemed an insurmountable task, both financially and because
of the time limitations imposed by the nearness of the trial
date. It seemed unfair that the government should take six
months to prepare this case, while we only had four weeks.
In spite of what seemed strong grounds justifying relief,
Judge Fay denied our request for an extension.

"We're being pushed to trial," Sandy complained.

"It'll make a good issue on appeal," I said, hoping to
placate her.

I considered the possibility of applying to an appellate
court for an extraordinary writ of mandamus requiring Judge
Fay to give us more time to prepare for trial, on the ground
that we were being effectively deprived of the right to
present a defense. I went so far as to have one of my Rutgers
students research the issue and draft a petition for mandamus. In the end, my student and I decided that we had
little chance of winning (since appellate courts rarely interfere with trial proceedings) and would only lose more of the
time which was so precious. The idea of a petition for mandamus was abandoned and I settled down to work on the
pre-trial motions.

I began by researching the statute under which Tim and
Sandy had been charged. It was part of the National Firearms Act, which was itself part of the Internal Revenue
Code. The statute set forth procedures by which application
must be made for permission to make, transfer, and/or
register a firearm and a tax paid. It was of recent vintage,
having been enacted in 1968. This meant that there were
likely to be few cases interpreting the statute, so I would be
covering new ground and might even be able to make new
law. The sections under which Tim and Sandy had been
indicted penalized possession of illegally made or unregistered firearms. Specifically, they were charged with possession of "destructive devices, commonly known as fire bombs,

consisting of cans with a wax like mixture of potassium nitrate and sugar." According to the relevant sections of the statute, "destructive devices" were defined as follows:

> (1) Any explosive, incendiary, or poison gas (A) bomb, (B) grenade, (C) rocket having a propellant charge of more than four ounces, (D) missile having an explosive or incendiary charge of more than one-quarter ounce, (E) mine, or (F) similar device . . . and (3) any combination of parts either designed or intended for use in converting any device into a destructive device as defined in subparagraph (1) . . . and from which a destructive device may be readily assembled.

To find out more about what Congress meant by the term "destructive devices," I went to the transcript of the legislative hearings that had been conducted when the bill was being considered by the Senate. The volume of testimony was almost 1,200 pages long. I took a deep breath and plunged in. It was dull stuff and it took me almost a week to read the entire volume, but it was worth it. The transcript of the hearings repeatedly referred to destructive devices as "military type weapons," "the heavy ordnance of war," "implements of war," and the like. It was apparent from the legislative history of the Act that it was meant to restrict the dissemination of surplus military ordnance and was not meant to apply to homemade incendiary devices. That explained why none of the definitions of destructive devices neatly fit the devices which were the basis of the indictment in this case.

When I researched previous cases under this new statute, I discovered none that involved devices like ours. The nearest equivalent were cases involving Molotov cocktails, which the courts had held to be "similar devices" to incendiary bombs and/or grenades. None of the Molotov cocktail cases confronted the legislative history of the Act, and it seemed to me that the judiciary had gone beyond the congressional intent that the Act apply to surplus military ordnance. Although these cases were not decisive for us, because our devices were not Molotov cocktails, they were troublesome nonetheless.

The statutory scheme of application and registration for permission to make or transfer a firearm also made it clear that the Act was never meant to apply to homemade incendiary devices. Possession or construction of a gun could be legal if there was prior compliance with the Act. But how could one go about applying for permission to make fire bombs? One could never legally possess a fire bomb, and permission would never be granted to make one. As I saw it, were the statute meant to apply to homemade fire bombs, it would be analogous to requiring prior application for permission to rob a bank.

Curious to know how the maker of a homemade fire bomb crazy enough to apply for a license might pursue the course set forth in this statute, I called the New York regional office of the Alcohol, Tobacco and Firearms Division of the Internal Revenue Service, which has jurisdiction over the enforcement of the Firearms Act. "How would one go about getting permission to make a fire bomb?" I asked the Firearms Coordinator.

His response was incredulous laughter. "Who is this?" he asked.

I explained that I was a lawyer. Since it was possible that A.T.F. personnel might be working with the prosecutor in preparing this case, I didn't want to mention that I was involved in litigation. I told the agent that I was writing a law-review article on the Firearms Act. "I don't understand how this Act can possibly apply to homemade fire bombs," I said. "Can you help me?"

"I confess that I don't know myself," he answered. "To my knowledge, no one has ever applied for a license to make a bomb." It was an interesting admission from a man responsible for enforcement of the Act, that he had no idea how a potential bomb maker would apply for a license. He was intrigued by the problem and agreed to look into it further. I arranged to meet him at his office the next day. When I appeared at the downtown office of A.T.F., the agent was expansive and helpful. Although he still hadn't figured out how one would go about applying for permission to make a fire bomb, he did give me various regulations relating to the Act, application forms, and copies of similar state statutes. Some of his colleagues were not so amused by my inquiries about fire bombs, however. One gun-toting agent was particularly suspicious. He kept asking why I was so interested in fire bombs. For which law review was I writing this article? Where did I teach? And finally, in tones which were only half playful, he asked, "You don't live anywhere near West Eleventh Street, do you?"

"If I did," I replied, "it's unlikely that I'd come to visit all of you, isn't it?" With that statement, he had to agree. West Eleventh Street was the site of the 1970 explosion which destroyed a town house that supposedly held a bomb factory staffed by members of the Weather underground, with a resulting conflagration that claimed several lives. It occurred to me that the reaction of the A.T.F. office engendered by my questions about fire bombs was more evidence of the fact that the statute was never intended to cover homemade incendiary devices.

I gathered together the legislative history, case law, and my experience with A.T.F. into an extensive motion to dismiss the indictment on the ground that the charges were outside the ambit of the statute. The reason I put so much energy into this motion is that it is difficult to defend a possession case. Government witnesses testify that the devices were in the defendants' possession; the defendants counter by saying they were not. It comes down to a question of whom the jury believes. And if it is a matter of uniformed police officers and F.B.I. agents versus long-haired radicals, you need an alternative defense. I was hoping that I could get Judge Fay to toss the case out before it reached the jury, by means of a ruling that the indictment went beyond the scope of the statute. There were never any responding papers from the prosecutor, and the motion was denied almost as soon as I filed it.

I also made a motion requiring the government to disclose whether the defendants or their attorneys had been wiretapped. In some jurisdictions, all you have to do is make an assertion of the possibility that there has been electronic surveillance, and the government is required to affirm or deny whether it has taken place. In the Florida federal court, a "mere assertion" of wiretapping was insufficient. I had to put in affidavits establishing reasonable grounds for belief that there had been tapping.

In this case, that wasn't too difficult. Sandy and Tim had both been under constant personal surveillance during the convention summer, by undercover agents of the Miami police department who had infiltrated the Zippies and whose cover had long since been blown. What Tim's affidavit characterized as this "unusual government interest in me" was one reason why we presumed that there had been electronic surveillance as well. In addition, Tim and Sandy were closely associated with numerous people the government had previously admitted were overheard, which made it likely that they too had been wiretapped. Among these "associates" were Abbie Hoffman and Jerry Rubin (whose taps surfaced during the Chicago Eight case) and Pun Plamondon, whose overhearing led to the decision in the Keith case. Tim and Sandy had often called them and/or used the same phones they had used, which was good reason to believe they too had been illegally overheard.

Repeated interference with their telephone service and suspicious noises on the lines also made it probable that their phones had been tapped. In describing his experiences with the phone which was installed at the house he stayed at during the conventions, Tim said:

> This phone worked very erratically. It often didn't ring; callers couldn't reach us; there was often whispering on the line. Almost every day, between the hours of two and five in the afternoon, the phone would be out of order. After two weeks, the phone was replaced with a noticeably heavier instrument, but the erratic service continued.
>
> On or about July 4th, I dialed this number from an outside line in the environs of Miami. Instead of ringing, I heard a loud "click." Then I could hear everything that was going on in the house, although the phone had never rung and no one had picked it up. I could hear the stereo playing and overheard several conversations in the house. The voices were so clear that I was able to identify several of them. About ten minutes later, there was another loud click and I was no longer able to hear what was going on in the house. The phone line was dead, so I hung up and dialed again. This time, it rang and I was able to complete the call without further interference. This sort of disturbance on my telephone lines leads me to believe that I have been the subject of electronic surveillance.

Sandy's affidavit included as an example of difficulties with the telephone the time, a few weeks before the Democratic Convention, when she had picked up her phone to make a call and there was no dial tone.

> Instead, I heard an unidentified man's voice say, "Shh, they're on the line." A few moments later, I got a dial tone and was able to complete my call. Although there was an extension of this phone in the attic, no one else was at home at the time this incident occurred, so it was clear that there was some sort of outside surveillance of the line.

In my own affidavit, I listed some of the clients I'd represented who the government had previously admitted were subjects of electronic surveillance, such as the Chicago Eight defendants. I also named several cases in which the government had admitted overhearing lawyers who were associates of mine. Most recently, the government had conceded that one of the attorneys representing the witness-contemners in the Texas I.R.A. case had been overheard. (The "Texas I.R.A." or "Fort Worth Five" case [In re Tierney] involved the refusal of five Irish-Americans from New York City to testify before a Fort Worth grand jury which was investigating suspected illegal gun running from the Southwest to the Irish Republican Army. After over a year and a half in jail, they were released without being forced to testify.) Center lawyers Jim Reif, Doris Peterson, and Bill Cunningham were counsel of record in that case. If clients and associates of mine were victims of wiretapping, then it was likely that I was too. Roger drafted an affidavit for himself along the same lines and we sent the motion papers to Florida.

The intensity with which I pursued this wiretap business was a direct result of the Supreme Court's decision in the Keith case. In Keith, the Supreme Court had held that warrantless electronic surveillance of suspected domestic subversives was illegal. The defendants in the Keiser-Birdsell case were obviously the sort regarded by the Nixon Administration as "domestic subversives." If they had in fact been the victims of warrantless wiretapping, the government might follow the same path as in the Sinclair case (the underlying case in Keith), Abbie Hoffman's Mayday indictment, the Detroit Weather case, and others; that is, refuse to turn over the wiretap logs and dismiss the proceedings against Keiser and Birdsell. That was what we hoped might happen.

I also filed motions relating to voir dire, a request for a bill of particulars, and other pre-trial discovery matters. Not long after I sent in the motions, they were denied. I protested to the clerk that I still hadn't gotten any answering papers from the government, so how could the motions be denied? The clerk told me that, according to the local rules, the prosecutor didn't have to file answering papers to defense motions.

One of the first things I do when I get a case outside the New York area is to check the local rules, and this case was no exception. I had looked at a copy of the federal rules for the Southern District of Florida that was in the Rutgers Law Library. You always have to watch out for local idiosyncrasies of practice and I didn't want us to be delayed by procedural mishaps. After my conversation with the clerk, I went back to the library and checked the rules again. To my dismay, I discovered that a page was missing, obviously the page outlining this interesting and unusual procedure. No doubt it was meant to save the prosecutors work. But it left me with the feeling that it was the defendants against the team of judge and prosecutor, and that the deck was stacked against us.

Then the judge surprised us by granting a wiretap hearing. I got the notice of his order in the Monday mail and the hearing was called for that Wednesday in Miami. Since I had to teach in Camden on Tuesday, that didn't leave me much time to prepare. And once my excitement at our victory wore off, I realized that I hadn't the vaguest idea what was supposed to happen at a wiretap hearing. The Keiser-Birdsell wiretap hearing was only the third or fourth that had ever been granted. Fortunately, I knew the attorneys in the Harrisburg Seven case, where a wiretap hearing had been ordered in connection with the proceedings against Philip Berrigan and other members of the Catholic left. I contacted Bill Bender, who had conducted that hearing. He told me that he had given Jim Reif a copy of the transcript, so that Jim could prepare for the possibility that a hearing would be granted in the Vet case. I rushed over to the Center to examine the available material, which was the only way I could become an instant expert on wiretap hearings. Once more, I appreciated how important our communal efforts were; the Center lawyers helped me to get ready for the wiretap hearing, as I was later to help them prepare the defense against the Firearms Act charges in the Vet case. It's the best way to practice law.

The purpose of a wiretap hearing at this stage of the proceedings was to prove the unreliability of the government's assertion that the defendants and their counsel had not been the subjects of electronic surveillance, by showing the insufficiency of the government's search of its records. I was particularly interested in the testimony of the F.B.I. agents who were subpoenaed to appear as witnesses at the Harrisburg hearing, because it pinpointed the sloppiness of government record-keeping practices. For example, one of the agents testified that the F.B.I. kept an alphabetical list of the names of the people who were being tapped, as well as the names of those who were overheard on that "installation," as the agent put it.

He was then asked: "Do you keep any index system other than an index by name of the person who has been overheard?"

"No," replied the agent.

"To be specific," Bender asked, "is an index kept by subject investigation; in other words, by investigation of a particular case?"

"No."

"Is there any index whatsoever kept as to place?"

"No."

"So what you are telling me then," Bender said, "is that the only way you can determine whether or not a particular individual has been overheard is to go to an index file by name, and alphabetically, and see whether or not his name appears?"

"That is right," the agent said.

The problem that this testimony pointed up was that when people use the telephone they don't necessarily identify themselves by their full names. "Hi, this is Felix," is a typical telephone greeting. If Felix Black thereafter made a wiretap motion, the government would probably be unable to tell from its records that the "Felix" overheard was the same person making the motion. This has actually occurred. In one of the cases involving the Jewish Defense League, a wiretap motion was made by Jeffrey Smilow. Initially, the government denied that he had been overheard. When the case reached the Supreme Court, the government admitted the possibility of illegal surveillance because wiretap logs revealed conversations of an individual identified only as "Jeff."

The point is that the presumption of regularity of government conduct has been overcome countless times in the course of wiretap proceedings. It was for this reason that the courts were beginning to grant wiretap hearings, in order to go behind the government's denial that there had been tapping of the participants in a particular case.

While I was considering this point, I suddenly realized that I was missing something crucial. In our case, there had been neither a denial nor an affirmance by the government of our assertion that there had been electronic surveillance. Once again, the government had not deigned it necessary to reply. This might be permissible with respect to the other motions I had made, but no local rules could evade the federal statutory requirement that the government respond to a wiretap motion. It was obvious from the government's actions in other cases that the government was aware of its responsibility to respond to a wiretap motion, because I had in my files affidavits which the government had submitted in these cases. In the Ellsberg-Russo case, for example, a member of the Internal Security Division of the Justice Department had sworn that inquiry had been made of eight federal agencies, including the F.B.I., the Departments of State and Defense, the I.R.S. (and its Alcohol, Tobacco and Firearms Division), and the C.I.A. The affidavit concluded:

That based upon the results of such inquiry [affiant] hereby
states that there has been no electronic surveillance of any
conversations of Anthony J. Russo or Daniel Ellsberg and
there has been no electronic surveillance of any conversations
occurring on their premises.

We were entitled to a similar affidavit denying or affirming
wiretapping in our case. I called Carol Anderson, the government attorney who was trying the Keiser-Birdsell case, to
ask her what had happened to the government's affidavits.
I assumed that they had gotten lost in the mail.

"I'm not filing any," she told me.

"You can't do that," I said. "You have a statutory duty to
respond."

"I called someone in the Justice Department," she said,
"and he told me there hasn't been any wiretapping in this
case, so I'm going to stand up in court and tell that to Judge
Fay."

"That's not a proper response," I said. "You have to file
an affidavit."

"That's not what my expert told me," she replied.

"Carol," I said, "you'd better get another expert. The government is required to put in affidavits. Just look at the files in
the Tierney, Ellsberg-Russo, Purcell, and Briggs cases and
you'll see what type of affidavit you have to get." She kept
insisting that I was wrong and that she didn't have to file
any affidavits. I hung up the phone and sighed. Here I was,
primed for a wiretap hearing, and it looked as though I was
going to have to go two steps back and argue about my right
to get affidavits.

The next day I went to Camden and spent the day teaching my students about the right to a fair trial, while wondering whether I was going to be able to get one for my client.
That night I flew from Philadelphia to Miami. Passing
through the airport security device, I set off the alarm. I
wondered what the inspector would think if he knew that

my luggage was filled with material on how to make fire bombs. The mechanical fuss was apparently occasioned by what the inspector called my "wired foundation garment." He waved me toward the plane and I was seated next to a two-year-old boy. "Is he a good flyer?" I asked his mother. "Oh, yes," she said. "He loves to fly, don't you dear?" By way of reply, the baby turned toward me and threw up, dousing both me and the legal papers I held in my lap. I hoped it wasn't an omen for the case.

After all the work we had done preparing the wiretap issue, the next afternoon was a letdown. We spent most of the time arguing about the government's responsibility to file affidavits. I pointed out to Judge Fay that the government had failed to make a proper response to our request for disclosure of electronic surveillance. Prosecutor Anderson's oral denial was insufficient, because she herself had not made the inquiries and because her statement was unsworn. It was settled practice for the government to respond to a wiretap motion by putting in an affidavit by someone in the head office of the Justice Department, attesting that he or she had made direct inquiries of the relevant government agencies, and affirming or denying electronic surveillance. I showed Judge Fay copies of affidavits the government had submitted in other recent political cases. He agreed that the government's response in our case was incorrect and ordered Mrs. Anderson to file an affidavit similar to the ones the government had filed in the cases I had cited.

Mrs. Anderson said that it would take at least two weeks to get an affidavit from Washington as to whether the defendants had been tapped. I interrupted to say such an affidavit would also be insufficient. We had a right to know whether Roger or I had been overheard, and I wanted her to check that out too, which the judge ordered her to do.

I had one more point to make. The government's wiretap affidavits customarily alleged that the affiant had checked with federal agencies to see whether there were any over-hearings. I urged that the government had the additional obligation to check to see whether the defendants or their lawyers had been overheard by any state or local authorities. "The alleged fire bombs in this case were originally seized by local authorities; namely, the Miami police," I said. "If that seizure was made because of information received from an unlawful tap by local authorities, then the evidence is tainted. The federal government cannot use the fruits of illegal electronic surveillance conducted by state or local governments as evidence against these defendants." I cited a few cases on the general question of tainted evidence and asked Judge Fay to order the government to inquire whether state or local authorities had conducted electronic surveillance of the defendants or their lawyers, and to submit an affidavit of its findings. He granted my request and told Mrs. Anderson to file all the required affidavits prior to the trial date.

When court adjourned, I went running out of the court-room to look for a phone. We had just gotten a great ruling and I was anxious to tell the Center lawyers representing the Vets what had happened. In all the other wiretap affidavits I had seen, the government had investigated only federal agencies. To my knowledge, this was the first time the gov-ernment had been ordered to investigate state and local agencies as well. I knew that there were wiretap motions in the Vet case scheduled for argument within the next few weeks. I hoped that the Vet lawyers would be able to use Judge Fay's ruling as precedent for getting a similar order in their case, where there had also been an initial seizure of demonstrative evidence by local authorities.

I finally found a pay phone in the middle of Flagler Street in downtown Miami, and from the open booth, surrounded by traffic and blaring horns, I called Doris to tell her the news. She was excited about the ruling and promised to tell Jim Reif, who was going to argue the wiretap motion on behalf of the Vets. A few weeks later, I heard that Jim's argument on that point had been successful. On the basis of Judge Fay's ruling in our case, Judge Winston Arnow had ordered the government to inquire whether there had been local electronic surveillance in the Vet case. I was delighted to hear about this. Having your case used as precedent in another proceeding is one of the most exciting things about being a lawyer.

Several months after the fire-bomb trial, Doris showed me the transcript of the Vet wiretap hearing. I learned for the first time that after Jim had made his motion Judge Arnow had called a recess. Fifteen minutes later, he returned to court and announced that he had "called Judge Fay, just to check back on that decision a little bit." I was amazed when I heard that, because it indicated that he did not believe what Jim had told him about the ruling in our case. (This sign of the lack of respect which the trial judge in the Vet case had for the defense lawyers presaged future difficulties they were to have with him. See page 299.)

"Judge Fay said that in effect what happened in that case," Judge Arnow said, "was that there were so many affidavits being filed back and forth he was getting tired of them and thought everybody was getting tired of them and finally just suggested to the Assistant United States Attorney, 'Why don't you go ahead and make inquiry of the Dade County people and let's get through with this thing.' And that is what occurred, so there wasn't any argument left with it."

I howled with laughter when I read that transcript. I had been so proud of my legal presentation to Judge Fay, so excited that I had convinced him to order the government to investigate the possibility of local surveillance. I didn't know how accurately Judge Arnow had recounted his conversation with Judge Fay, nor what was meant by "affidavits being filed back and forth," since the government hadn't filed any affidavits at all at the time I made my argument. Still, it appeared that Judge Fay had been less impressed with the intellectual weight of my oral argument than with the actual weight of the motion papers I had submitted to him. So much for my expanding ego. Anyway, even Judge Arnow had to admit that I'd established good precedent, because he'd ordered the government to make the same investigation in the Vet case.

In the Keiser-Birdsell case, our victory was pyrrhic. Government mills ground so slowly that we never received a complete set of answering affidavits, and because of this, we never got to hold a hearing to explore the question of wiretapping. We were all disappointed, especially Sandy and Tim. They were convinced that we would have been able to prove that they had been the subjects of illegal electronic surveillance, which might have been grounds for dismissal of the case.

On the day the wiretap hearing was supposed to have been held, we renewed our motion to dismiss on the ground that the statute did not cover the crime charged, and it was once more denied. We again requested that the trial date be put off, to give us more time to locate witnesses and prepare a defense. Judge Fay remarked that defense lawyers usually complain about the lack of a speedy trial, which certainly wasn't the case here. "A speedy trial is one thing," I responded. "But not at the expense of the right to prepare a defense." The motion for an extension was again denied.

After the abortive wiretap hearing, Roger returned to New York, while I remained in Florida to work on the case. There were two more pre-trial hearings to prepare for, which were to be held the next week. The most important hearing was on our motion to suppress the cans that were the basis of the charges, on the ground that they had been illegally seized from the truck. This was a near impossible motion to win, but we had to try. And even if we lost, we would have an opportunity to examine the police officers who stopped the truck and get an idea of the government's case.

Sandy and Roger came down from New York for the suppression hearing. The day it was scheduled, Sandy and I walked into the courtroom together. On a table in front of the bench were several large packages marked "fragile," "explosives." (We later moved successfully to have these labels removed, so as not to prejudice the jury.) We watched curiously as an F.B.I. agent unwrapped the packages and set three cans out on the table. With his permission, we moved closer to examine them. There was one large can overflowing with wax, with a cigarette stub sticking out of the wax. The two smaller cans contained a substance that looked like marzipan. "That's the candle I told you about, the one I found on the floor of the truck and used as an ashtray," Sandy whispered, pointing to the largest can. "See, there's my cigarette."

Then we turned our attention to the other two cans. As Sandy reached out toward one of them, I grabbed her arm. "Don't touch anything. We haven't received any fingerprint reports yet."

"I've never seen either of those two cans before," Sandy said.

We returned to the defense table, and the suppression hearing began. Officers Eades, Horvath, and Sewell of the Miami police department were called to testify about the seizure of the cans. They were part of the fifteen- to twenty-man unit detailed to patrol the convention area on their motorcycles. As Officer Eades put it, "The Department had received word that possibly the [Lincoln Road] Mall was going to be destroyed or burned or looted that night. We were over there to protect the Mall."

While patroling near Meridian Avenue and Lincoln Road,

the policemen saw a large truck traveling north on the wrong side of Meridian Avenue. The truck was stopped and the driver, subsequently identified as Tim Keiser, was arrested for careless driving and driving without a license. A second man was also arrested for driving without a license. The truck was released to a man named Piper, whom all three officers identified as the third passenger in the cab of the truck.

When the driver stepped out of the truck, arresting officer Eades saw "a can on the seat between the driver and a female passenger sitting on the front seat of the vehicle." He described the can as having what "looked like a rope wick or something coming out of the top. It appeared to have a wax substance it was sitting in." He took the can from the truck, put it on the curb, and called for a departmental bomb expert.

Officer Horvath then took the stand. He testified that he had been standing on the opposite side of the truck from Officer Eades. "On the floorboard of the truck, alongside of a white female who was sitting in the middle, were two cans. One was a sort of a fruit can and the other looked like a large tuna-fish can. There was a waxy substance inside the can with matchheads sticking in the substance." He said that he had taken the two cans and put them on the curb next to the can that had been seized by Officer Eades.

Another member of the Miami police department, criminalist Thomas Brodie, was the officer who had responded to the call for a bomb expert. A member of the department's bomb-disposal squad, he had taken the three cans into custody. While still on the scene, he had made a pea-size cut into the material in one of the cans and had burned it with a match.

"What happened when you put a match to it?" Roger asked on cross examination.

"It flared up," was Officer Brodie's simple answer.

After hearing the testimony, we urged that the cans had been illegally seized: they looked like ordinary homemade candles and the officers had no reasonable grounds for belief that they contained dangerous materials. The fact that Officer Eades had testified that he had heard general, unconfirmed rumors that Lincoln Mall might be bombed was insufficient grounds to uphold the seizure.

"Let me ask you some questions," Judge Fay said during my argument. "Don't you believe, under the circumstances that are known to everyone that has lived in this country and read the newspapers or watched TV, that anyone, any reasonable person, would have reasonable cause to believe that there might be some disruption at any political convention of a national political party in this country?"

"Are you asking me to admit," I said, "that because there was difficulty in Chicago in 1968, for example, which difficulty the Walker Report clearly pinned upon a 'police riot'—"

"The only reason I asked the question," Judge Fay interrupted before I could finish my response, "is that the basis for my ruling would be that any police officer on duty, either in Chicago, if you want to relate it to Chicago, or Miami Beach, or anywhere else where a national political convention is going to be held, had better be particularly alert and particularly astute for anything that might be a dangerous weapon and that might cause him or those around him bodily harm."

Judge Fay said that the officers had "an absolute right" to seize the three cans. "They were not candles and they were not ashtrays and they didn't look like candles or ashtrays," he said.

I then told him that the government had turned over to us the F.B.I. reports analyzing the contents of the cans and that the first can, the so-called ashtray, contained no incendiary material. "Its mere appearance is wax and wick," I said. "Wax plus wick equals candle."

Judge Fay remarked that it didn't look like a candle to

him, and that "if a young lady wants to carry that type of candle in that type of can in the front seat of a truck at a political convention," the police had an absolute right to take it.

Hearing that, I turned and walked back to the defense table. "He just ruled that the Fourth Amendment protections against illegal searches and seizures are suspended during political conventions," I said.

Roger nodded grimly. Neither of us had felt that there were strong grounds for suppression, but the comments that went along with this ruling seemed unnecessarily harsh and we saw no point in arguing further. Our motion to suppress was denied, but at least we had accomplished one of our objectives, which had been to get an idea of what the police testimony at the trial was going to be.

When I left the courtroom after the hearing, I was accompanied by my Grandmother and Grandfather Weisenthal, who lived in Miami Beach, and had come to see me perform in court. That they sat through four hours of what for them must have been extremely tedious proceedings was a measure of their devotion to me. As we walked down the courthouse corridor, my grandmother turned to me and said, "That judge, he's such a nice fella."

"Why do you say that, Grandma?" I asked.

"He's so nice and he always smiles and he complimented you on how beautifully you spoke," she said.

"Grandma," I said, "we lost this afternoon."

"What do you mean?" she asked.

"Well, everything that I asked the judge to do for me, he refused to do."

My grandmother's eyes narrowed, her brow wrinkled, and with a passion of which only grandmothers are capable, she muttered, "The bum!"

My grandmother's initial reaction to Judge Fay illustrates a difficulty which faced us. There was no doubt that Judge

Fay was one of the most finely temperamented, courteous judges I'd ever met. But his graciousness could turn out to be a problem. A nasty judge might make the jury sympathetic to the defense; a judge who constantly denied our motions with a smile could be dangerous. Because of this and also because we were disturbed by his comments about conventions, we once again considered asking Judge Fay to recuse himself. But it was still so unlikely that the request would be granted that we didn't bother making it.

Roger again went back to New York to work on his other case, and I continued to prepare this case for the trial, which was less than a week away. One day Roger phoned with the suggestion that we consider getting a truck like the one the rock group had rented. We needed interesting demonstrative evidence to capture the jury's fancy and to compete with the cans that the government would introduce into evidence. No doubt we would have difficulty convincing the judge to let the jurors view the truck, so we had to think of a way to make it relevant. It occurred to me that the cans might have been under the seat in the cab of the truck, which would explain why Sandy and Tim hadn't noticed them. I wanted to look at a similar truck to see if that was possible, so Sandy and I drove over to the truck-rental lot one balmy afternoon.

I thought it likely that the manager of the rental office would react adversely if he knew we wanted to see the truck for reasons relating to a court proceeding. If he was smart, he might insist upon calling the company lawyers, to protect himself. This would result in delay, and that was one thing we couldn't afford. To prevent this from happening, my inventive client told the manager that we were part of a street theater group interested in renting a truck for use as a stage. He was a congenial fellow and he and Sandy carried on a flirtatious conversation about the type of plays we presented (Westerns and comedies), how long we had been actresses (three years), who else was in the troupe (two other women and three men). That guy must have thought I was a half-wit, because at this point I was too convulsed with suppressed laughter to look at him, let alone participate in the conversation.

"What part do you play?" he asked me.

"I play a clown," I said. It was no use. As soon as I opened my mouth, a series of giggles came out. What the heck was I doing here? Why didn't I have clients rich enough to hire an investigator?

"A clown?" the manager repeated. "Well," he said cordially, "you certainly have a nice enough laugh."

At that, even Sandy broke down and snickered. The manager looked at us strangely. "Are you two being hazed for a sorority or something?" he asked. We denied it, but I don't think he believed us for a moment. Still, he was sweet to play along and he even volunteered to join our troupe.

I examined the truck to which he led us, and took various measurements of the cab ("to see whether our make-up kits will fit under the seats," I explained to the watching manager). In the end, I decided that the truck would not be useful at all, but our afternoon adventure was definitely worth it for the comic relief it provided during the intense period before trial.

On the Saturday prior to the trial date, I flew up to central Florida to interview several members of the rock group The Cowboys. I was especially anxious to speak to Randy Piper, the lead singer of the group and the one who had been responsible for renting the truck. Since the summer, he had clipped his hair short, shaved his beard, and taken a straight job. Now he was afraid that his job would be endangered if he was involved in the trial. At first, he refused to see me. After a personal plea from Sandy ("I might go to jail, Randy. You've got to help us. This is serious"), he made an appointment, and then didn't keep it.

After two false starts, I tracked him down at his office. I showed him the photographs I had taken of the three cans the Miami police claimed to have found in the cab of the truck. Although he had been in and out of the cab when the truck was in Flamingo Park, he said he had never seen any of the three cans. Of special importance to our case was his absolute certainty that when the truck was proceeding to the convention hall he had been riding on the flatbed, singing with his group. He had definitely not been the third passenger in the cab. At the suppression hearing, all three police officers had testified that Piper was the third passenger. They were wrong, most likely confused because it had been Piper who had driven the truck away after the police arrested Tim Keiser.

Piper's testimony would be useful to impeach the credibility of the police officers. But his nervousness ("I'm afraid I'll lose my job if they find out about this") was too apparent when he talked about the case. And I wasn't certain that his agitation related entirely to his employer. As I talked to him, I became convinced that he knew more about the origin of the cans than he was saying. After all, it was his truck and his rock band. Sandy had told me that the rock group had a number about Lieutenant Calley and My Lai, during which they set off some sort of canisters that emitted smoke, to simulate the battle. She had never seen them, but I was beginning to think the government's "fire bombs" might be just stage props and that Piper knew it and was too terrified to admit it. It was just possible that his disquietude stemmed from what he regarded as his "lucky escape" from indictment.

Whatever the reason, I had strong doubts as to how his demeanor would impress the jury. I discussed the matter carefully with Roger and we agreed that we would not subpoena him. Our strategy was to bring out his corroborative testimony favorable to the defense while cross examining him as a government witness.

While in central Florida, I also met with Brett Hotchkiss, the equipment manager of the rock group. He turned out to be a lawyer's dream of a witness. Only twenty years old, he was a solid and responsible person who held two jobs, one of which was with the county. He was married and the father of a child, lived with his parents, was nice-looking and personable, and was sure to impress the jury favorably. Hotchkiss told me the details he remembered about the afternoon of the twenty-third. Most important, he confirmed that it was he, not Piper, who had been the third passenger in the cab of the truck. When I showed him the photographs of the cans, he said that he had never seen any of them. This was disappointing. I had hoped that he might be able to confirm my theory that the "fire bombs" were stage props. I subpoenaed Hotchkiss and told him that he would probably be called as the first witness for the defense.

There remained one other problem in the preparation of the defense. This was solved by Roger, who located an expert witness who knew about bombs, organic chemistry, and the like, to testify on behalf of the defense. But the expert was not available until the day the trial was scheduled to commence. We explained the problem to Judge Fay. Since we were entitled to have our expert make his own analysis of the contents of the cans prior to trial, the judge reluctantly granted a two-day extension on the trial date. I informed an ecstatic Sandy that Mercury would no longer be retrograde, and she would not have to bring her toothbrush to court.

18

Defusing the Opposition

I awoke at five-thirty the morning the trial was to begin. For the next two hours, unable to sleep, I lay in bed and conducted cross examinations in my head. This was typical. I am always restless before an important courtroom appearance. It doesn't interfere with my ability to work. On the contrary, like most litigators, I find the adrenaline flow crucial if I am to be at my best in court. I remember one time before an appellate argument when the tension was inexplicably missing. I always felt that was one of my least effective performances in court. Anyway, the nervousness disappears as soon as I say my first words to the judge.

After the others had eaten breakfast, I joined them in the coffee shop and quickly drank a glass of chocolate milk before going off to court. I never eat much breakfast, but when I am on trial, my normally erratic eating habits become totally eccentric. The combination of tension and forgetfulness always results in a loss of several pounds. While preparing the Keiser-Birdsell case, I dropped eight unnecessary pounds in six weeks, a source of great consternation to Sandy's mother. She sent me a large box of candy to see me through the pre-trial motions and made sure that I was well

supplied with chocolate bars to eat during the trial recesses.
"I don't want you to collapse from lack of energy in the
middle of Sandy's defense," she explained. What she didn't
understand was that I was running on energy that no food
could provide.

Trial was scheduled to begin at nine o'clock in the morning. Judge Fay had wanted to begin at eight, but after I
confessed with horror that I was a night person and was
barely functional at that hour, he agreed to open the trial
at nine. As we walked into court for the first day of trial, a
beaming Judge Fay peered down at me from the bench and
said playfully, "Well, Miss Schwartz, how did you like our
Florida sunrise?"

"Your Honor," I responded, not about to admit that I had
been up early enough to see it, "this is cruel and unusual
punishment and my client is being deprived of her right to
the effective assistance of counsel, and I'd be grateful if you
wouldn't mention it any more."

After this relaxing badinage, we began to pick a jury.
Judge Fay introduced Mrs. Anderson to the venire and asked
whether any of them knew her, which they did not. He introduced Roger and me, saying that it was unlikely that any of
them knew us, as we were both from New York. Roger wag-
gishly complained that he didn't want the jurors to think
he was a carpetbagger. I volunteered the information that my
entire family lived in the Southern District of Florida, which
made me at least a kissing cousin. As it turned out, one of
the jurors had met me a few days before, when we had
shared a seat on a long bus ride. She was dismissed for other
reasons, but I was glad to know that we "foreigners" had a
friend in court.

Federal judges usually question the jurors themselves, but
Judge Fay allowed the lawyers to conduct the voir dire. We
asked questions about reading habits, to see whether any
members of the venire read right-wing publications. We

asked whether any of the potential jurors had attended activities sponsored by the non-delegates or had participated in any of the demonstrations. One woman said that her daughter had gone to Flamingo Park and had been "disgusted" by what she saw there. We used one of our peremptory challenges to excuse her.

We inquired about the prospective jurors' backgrounds in chemistry. We did not want a self-appointed expert in the jury room, who might interfere with the jurors' evaluation of the testimony of expert witnesses. We decided to keep those who had studied chemistry in high school, figuring that they wouldn't remember enough to make them troublesome. But we did excuse a retired New York City fireman who had taken a special course in explosives. We also excused a security guard and several people who had close associations with the Miami police department, quite a few members of which were going to testify as government witnesses. One man admitted that his best friend was a police undercover agent, but after ascertaining from Mrs. Anderson that the man's friend was not going to appear as a government witness, we decided to keep the juror anyway. He seemed open-minded and intelligent and turned out to be one of my favorites on the jury.

For its part, the government dismissed all jurors with Jewish-sounding names. We had been warned that this was a familiar prosecutorial ploy in this district, as Jewish jurors were felt to be "too liberal" in criminal cases. Roger made an objection for the record, but it was denied and the jury was sworn.

The first witnesses called by the government were the three motorcycle policemen and Thomas Brodie, the bomb-squad expert who had been called to the scene. Their testimony was roughly the same as it had been at the suppression hearing, except for one interesting discrepancy which surfaced during my cross examination of Officer Eades, the policeman who had taken the can that Sandy had been using as an ashtray.

A few minutes before we entered the courtroom, Mrs. Anderson had given me what is known as "3500 material." This is the grand jury testimony and statements made to F.B.I. agents by people the government intends to call as witnesses. A federal statute (18 United States Code §3500, hence the nickname "3500 material") provides that defense attorneys are to be given this material after the witness has testified on direct. The material can be extremely useful on cross examination, because you can sometimes impeach a witness by showing that he or she has made a prior inconsistent statement to the grand jury or the F.B.I.

I got six-inches-thick worth of statements and transcripts only moments before the trial began, and I had to read it while the trial was going on. As a general rule, I do not like to ask for recesses in a jury trial. Jurors are alienated by what they regard as "delaying tactics." They get bored sitting in the jury room and you run the risk that the boredom will translate into antipathy toward you or your client, since you are the one who asked for the recess. So I had to try to scan the material while Mrs. Anderson was examining on direct. In addition, I had to listen to the testimony of the government witnesses, so I could object to improper questions, and I had to take notes on the substance of the testimony, so that I could prepare my cross examination. And I had to watch the jurors' reactions to the witnesses' demeanor and to the substance of the testimony. After a while, you can do most of these things at once, somewhat like a person who steers a car while watching the road for other cars, stop signs, little children, etc., all at the same time.

The sad thing is that the problem with 3500 material could so easily be solved. Prosecutors are understandably reluctant to give away their case before trial. But since Congress decided that defense lawyers are entitled to see 3500 material, the intent of the statute might as well be made meaningful by allowing the defense attorneys some time to read the statements and transcripts. The present procedure is a farce. We get the stuff, but we can't really utilize it. These difficulties could be disposed of if only the courts would uniformly agree that defense counsel should be served 3500 material twenty-four hours before trial. This would maintain the secrecy of the government's case until the day before trial, while allowing defense lawyers adequate time to prepare for cross. Some jurisdictions follow this procedure, but most don't—the federal court in Florida being among the latter.

Still, while flipping through the grand jury testimony of Officer Eades, I did discover something interesting. When my turn came to cross examine him, I set him up for impeachment by reviewing his testimony that he had taken the can because he believed it to be a dangerous weapon and that was why he had called the bomb squad. I then took the minutes of his grand jury testimony. "Did you testify before the grand jury?" I asked. He replied that he had done so. Reading from the grand jury transcript, I then asked: "And were you not asked, 'Question: What was your first reaction when you saw this can?' " Officer Eades replied that he may have been asked that question, but he did not remember.

"And did you not respond," I continued, " 'I thought it might be an incense can or something'?" The witness equivocated, said he couldn't remember, but I hoped that the jury had gotten the point and that it wasn't buried in a morass of other less important cross examination. This was likely to be the first officer in the history of the Miami police department who seized what he thought was a can of incense and called for help from the bomb squad.

This incident also illustrates the unfairness of our not having the grand jury testimony at the pre-trial suppression hearing. If Officer Eades thought (as he had testified before the grand jury) that the can held incense, then he was obviously lying when he testified at the suppression hearing that he thought it was a bomb. He had no reasonable grounds for belief that the can was dangerous, and he should not have seized it. If we'd had his grand jury testimony at the pre-trial hearing, the can would have been suppressed because its seizure was illegal.

After the police officers testified, the prosecutor called Gerald Rudoff to the stand. Sandy leaned over toward me and whispered, "He's one of the undercover agents who followed us around all summer." I had already recognized his name and I was tense with anticipation. For an undercover agent, Rudoff was practically a celebrity. His appearance raised sensitive issues that could determine the outcome of this trial.

The government's use of informers and undercover agents, which is so prevalent in political cases, raises strategic defense problems of great magnitude. Before discussing these problems, I should note that there is a difference between undercover agents and informers which in itself makes for different issues at trial. Undercover agents are law-enforcement officers who hide the fact that they are employed by the government and infiltrate or otherwise surveil the people or organizations they are investigating. Informers are not official law-enforcement officers, although they are often paid by the government. They are usually people who are friends or associates of the group or individuals under investigation who, for one reason or another, decide to work with the law-enforcement agencies. Sometimes they do it for money, sometimes for a softer sentence (since they might be just as guilty as the people they are informing on). Informers are often motivated by malice, and particularly in political cases, they may turn state's evidence because they are disillusioned by the politics or personalities of their former co-workers. An informer's motives are far more complex than an undercover agent's.

If you have reason to suspect that the government has gotten hold of an informer, special discovery techniques are necessary and cross examination must be carefully prepared. The informer's emotional make-up and motivations must be closely questioned. For example, William Lemmer, an ex-paratrooper who turned informer in the Vet case, had supposedly been offered a psychiatric discharge from the army, and was alleged to have a history of mental instability. He was reported to believe that the Vets were responsible for his separation from his wife, and to have written letters to her vowing "vengeance" on the group. When facts like these are brought out on cross examination, a jury should be less inclined to believe the testimony of what is often the government's star witness.

Undercover agents, who are usually police officers or F.B.I. men, have far more credibility than informers, and it is more difficult to impeach them on the ground of motive. The important thing to do if you think the government intends to call undercover agents (or, for that matter, any law-enforcement officials) is to question the jurors closely on voir dire. Since we knew that almost every government witness in the Keiser-Birdsell case was either a local or a federal law-enforcement officer, we asked the prospective jurors whether they recognized that the mere fact that a witness is a law-enforcement officer does not automatically entitle that person to greater credibility. If the jurors weren't previously aware of their "prejudice" in favor of police witnesses, they would be "educated" by the questions and (we hoped) would lean over backward to judge police witnesses fairly. This educative process is just as important a function of voir dire as is finding out whether jurors are prejudiced and dismissing them if you think they are or might be.

Although there have been numerous attacks on the use of informers and undercover agents (on the ground that they are violative of constitutional rights), the courts have generally upheld the government's use of this investigative technique. Still, the government runs risks when it uses informers or undercover agents, since the technique often allows for the defense of entrapment. Basically, the defendant argues that were it not for the informer, the crime never would have been committed. In the Camden 28 case, the defendants were accused of raiding a draft-board office. They testified that they had made plans to do this, but had abandoned them—among other reasons, for lack of funds. A government informer, Robert Hardy, admitted that he had "provided ninety percent of the tools necessary for the action. They [the defendants] couldn't afford them, so I paid and the F.B.I. reimbursed me." Were it not for the informer, the raid never would have taken place. The Camden 28 defendants were acquitted, and most people believe it was because of a successful entrapment defense.

Sometimes, although not actually entrapping the defendants, an informer or undercover agent functions as an *agent provocateur,* seeking to escalate legal activities to a more serious, perhaps criminal, level. When the Vets were planning their anti-war demonstrations in Miami Beach in the summer of 1972, it was the informant Lemmer who supposedly urged the use of violent tactics, including shooting and bombing.

While on this subject, I should mention that prior to the Keiser-Birdsell trial Sandy showed me a photograph of two of her fellow Zippies at the Miami demonstrations. The one on the left had a bushy blond beard and moustache and shoulder-length hair. He was wearing a black-brimmed hat with a flowered band around it, a gray T-shirt and cut-off dungarees. The other had on a floppy brown suède hat, bleached dungarees, a tan vest that looked like an army shirt with sleeves cut off, and a red-and-blue-striped T-shirt. He too had a beard and moustache and shoulder-length blond hair. They looked like the perfect dropouts. They were members of the Dade County Public Safety Department, the local police in Miami.

These stalwarts of law enforcement had infiltrated the Zippies' activities and were among the half dozen or so undercover agents who had Tim and Sandy under close personal surveillance for most of the summer. On the occasion that the photo was taken, they were carrying a toilet bowl to an open meeting of the Miami Beach City Council. It was their idea to go to the meeting bringing this symbol of what the demonstrators thought of some of the Council members. That, on an innocuous level, is what is known as being *agents provocateurs*. They were not merely observing what the demonstrators were doing; they were contributing to the plans and escalating them. Their "contributions" reached their peak when the two men revealed themselves as police officers the day after the convention, and arrested several of their Zippie "compatriots" on charges of possession and sale of marijuana. This was perhaps the ultimate irony As part of their "role playing," undercover agents are often among the most enthusiastic pot smokers.

Jerry Rudoff, who had now unexpectedly appeared as a witness in our case, was another member of the Dade County Public Safety Department who had infiltrated the demonstration organizers during the summer of 1972. He had been revealed as a law-enforcement officer at pre-trial hearings in connection with the Vet case. Now he had come to haunt us. If Rudoff were allowed to testify about some of the Zippies' more colorful stunts (nude swimming in hotel fountains, marijuana smoke-ins at the City Council meetings), he would no doubt mesmerize the jury, but it would be very prejudicial to us.

Officer Rudoff testified that when the truck was stopped, he took pictures of the ensuing events. The prosecutor introduced these into evidence, including one of a surly-looking Sandy sitting in the cab of the truck and one of Tim in the police car after his arrest on the traffic violation. Mrs. Anderson asked Rudoff whether he had ever seen Sandy before this incident, to which he replied that he had. She then inquired how he knew Sandy and it was obvious that he was about to tell the entire story of his summer undercover operation. Roger and I were on our feet, strenuously objecting on the ground that this was a possession case and any prior activities of either of the defendants were irrelevant. We had expected trouble excluding the testimony about the Zippie stunts and were prepared with case citations and impassioned rhetoric. It was almost anticlimactic when, after a minimum of argument, Judge Fay said that he agreed with us and sustained our objection. He precluded Rudoff from testifying about anything other than what happened on August 23, when the government alleged that the devices were taken from the truck.

The rest of the government witnesses were F.B.I. agents, most of them experts who testified about the qualities of the material in the cans. Their tests showed that the material in the first can, the so-called ashtray, was wax with a charred wick and contained no incendiary chemicals. The material in the other two cans was identified as "a wax like substance containing potassium nitrate and sugar," which was "easily ignited." "Based on our tests," one of the F.B.I.'s chemistry experts testified, "the cans could be used as incendiary devices to ignite combustible materials in contact with the incendiary mixtures."

"In other words," said Roger, "they burn."

"That is correct," the agent answered.

"Well, so does a match," Roger responded.

The fourth F.B.I. witness, Special Agent Smith, was qualified as an explosives expert. He testified that he had taken the cans to a field to test them. After several unsuccessful attempts with fuses (how dangerous could these devices be?), he had managed to ignite the material in the two smaller cans, using matches, and it had flared briefly.

"Are they bombs?" Roger asked on cross examination.

"No, they are not," Agent Smith replied.

Roger had the good sense not to risk eroding the impact of Agent Smith's testimony by asking further questions, and, for the same reason, I declined altogether to cross examine him.

With that startling concession from her own expert, Mrs. Anderson moved for admission into evidence of the three cans. We objected to the admission of the two smaller cans, on the ground that the government's own expert had just testified that they were not bombs, and therefore they were outside the purview of the statute. I doggedly renewed our motion to dismiss the indictment on the same grounds. Both these motions were denied.

The large can, or "ashtray," was another matter. "The F.B.I. reports make it clear that there are no incendiary chemicals in the wax in the large can," I argued. "This is nothing more than an ordinary candle. If we've reached the point where you can get indicted for possession of a candle, then all the housewives in Florida had better beware." Judge Fay agreed and granted our motion to exclude the large can from evidence. The two smaller cans were admitted into evidence and the government rested its case.

One of the mysteries about the government's case was the failure to call Randy Piper as a witness. I knew that Mrs. Anderson had at one time intended to call him; he had shown me the government's subpoena. I couldn't understand why she decided not to call him. Maybe she too was unimpressed with his demeanor and didn't want to have to vouch for his credibility.

A recess was called after the government rested, and I wandered out into the hall. There I found an hysterical client. "How could you have been so stupid?" Sandy screamed at me.

"What are you talking about?" I asked.

"Why didn't you subpoena Randy for us? Now he isn't going to appear at all, and we're going to lose."

"But I told you that I didn't think we should have to vouch for his credibility," I said. "He'd make a lousy witness. We're better off without him."

"I'm going to jail for twenty years, and it's all your fault," Sandy said, "just because you were too dumb to subpoena him." She was shouting and people were beginning to stare at us. Her parents tried to quiet her down. "How can you say things like that to Helene when she's done so much for you?" her father asked.

She was understandably tense, as anyone would be when facing the possibility of twenty years in jail and a $20,000 fine. Still, I was just as tense as she was, since I bore responsibility for her future. Trying to explain my strategy while she was so distraught would only upset us both. I have had clients who ripped me off by not paying my fee or expenses, who failed to thank me, not shown up for trial dates, and annoyed me in the various ways that clients choose to addle their lawyers. But never before had I wanted to take a client's head and squish it face down into the sand. For the moment I'd had enough of Sandy and her tantrum, so I moved away without saying anything more.

Actually, I was pleased by the way things had turned out, and when Sandy calmed down and I explained things to her, she agreed that we couldn't have been in a better position if we'd maneuvered it ourselves. It was logical for the government to call Piper as its witness, and it was inexplicable that, having gone so far as to subpoena him, the government did not put him on the stand. I planned to make the most of this in my closing argument. It was Piper's truck and Piper's rock band. Why hadn't he been indicted? Let alone called as a witness? The inferences which could be drawn from Piper's absence (e.g., selective prosecution, bad faith on the part of the government, etc.) were more valuable for us than his testimony could ever have been.

On the evening after the government rested, we convened

to discuss our strategy for the defense case. Perhaps the most important decision facing us at this point was whether to put the defendants on the stand. As a rule, unless a defendant is totally inarticulate, not credible, has a police record, or is really obnoxious, he or she should be called as a witness. Jurors expect to hear first-hand from the defendant, and they tend to be suspicious when the defendant does not take the stand. Tim and Sandy were both anxious to have their day in court. I had worked closely with Sandy, as Roger had with Tim, preparing her to take the stand in her own defense. I planned to have her testify on direct examination for at least an hour, detailing her background and schooling, the reasons why she had gone to Miami Beach, the various convention activities of a less zany nature which she had organized and participated in, and a complete exposition of what had occurred on August 23, the day the truck was stopped. Tim's testimony was to be in the same pattern.

The attempt of the government to introduce evidence from undercover agent Rudoff forced a sudden change in this strategy. If Tim and Sandy testified as fully as we had planned, then the government might be permitted, as part of its case on rebuttal, to recall Officer Rudoff to the stand. Through him, all the evidence of the Zippies' outlandish activities the summer before, to which we had successfully objected when Rudoff had originally been called to the stand, could be introduced, as a fair response to the testimony of Tim and Sandy. To avoid this disastrous possibility, Roger and I agreed that it was necessary to sharply curtail Tim and Sandy's testimony. We decided to offer the whole story of what had happened on August 23 through the testimony of Brett Hotchkiss, the third occupant of the cab. Our clients were both dismayed by this decision, but they knew that we could not risk opening the door for detailed testimony by Rudoff.

When court reconvened the next morning, the first witness

called on behalf of the defense was Brett Hotchkiss. He told
the jurors what had happened from the time the truck was
in Flamingo Park to the time it had been stopped by the
motorcycle police. He said there had been hundreds of
people on the Flamingo Park campsite, any one of whom
could have put the cans in the truck. He confirmed that
homemade candles were in use all over the park. He con-
tradicted the testimony of the police officers and swore that
he, not Randy Piper, had been the third passenger in the cab.
In fact, he was still sitting in the cab when he was arrested for
driving without a license. He had tried to show Officer Eades
his license, but the policeman would not look at it. As soon
as he was brought to court that night, Hotchkiss produced
his license and was released from custody.

Hotchkiss also testified that the rock group had a trunk
full of props, including flash powder that was used as a
theatrical effect when the group sang its song about Lieutenant Calley and My Lai. He had never noticed any of the
cans which the government claimed were found in the cab
of the truck, but it was possible that they were stage props.
He remembered that there was a can of black flash powder
on the truck when the police searched it, but this had not
been seized. I concluded my direct examination of Hotchkiss by eliciting the information that he had been questioned
by the F.B.I., that he had told the agents the entire story,
including the fact that he, not Piper, had been riding in the
cab with Tim and Sandy. In spite of this, he had not been
indicted or even subpoenaed to appear as a government
witness.

On cross examination, Mrs. Anderson tried to intimate
that Hotchkiss was a good friend of Tim's and Sandy's, but
as he had only seen them on one occasion other than the
time they rode together on the truck, I didn't think this
tack was successful. I could only hope that the jury found
Brett Hotchkiss as impressive as I did.

Then Sandy took the stand. She gave her name and address and told the jurors that she lived with her parents.

"Where were you on August 23, 1972, in the late afternoon?" I asked.

"Riding in a truck in Miami Beach," she replied.

"Was the truck owned or rented by you?"

"No, I was just hitching a ride."

"Had you ever ridden in the truck before?"

"No."

"I show you government exhibits 4B and 4C," I said as I brought the two smaller cans toward the witness box. "Did you ever see these in the truck?"

"No, I didn't."

"Prior to the time you saw these in court, had you ever seen them before?"

"No, I never saw them before in my life."

"Cross examine."

The direct examination of the defendant Birdsell was so short and ended so abruptly that it seemed to take the prosecutor by surprise. "No questions," she said.

Roger then put Tim on the stand, and his testimony, only slightly longer than Sandy's, covered approximately the same ground. Then Tim was turned over for cross examination. "Mr. Keiser," the prosecutor asked, "is Sandy Birdsell your girlfriend?"

"I object," I said.

"We're not going into anybody's personal life here," Roger added. "This is a possession case."

"I think the question might be proper. I will overrule the objection," Judge Fay said.

The question was repeated and Tim responded that Sandy was not his girlfriend. "Has she ever been your girlfriend?" Mrs. Anderson asked.

"It depends on how you define 'girlfriend,'" Tim replied. "Define 'girlfriend' for me and I'll be glad to answer."

Tim was sometimes unpredictable and I hoped that he wasn't going to be a smarty-pants on the stand. It would alienate the jury, and since she was his co-defendant, it would hurt Sandy. Fortunately, Mrs. Anderson decided that she didn't care to pursue that semantic distinction, so she rephrased her question. "Did you introduce her as your wife?"

"No, I have never introduced her as my wife."

"Have you ever introduced her as your girlfriend?"

"I may have. I don't recall ever doing so."

"During the time that you were down here in July and August of 1972, were you and Sandy together all the time?" the prosecutor asked. I did not see the relevance of that question, but I said nothing.

"No."

"Were you living together?" she asked.

"Objection. Good heavens!" I said.

"Sustained," said Judge Fay.

"Does Sandy more or less follow you around?" Mrs. Anderson asked.

"Good heavens," I protested as I rose to my feet once more. "Objection. She is not a sheep!"

Sandy later insisted that this was "by far one of the best lines in the whole trial." She thereafter referred to herself as "your client, the sheep." Roger, on the other hand, complained that he'd never before had co-counsel who began objections by saying, "Good heavens!" "Well, at least the objections were sustained," I said by way of justification. Teasing aside, we both knew that the damage had been done merely by the asking of the questions, and Mrs. Anderson knew it too. I asked for a bench conference and moved for a mistrial, but it was denied.

After Tim's cross examination was completed uneventfully, we called Herbert MacDonell, Professor of Criminalistics at Elmira College, to the stand. His qualifications as an expert witness on bombs and explosives included experience as a teacher, researcher, and associate of law-enforcement agencies across the country. In fact, most of the staff members of the Miami police lab had at one time studied with Professor MacDonell. Deftly questioned by Roger, the witness discussed the properties of the contents of the two smaller cans—the large can or "ashtray" having by this time been excluded from evidence. He described the tests he had performed on the contents of the cans. The material did not easily ignite, he said, but burned brightly when matches were applied to it. Professor MacDonell also testified that if one wanted to make a fire bomb, black powder, which was easily obtainable in any gun store and which could be possessed without danger of violation of the Firearms Act, would make a better ingredient than the potassium nitrate and sugar in the cans.

I listened with interest but not much understanding (I have never studied chemistry) to MacDonell's complex testimony about chemicals that provide their own oxygen when they burn, about temperature, burning rates, and the like. I wondered whether it might not be over the heads of some of the jurors too; it occurred to me that the expert's testimony could be simplified. Since MacDonell was appearing as a witness for both defendants, Judge Fay allowed me to question him on direct. When my turn came to examine, I stood up and, pointing to the two small cans, asked: "Professor MacDonell, I am going to read to you from the statute under which these defendants have been indicted. Are these devices, quote, 'explosive, incendiary or poison gas bombs,' unquote?"

"No, they are not," Professor MacDonell replied.

"Are they, quote, 'explosive, incendiary or poison gas grenades,' unquote?"

"They are not."

"Are they, quote, 'explosive, incendiary or poison gas

rockets having a propellant charge of more than four ounces,' unquote?"

"No."

"Are they, quote, 'explosive, incendiary or poison gas missiles having an explosive or incendiary charge of more than one quarter ounce,' unquote?"

"They are not missiles."

"Are they, quote, 'explosive, incendiary or poison gas mines,' unquote?"

"Of course not. They are not mines."

"Are they, quote, 'similar devices,' unquote, to any of those I have just described?"

"They are not."

"Thank you very much," I said. "Cross examine."

As Mrs. Anderson walked toward the lawyers' podium, she pointed out, with a note of triumph in her voice, that I had neglected to ask the witness about one relevant section of the statute. I looked down at my copy of the statute. She was right. I had inadvertently skipped section three. If MacDonell testified that the devices fell within that defini-tion, it would look awful, as though I had tried to deceive the jury and Mrs. Anderson had caught me. "I am quoting from subsection three of the statutory definitions," Mrs. Anderson addressed the witness. "Professor MacDonell, are these devices, quote 'any combination of parts either de-signed or intended for use in converting any device into a destructive device . . . and from which a destructive device may be readily assembled,' unquote?"

"No, they are not."

Mrs. Anderson looked disappointed. No doubt, I looked relieved. The defense rested.

On rebuttal, the prosecutor recalled undercover police officer Rudoff to the stand. She again attempted to introduce evidence of the activities of Tim and Sandy and the other Zippies during the months preceding the Republican Convention. Our objections were sustained, which showed that our strategy of restricting the direct examination of the defendants had been correct.

The jury was then taken from the courtroom and counsel approached the bench to discuss Judge Fay's proposed instructions to the jurors. I commented once again that I didn't see how the jury could find the defendants guilty of possessing fire bombs, as charged in the indictment, when the government's own experts had testified that the devices were not bombs. It seemed clear that the cans did have some incendiary qualities, but this was not enough to bring them within the ambit of the statutory definitions of "destructive devices," as our expert had testified.

After repeatedly denying our motion to dismiss on these grounds, made at various times during the trial, Judge Fay suddenly did a turnabout and evinced interest in that issue. He requested argument from Mrs. Anderson on the applicability of the statute. She was, understandably, not prepared to argue a question which we all assumed had been decided long ago, when our initial and continuously renewed motions to dismiss had been denied. She requested a short recess to gather her thoughts and confer with her colleagues.

"What have you got to enlighten me?" Judge Fay asked when court reconvened. Mrs. Anderson began her argument by urging that the devices really were bombs. She said that, over the recess, she had discussed the question of the definition of a bomb with Mr. Brodie, the bomb expert from the Miami police department. Before she could go any further, I interrupted. It appeared to me that she was trying to impeach the testimony of her own witness, the F.B.I. agent who had testified that these cans were not bombs.

"Your Honor," I said, "I must object to this. The government's case is closed and there can be no further testimony as to what these items might be."

"I want to point out," Mrs. Anderson said, "that these

particular devices not only could be considered in certain instances as incendiary devices or fire bombs, but they could actually be considered to be a device similar to a grenade, an incendiary grenade, because if thrown, they would, in fact, be just that." She was doing a fine job of arguing, but the statute had her boxed in.

"Your Honor," I said, "I specifically asked Professor Mac-Donell that question, and he answered no, this is not in any way, shape, or form similar to an incendiary grenade."

"Also, I prefer Mr. Brodie's testimony under oath, as to what he says," Roger said, objecting to the prosecutor's attempt to base her legal argument on unsworn new facts.

"If your Honor would allow me to reopen my case," Mrs. Anderson said, "I would call Mr. Brodie, because I think I could . . ."

"Your Honor," I interrupted, "I must object strenuously. Our expert has been dismissed."

"Sustained," Judge Fay said.

The government then urged that the cans, or "incendiary devices," as Mrs. Anderson referred to them, if not actually bombs, were "similar devices" to bombs, grenades, and other destructive devices (under section 1(f) of the statute). "Do you suggest," Judge Fay asked Mrs. Anderson, "that if somebody took a piece of paper and rolled it up and set one end on fire, that it would come within the meaning of this statute?" Judge Fay went on to say that to him a bomb was something that exploded. There was no testimony whatever that these devices exploded. "Now if somebody has a can of gasoline and they soak a building with gasoline," he said, "and they toss a rolled-up newspaper or fire into it and burn down the building, maybe they have committed arson. But I don't think that they have violated the firearms statute."

At that point, a hopeful Sandy put her hand on mine. "It isn't over yet," I whispered. "Not until you hear him say the word 'acquit.'"

"There was testimony," Mrs. Anderson continued, "that if this were thrown into gasoline, it would be able to ignite gasoline."

"It could be used to light gasoline," Judge Fay agreed. "So could a newspaper, so could a match, so could any other device that would hold a flame. That would not make them a violation of a firearms statute, within the definition of destructive devices."

"Your Honor," said Mrs. Anderson, "I have not been able to get the legislative history."

"Your Honor," I said, "if she had read our motion to dismiss, she would have. I spent time reading 1,189 pages of the most boring Senate hearings I ever read in my life. It is all set forth in our motion to dismiss. The legislative history makes it clear that the destructive-device section was meant to apply to military ordnance."

"It might have been read prior to presenting this case to the grand jury," Roger remarked.

Mrs. Anderson asked that the record reflect that she had not been the person who drafted the indictment. I couldn't blame her for not wanting the credit for this one.

"The Court feels," Judge Fay finally announced, "that it must grant the defendants' motions for judgment of acquittal."

"Now," I said to Sandy. She fell into my arms, hugging me with relief, as the judge continued with the formalities of dismissing the case.

In his concluding remarks, Judge Fay admitted that he had been "alerted to the problem" by defense counsel. He said that he had denied our previous motions to dismiss because he had wanted "to allow a full and complete presentation of all of the evidence." That was probably the most conservative way to proceed, and was understandable from his point of view. But why didn't he dismiss at the end of the government's case, after Agent Smith's admission that the devices were not bombs? Still, we couldn't complain much about an acquittal.

Although the government's use of the National Firearms Act against political activists was limited by the decision in the Keiser-Birdsell case, there were other cases pending in which dissident defendants were charged with violations of the Act. Center lawyer Mark Amsterdam had a case involving Puerto Rican nationalists who were charged with possession of Molotov cocktails, and he was also working on several Wounded Knee cases arising under the Act. But the case on which the Keiser-Birdsell decision would probably have the greatest impact was the Vet case, in which the defendants were alleged to have possessed illegally made fire bombs of potassium permanganate and glycerin, devices similar to the so-called fire bombs in the Keiser-Birdsell case. Judge Fay's decision that the devices in our case were outside the ambit of the Act was vital to the defense in the Vet case.

Because an oral opinion announced from the bench has less persuasive force than a decision that is officially published in the law reports, the Vet lawyers and I were anxious that Judge Fay write up and publish his opinion. The problem was, he had a reputation for not liking to write opinions. One of my students had sought a clerkship with him, and during an interview Judge Fay had said that the duty of a trial judge "was to try cases, not to write opinions." I knew that I would have a hard time persuading the judge to publish his decision, but in the interests of the Vet defendants, it was worth a try.

I wrote Judge Fay a long letter detailing the new and important aspects of his decision which, to my knowledge, had not appeared in any reported cases. I did not mention the pending Vet case, but I did tell him that a colleague and I were considering writing a law-review article on the Firearms Act (which we began but never finished), and that it would be helpful if he would publish his decision, and a shame if it remained buried in the stenographic roll. At the end of the letter, I wrote:

> My final plea is perhaps a bit low. If I could adjust to getting up with the Florida sunrise, would you write an opinion this once?

I mentioned the letter to a few of my colleagues and they reacted with dismay. "How could you write a letter like that to a judge?" one of them asked me.

"What's wrong with it?"

"It's disrespectful."

At first, I didn't see what was disrespectful about it. After all, Judge Fay had been the one to initiate the teasing about Florida sunrises. But after two weeks passed and I didn't get a response to my letter, I began to worry. Maybe my letter had been a bit indecorous. I made up my mind that the next time I was in the Miami area I would stop in at the judge's chambers and apologize.

Then, at last, I received a reply to my letter. It began with a refusal of my request: "Despite your most persuasive and enticing letter, I must decline to publish any opinion." There followed a predictable lecture on the duty of trial judges to try cases, not write opinions. The judge's response was disappointing, but when I read his closing words, at least I knew that my letter had not offended him.

> It was a pleasure having you appear in this case [he wrote] and I will look forward to seeing you again soon. Who knows, in the future you may come to enjoy sunrises and sunsets!

Many disturbing questions were left unanswered at the conclusion of the Keiser-Birdsell case. If the Florida police had originally seized the devices, why was the case brought by the federal government, as a violation of the National Firearms Act? Florida state law is almost exactly the same as the Firearms Act, and possession of the devices would be equally illegal under the State Act, so why wasn't the case kept under local jurisdiction? How and why were the devices given to federal authorities? Why was the case prepared by the F.B.I., when responsibility for enforcement of the federal statute involved rested with the Alcohol, Tobacco and Firearms Division of I.R.S., which had its own agents? Why, out of the thirty-odd people who had been on the truck, had Tim and Sandy been singled out for prosecution? Why not Randy Piper, who had rented the truck and who the police thought had been the third occupant of the cab? Why not Brett Hotchkiss, who had actually been the third passenger in the cab and who had admitted this to the F.B.I.? If the devices were seized in August, during the convention, why weren't the defendants arrested at once? Why wait six months to indict them? After lab reports were received from the F.B.I. which made it clear that the devices were not bombs, why did the indictment specifically allege that the defendants had possessed "fire bombs"? Finally—and especially when one considered the timing of the indictment and the totality of suspicious circumstances about the case—were the defendants victims of Watergate-related political considerations, as they claimed? We could still only guess about the answers to these questions.

19

Some Issues without Answers

Little over a month after the decision in the Keiser-Birdsell case, the defendants in the Vet case filed a motion alleging "that the prosecution herein was designed, timed and concocted for the purpose of giving credibility to the Watergate cover-up plan." Whereas we could only speculate about the question of selective prosecution in the Keiser-Birdsell proceeding, facts were now surfacing, both through newspaper investigations and in the Senate Watergate hearings, which supported a defense of discriminatory prosecution in the convention cases.

Jeb Magruder (subsequently an admitted member of the Watergate cover-up team) had previously testified at the trial of the Watergate burglars that the major intelligence assignment given to Gordon Liddy had been to learn "the plans of potentially troublesome demonstrators both at campaign appearances around the country and at the Republican National Convention," and that "some $250,000 had been budgeted for Mr. Liddy's work." And Gerald Alch, counsel to James McCord, had attempted to justify his client's actions on the ground that McCord had acted to forestall violence against President Nixon and other Republican officials by various peace groups and leftist organizations. Of course, we had been aware of this when Keiser and Birdsell were indicted, and it was stories like this that made them and their supporters certain that their indictment was politically motivated. But we'd had no proof of the allegation.

On May 2, 1973, the lead story in *The New York Times* stated that the talk about violence at the conventions was mere invention by the participants in the cover-up. Those of us who had worked with the demonstration organizers had always known this, but now for the first time there was public recognition of the fairy tales which had developed about the convention activities of the non-delegates. The *Times* story gave details of the cover-up plot allegedly engineered by Mitchell, Haldeman, Ehrlichman, Magruder, and Dean, among others. According to the article:

> Perhaps the grossest fabrication, sources said, was the co-ordinated account provided to the Federal prosecutors, and used by them as a bulwark in the subsequent Watergate trial, of the initial rationale behind the cash payments to G. Gordon Liddy. . . . The Government was told by a number of re-elected committee officials that the $100,000 given to Liddy was to pay 10 intelligence agents $1,000 a month each for ten months in 1972, to find out if anti-Republican demonstrations were planned . . .
>
> "That was a complete fabrication," one investigator said. "Just a complete lie."

As the *Times* article made clear, the aim of the fraudulent cover-up plan was, as the Vet motion papers put it, "to attribute the expenditure of large sums of cash and the 'bugging' of the Democratic National Committee to the need for protecting the Republican convention from violent demonstrators."

While the motion papers were being prepared, James McCord was testifying before the Senate Watergate Committee. He stated that he had been getting information from the Internal Security Division of the Justice Department. Among the intelligence reports passed on to him were several concerning the Vets, according to which the Vets "were planning violence at the Republican National Convention involving danger to, threats to life of individuals" [sic]. To the Vets, McCord's testimony was further evidence that the cover-up plan was continuing and, as they put it, "that is why this prosecution of an alleged conspiracy to disrupt the Republican Convention is still being pressed by the administration, whose record of trying to corrupt the entire democratic process is now being daily exposed to the public." An affidavit from McCord, verifying his testimony before the Senate, was attached in support of the selective prosecution motion.

The Vets also noted in their moving papers that it was "significant" that the grand jury investigation in their case had been conducted, not by members of the staff of the United States Attorney's office in Florida, but by attorneys from the Department of Justice in Washington. The same had been true of the Keiser-Birdsell case, in which a Department of Justice lawyer had come down from Washington to present the case to the Miami federal grand jury. In addition, the Washington attorneys in charge of the Vet case were Guy Goodwin and Stark King, both of whom were associated with the Internal Security Division of the Justice Department. Up until March 1972, the I.S.D. had been headed by Robert Mardian. In that month, Mardian had become political coordinator of the Committee for the Reelection of the President, and he was subsequently indicted as one of the participants in the Watergate cover-up. Moreover, the fact that McCord, a political operative, testified that he was, with Mardian's connivance, receiving intelligence reports from the I.S.D. was another convolution that warranted investigation in the Vet case.

The Vet defendants also noted the parallels between the

governmental misconduct uncovered in the Ellsberg-Russo case and suspicious occurrences in their own case. For example, in the Pentagon Papers prosecution, the office of Ellsberg's psychiatrist had been broken into by Messrs. Liddy and Hunt while they were on the White House payroll. In the Vet case, the office of one of the attorneys for defendant Scott Camil had been burglarized the day after he was served with a grand jury subpoena in this case, and the only thing removed from the office was the file of the defendant Camil. The pattern of governmental misconduct in other political cases made necessary further inquiry into similar incidents in the Vet case.

The Vet defense attorneys filed extensive affidavits and exhibits in support of their selective prosecution motion. They asked that the Court schedule an evidentiary hearing at which the following questions would be investigated:

> a—Whether and to what extent representatives of the White House and the Committee for the Reelection of the President (CREP) participated in the determination to prosecute the defendants;
>
> b—whether and to what extent the prosecution herein was undertaken to give credibility to the cover-up theory which was developed in respect to the Watergate break-in;
>
> c—whether and to what extent employees or agents of the White House, CREP, the FBI, the CIA, military intelligence, or other agencies of the government participated in espionage, infiltration, sabotage, provocateurism and electronic surveillance of the defendants or the Vietnam Veterans Against the War (VVAW), the organization with which the defendants are affiliated;
>
> d—whether and to what extent employees or agents of the White House, Secret Service, CREP, the FBI, the CIA, the Treasury Department, the Interior Department, military intelligence, or other agencies of the government were responsible for the break-in at the office of the attorney for the defendant Camil and the theft of files

> from that office relating to said defendant, or to what extent any such agencies or their employees have knowledge of such break-in;
>
> e—whether and to what extent government files which may have affected the defendants or the prosecution herein have been lost or destroyed.

I was impressed with the moving papers and I eagerly awaited the hearing, because I was sure that, in the course of the investigation of the motives for prosecution of the Vets, information would surface about the decision to prosecute Keiser and Birdsell as well. I was hoping that we might at last get answers to some of the issues left dangling at the end of that trial.

To everyone's surprise, Judge Winston Arnow ignored the allegations about Watergate and ordered a hearing limited to the break-in at the office of Camil's attorney. After abortive testimony from the lawyer and the local police chief, the judge ruled that the attorney's evidence was not "credible" and that there was no basis for belief that the federal government had been involved in the break-in.

It was sad enough that the judge refused to make a full and energetic inquiry into the issue of selective prosecution. Worse still, he held that in making their selective prosecution motion, the defense attorneys had acted "unreasonably and vexatiously." On his own motion, he entered an order requiring the defense attorneys to show cause why the costs incurred in connection with the hearing "relating to the alleged break-in and burglary" should not be taxed against them.

When this order was entered, there was an uproar from other members of the bar. There was no doubt that the trial court was the proper forum in which to raise the issue of governmental misconduct, and the Vet lawyers would have been seriously remiss in their duty to their clients if they had failed to move for a full evidentiary hearing. A vigorous defense, particularly with grounds as strong as those in the Vet moving papers, should not be met with intimidation and harassment from the trial judge. Center lawyers Doris Peterson, Nancy Stearns, and Morty Stavis were among those on the receiving end of this order. At their request, I appeared before Judge Arnow to argue against the imposition of costs. Whether it was the commotion engendered by his order, or merely a realization that he had gone too far, Judge Arnow backed off. He made a new finding that perhaps the hearing testimony of Camil's ex-attorney was more credible than he had thought at first, and he held that the defense lawyers were, after all, not accountable for the costs of the hearing.

We were all disappointed by the judge's denial of the selective prosecution motion and his failure to order a full-scale hearing. For the Vets, it meant loss of the opportunity to prove governmental misconduct of a magnitude great enough to warrant dismissal of the charges against them. As other recent political cases have made clear, unconscionable activities by the government in order to obtain convictions of those whom the administration regards as dissidents have been all too common.

Among the incidents of governmental misconduct which surfaced during the course of the proceedings in the Ellsberg-Russo case were: the break-in at the office of Ellsberg's psychiatrist, planned and executed by Gordon Liddy and Howard Hunt while they were on the White House payroll; the unsubtle attempt to influence Matthew Byrne, the trial judge, by bringing him, in the midst of the proceedings, to San Clemente to meet with John Ehrlichman and President Nixon to discuss his possible appointment as director of the F.B.I.; illegal wiretapping by F.B.I. agents whose conduct was approved by John Mitchell and "closely supervised" by Robert Mardian; the belated disclosure, a year after the defendants' initial wiretap motion, that Ellsberg's telephone calls were tapped and that the records and transcripts of the overhearing had disappeared from the F.B.I. files.

The wiretap revelations were the latest in a pattern of what Judge Byrne himself characterized as "improper government conduct shielded so long from public view." When he dismissed the case "with prejudice" (meaning that the defendants could not be tried again), he said that "we may have been given only a glimpse of what this special unit [the White House plumbers] did."

Similarly, the Wounded Knee prosecutions against American Indian Movement leaders Dennis Banks and Russell Means were dismissed before going to the jury, on the ground of prosecutorial misconduct. In this case, the misconduct involved illegal wiretapping (which the government had at first denied and later admitted); insufficient pre-trial interrogation of an informer whom the government should have known to be of questionable credibility; failure to inform the Court that the informer was allegedly involved in a rape incident while under the "protection" of the F.B.I., and that the F.B.I. was said to have influenced the Wisconsin prosecutor to drop the charges, in exchange for which the informer gave testimony favorable to the government; failure to make timely disclosure of contradictory statements previously made to the F.B.I. by another government witness; dilatoriness in searching for information about and possible cover-up of the extent of unlawful military involvement during the Wounded Knee occupation.

In dismissing the charges against the defendants, Judge Fred Nichol held that he was "forced to conclude that the prosecution acted in bad faith at various times throughout the course of the trial and was seeking convictions at the expense of justice." It was a poignant moment in court when he admitted, with obvious sadness, "I guess this has been a bad year for justice."

20

About Yesterday—
and the Tomorrow
That Has Found Us

Actually, it had been a bad six years for justice. The power to prosecute became the power to persecute. Constitutional dissent was equated with subversion. The power to investigate became license for invasions of the Constitution by the very men who were sworn to uphold it. What we had witnessed during the Nixon era was the politicization of the Justice Department and the repeated use of the courtroom and legal processes to intimidate dissent. Which is not to say that this had never before happened in our country's history; from John Peter Zenger to the "Red" scare of the nineteen-forties and fifties, there have been trials with political overtones. But rarely had a pattern of executive misconduct been shoved in our faces with such offensive regularity, on the assumption that we would accept it as a legitimate use of governmental power.

Conversely, rarely had there been such a public reaction of distaste to the excesses of government. The jury verdicts in favor of the defendants (e.g., in the Vet and Camden Twenty-Eight cases), judicial reversal of the Department's few jury victories (e.g., in the Spock and Chicago Eight cases), and trial court dismissals before verdict (e.g., "Keiser-

Birdsell" and Wounded Knee) testify to the rejection of the policy of executive overreaching in the courtroom.

It would be a mistake, however, to assume from these defeats that the use of legal processes to intimidate dissent was a failure. On the contrary, in some ways it was a resounding success. The defendants were subjected to painful, exhausting, and financially devastating proceedings, and their energies were tied up in the courtroom and directed toward the leadership of defense committees rather than of street demonstrations against the government's policies. That, in itself, was a victory for the executive.

It would also be erroneous to believe that the depredations of the last few years will disappear as the men who practice them are torn from power. A few trials are not enough. The resignation, incarceration, or disgrace of the men guilty of misconduct are distractions from the real issue. What should be remembered is that these men plotted as they did because they had a particular philosophy which led them to think themselves above the law. What we must continue to examine is the effect that this philosophy had on their exercise of power. We are not so firmly grounded in the rule of law that individual excesses cannot tumble us. We are only as strong as the people who make, interpret, and execute our laws; when those in power choose to twist the law, then we are weak.

One of a lawyer's tasks is to expose these weaknesses and contradictions as they infect the judicial system, to enable the courts to perform, as a recent decision put it, their long-recognized "basic responsibility for protecting individuals against unconstitutional invasions of their rights by all branches of government." Currently, the efforts of defense lawyers in this direction have been largely concentrated on the problem of prosecutorial misconduct. But whether the issue has been the possibility of selective prosecution or the sufficiency of the government's response to a wiretap motion, defense lawyers have had to overcome the legal presumption of the regularity of government conduct. It was this presumption that the judge in Gainesville hid behind when he refused to explore the motives for the prosecution of the Vietnam Vets. What might we have learned about the effect on our system of justice of the Watergate philosophy that the executive was above the law, had that judge played his appointed role?

If we have learned anything from our recent history, it is that the presumption of the regularity of government conduct is unwarranted. The practical effect of this lesson is that in some cases judges have become more responsive when the specter of prosecutorial misconduct is raised. An example, in the Attica-related murder trial of John Hill and Charles Pernasilice, is the post-trial hearing to investigate charges of invasion of the defense camp by F.B.I. informer Mary Jo Cook. Irrespective of the outcome, just getting a hearing on the issue of governmental misconduct can be a victory. And when the misconduct is proven, the result can be dismissal of the underlying case. As Judge Fay recently said when he threw out verdicts of conviction in a drug case because of the prosecutors' misrepresentations and suppression of evidence, there are times when the misconduct of the government "is just too much."

I'd often wondered how all this looked from the perspective of the government. Not too long ago, I had a chance to find out, when someone gave me a report written by the Office of Policy and Planning of the Justice Department. From its content, it is clear that it was written after President Nixon's resignation. Entitled "Disruption in the Courtroom and the Publicly Controversial Defendant," it is drafted as though in answer to the question "Why has the government lost all those politically important cases?"

The report begins with an accusation that "the purpose of

defense counsel appears to be to make the case untriable, by orchestrating the activities of the defendants, spectators, and themselves to constitute a purposeful interference with the orderly processes of trial." That is the theme: that the cases were lost, not because of any fault of the government, but because of a nefarious conspiracy by defense counsel. Among the tactics allegedly utilized by defense lawyers to achieve this end are "dilatory argument and delaying motions" designed to disrupt the trials. As an example of this "technique of disruption," the memorandum cites motions "to dismiss the judge for prejudicial remarks." But was it improper to ask for a mistrial on the grounds of judicial misconduct in the Chicago Eight case, when the Seventh Circuit held that Judge Hoffman's misconduct was grounds for reversal of the convictions? Failure to make the motion at the trial level would have constituted waiver of the right to raise the issue of his misconduct on appeal.

Should the wiretap motions which uncovered monumental infractions of constitutional rights at the highest level of the executive, and led to the Supreme Court's decision in the Keith case, not have been made? Was it "dilatory" to urge that the charges in the "Keiser-Birdsell" indictment were outside the ambit of the statute, and to renew the motion to dismiss half a dozen times throughout the case, when it was ultimately granted and the case dismissed before going to the jury? Or is what the report complains about vigorous advocacy, which is the essence of the constitutional right to the effective assistance of counsel?

The report castigates the spectators—"orchestrated" by the defense lawyers—whose "outbursts" "disrupted" several controversial trials. "At Wounded Knee," the report notes, "when a chief prosecution witness was on the stand, spectators would answer his testimony with whispers of 'liar, liar, liar' building to a roar." What the report does *not* say is that the chief prosecution witness *was* lying on the stand, that the government knew this at the time and said nothing, and that this was one of the reasons why the charges against Dennis Banks and Russell Means were thrown out of court.

The report deplores defense attempts "to introduce evidence on the question of the motive for the alleged crime." An example cited is "evidence relating to the propriety or legality of the Vietnam War." But where the charges are based on the defendants' activities as members of the antiwar movement, and the basis of the statute involved is "intent" to incite a riot, the motives of the defendants—i.e., why they came to Chicago or Miami Beach to participate in convention demonstrations—are the essence of the defense.

"Rarely," says the report, "has the conduct of the prosecutor been a significant factor in courtroom disruption." Yet the Seventh Circuit concluded that the misconduct of the prosecutors in the Chicago Eight case "would require reversal if other errors did not." And at Gainesville, Justice Department lawyer Guy Goodwin testified under oath that there were no government informers in the defense camp, when it was later revealed that Emerson Poe, close friend of defendant Scott Camil, was working with the F.B.I. This and other prosecutorial misconduct in the Vet case is the basis of a pending civil suit for damages by the defendants. As to the government misconduct at Wounded Knee, the report notes "no evidence of the truth or falsity of these allegations. . . . We understand that the F.B.I. is conducting a further investigation into the matter." In other words, the F.B.I. is investigating its own misconduct. *"Res ipsa loquitur,"* as we lawyers would say: The thing speaks for itself.

In some ways, the heart of the memorandum is a paragraph which complains that it was

> also notable that while prosecutorial staffs changed with each trial, defense staffs maintained some overlap. In many of these cases, defendants were represented either at trial or on appeal by lawyers affiliated with the National Lawyers

Guild or the Center for Constitutional Rights. There was thus a recurring group of experienced personnel for trial work and research.

It is true that many of the lawyers representing defendants in these cases were associated with the Guild or the Center. This does not imply a conspiracy so much as it suggests a willingness on the part of the lawyers in these groups to represent controversial and financially unrewarding clients. Nor is the fact of shared expertise and experience indicative of a plot, but rather, the essence of good lawyering. In fact, the Justice Department has its own cadre of highly trained lawyers supervising "political" judicial proceedings. The Washington, D.C., staff was involved at every level of these cases, from grand jury to appeal. Moreover, the Justice Department has computerized its briefs and canned material is available at the press of a button. There was plenty of "overlap" and "experienced personnel" on the prosecutors' staffs as well.

The report concludes that "disruption itself was not a major cause of the government's failure to obtain convictions in many of these trials." Rather, the cases were lost

> because they were tried before juries at least partially composed of people willing to be convinced of government misconduct. . . . The defense sought, and was able to evoke, the sense that the government used the legal system to legitimize or enforce unpopular policies or decisions.

The authors of the report found "no evidence" that "political rather than legal motivations lay behind the decision to bring the charges" in these cases. Mention was made of law-enforcement techniques such as "the use of electronic surveillance, mail surveillance, and undercover informants." The report admitted that these techniques "are probably much feared by a significant segment of the populace," but made no reference to the questionable constitutionality and/

or outright illegality of the "law-enforcement techniques" used in most of these cases. In all, the report fails to deal with the real reasons why the government lost so many of the "controversial" cases. The truth is that some of those defendants should never have been indicted in the first place; some were tried in a manner inconsistent with our Constitution; and still others were victimized by investigative techniques that were so far removed from the law that the courts were offended. The saddest thing about the Justice Department report is that if it is evidence of the thinking of those who remain in power, then obviously they have yet to learn from the bitter mistakes of our recent history.

In one way, however, our recent history has improved upon our past. I, for one, no longer feel put upon in my work because I am a woman. I have continued to teach and to practice law. On that rare occasion when I have heard a patronizing remark about the role of woman as lawyer, I have felt as though my life has been touched by an antediluvian throwback. Today the possibilities are unlimited. A woman can choose what is right for her. So, if a woman is hesitating about going back to school, trying for that promotion, or wondering about that raise, she should ask herself this: If not now, then when?